The Werewolf Complex

Global Issues

General Editors: Bruce Kapferer, Professor of Anthropology, James Cook University and John Gledhill, Professor of Anthropology, Manchester University

This series addresses vital social, political and cultural issues confronting human populations throughout the world. The ultimate aim is to enhance understanding – and, it is hoped, thereby dismantle – hegemonic structures which perpetuate prejudice, violence, racism, religious persecution, sexual discrimination and domination, poverty, and many other social ills.

ISSN:1354-3644

Previously published books in the series:

Michael Herzfeld
The Social Production of Indifference: Exploring the Symbolic Roots of Western Bureaucracy

Peter Rigby
African Images: Racism and the End of Anthropology

Judith Kapferer
Being All Equal: Difference and Australian Cultural Practice

Eduardo P. Archetti
Guinea-pigs: Food, Symbol and Conflict of Knowledge in Ecuador

The Werewolf Complex

America's Fascination with Violence

Denis Duclos
Translated by Amanda Pingree

BERG

Oxford • New York

English edition
First published in 1998 by
Berg
Editorial offices:
150 Cowley Road, Oxford, OX4 1JJ, UK
70 Washington Square South, New York, NY 10012, USA

Published with the help of the Ministère français chargé de la culture.

Originally published in French as *Le Complexe du loup-garou* by Éditions La
Découverte, Paris, 1994. © Éditions La Découverte, 1994.

English Edition © Denis Duclos 1998

Berg is the imprint of Oxford International Publishers Ltd.

Library of Congress Cataloging-in-Publication Data

A catalogue record for this book is available from the Library of Congress.

British Library Cataloguing-in-Publication Data

A catalogue record for this book is available from the British Library.

ISBN   1 85973 146 5 (Cloth)
       1 85973 151 1 (Paper)

Typeset by JS Typesetting, Wellingborough, Northants
Printed in the United Kingdom by Biddles Ltd, Guildford and King's Lynn.

Contents

Prologue

This book examines the collective *mise-en-scène* of a cast of characters who represent violence and death.

Since our so-called postmodern society believes it has discovered how to channel human energy through automation, violence should be destined to gradual extinction, in which it would succumb to an abundance of goods, free-market transactions, and rational "risk management." But, although violence has been removed from the lives of the upper middle class, it is making an increasingly dramatic comeback in popular fiction and the press, where it is often associated with "outsider" groups. Scenes of automated security and comfort are contrasted with a mirror image of violence, as if the one necessarily conjured up the other and as if the ideal of a perfect society and the extreme savagery of the "killer instinct" shared a hidden mutual bond, a secret natural affinity.

The fact that the United States is an especially fertile ground for these mirror images is not due to any ethnic characteristic, but rather to the headway which the New World has made in realizing the postmodern ideal. Although my main focus in this book is on the United States, readers should interpret this as a reference to "modern society." For the horrifying nightmares which American fiction serves up ad nauseam are merely the symptoms of a worldwide ill that is linked to the consequences of creating a global village, which, while it codifies human beings' influence over each other, also has a tendency to stir the soul into a state of turmoil.

Introduction: Warriors, Werewolves, and Serial Killers

The Emergence of Serial Killers

For years, the media have been suspected of propagating crime by offering up a spectacle of violence for young audiences. This has become a heated topic of discussion in the United States, where the current criticism of media violence echoes an upswing in crime that surpasses that in other Western countries.[1]

The figures found in American sources speak for themselves[2]: 21,600 murders were recorded in the United States in 1995, making a per capita rate of 8 per 100,000, versus 4 in France and 2 in Canada. Despite a decrease from 1994, this works out at a 100 percent rise since 1966 and a 5 percent rise since 1986. The majority of the slayings (15,118) were committed with firearms, but this has not dissuaded the National Rifle Association from suing groups who have contested the constitutional right to bear arms[3] on the grounds that it increases the number of deaths by shooting.

This explosion of deadly acts coincides with an increasing lack of efficiency in formal investigations. According to VICAP,[4] whereas the circumstances of only 6 percent of criminal cases in 1966 were reported to be unknown, the figure rose to 25 percent in 1990 and 34 percent in 1992, an increase eight times that of the rise in crime in general.

Since 1984, a new factor has been used to explain, at least in part, the police's apparent ineffectiveness, and that is the growing number of crimes committed by the same criminals, who are considered to be real recidivist "professionals." This marked the beginning of the serial killer decade, which does not show any sign that it is coming to an end.

This hypothesis relativizes the theory that the increase in violence is due to the media or the sale of arms on a massive scale. It indicates instead that there is a limited number of hardened criminals who are veterans of heinous crime. According to unofficial estimates that circulate within the

1

United States Department of Justice, less than one hundred such serial killers are responsible for several thousand deaths annually.[5] Unlike one-time murderers, these highly mobile "specialists" know how to play on the weaknesses of the American justice system; and indeed the 16,000 local police in charge of conducting murder investigations find it difficult to work cooperatively to compare murders which are committed in different jurisdictions that may be thousands of miles apart.

The problem thus takes on a new perspective. Rather than wondering if children who watch television are future assassins, or if new owners of .44 Magnums are likely to kill one of their neighbors within the year, we are prompted to ask another sort of question.

For example: why does American culture seem to breed so many monstrous, cunning, and determined criminals, who have fallen together like an army of snipers operating country-wide? On the face of it, there is nothing unusual about the United States to indicate that this phenomenon is more natural here than in the other large countries of the Old or New Worlds. Poverty does exist, but no more than in many other countries, and a chaotic moral situation has become the common lot of quite a few modern societies.

One might also think that serial killers were invented as a sort of diversion. As the new link in the chain of "natural born killers" and "criminal types" (two falsely scientific approaches that have been revived to justify theories of "inbred" delinquency[6]), they turn attention away from a violence that has become "banalized" and which discredits America in her desire to set an example for the rest of the world. By creating an image of killers who do not fit the norm and whose abominable acts are underscored by the clinical style with which researchers describe them, one can concentrate public indignation on freak criminals, thus turning it away from the mass violence that is spreading through poverty-stricken, riot-ravaged streets from coast to coast.

A Society's Fascination with Criminals

There is an element of truth in this interpretation, but it would be a mistake to consider it complete. Diversion or not, the visible number of multiple murderers seems to be higher in the United States than elsewhere. The question remains: why?

To find the answer, we must first consider the problem from a different angle by looking for the connection that links this type of killer to a society which is more conducive to the phenomenon than others. For, if the secret to the fiercest psychological profiles lies neither in the genes, the facial features, nor the circumference of the skull, it must be found in their common culture.

One wonders why American culture is fascinated with murder and violence and why it has so easily become caught up in the generous supply of criminal acts provided on television, in the movies, and in crime novels. One thing that strikes readers of the abundant Anglo-American literature on murderers is that novelists and film directors rarely have to invent their own characters. Only rarely do detective or horror stories spring from the writer's pure imagination. Most of them are copied from the news. The influence may not always be reciprocal (as it is doubtful that criminals are driven to act by what they see in the media), but fiction writers are fascinated by the unbelievable examples they find in real-life crime.

The audience that blood crimes are able to command in the American public debate is reminiscent of the followers of the ancient oracles. Sketching a killer's profile based on that of his predecessors has become a technique in investigation. FBI agent Robert K. Ressler[7] writes: "My own actions could be called 'serial'. I now hoped to perfect my crimes by doing still more interviews before I had to face the paper hangman."[8] If this is true, why not hire convicted murderers to explain the unknown motives which the police are searching to discover?

The criminal is also a cop: for twenty years American culture has been honing this old idea, which Victor Hugo immortalized in his character Javert. The quasi-psychotic detectives invented by Jim Thompson and James Ellroy have added spice to the genre. And, with Tom Harris, another level was attained: his book, which later became the movie *The Silence of the Lambs*, directed by Jonathan Demme and winner of the 1992 Oscar for Best Movie, has become a cult film of the 1990s, not so much for its portrait of a cannibalistic psychiatrist but because this cannibal happens to be a special consultant for the police. Harris's novel starts with an excerpt from an imaginary article:

INSANE FIEND CONSULTED IN MASS MURDERS BY THE COP HE TRIED TO KILL, by Freddy Lounds. (Chesapeake, MD) Federal manhunters, stymied in their search for the "Tooth Fairy", psychopathic slayer of entire families in Birmingham and Atlanta, have turned to the most savage killer in captivity for help. Dr. Hannibal Lecter, whose unspeakable practices were reported in these pages three years ago, was consulted this week in his maximum-security-asylum cell by ace investigator William (Will) Graham [...] He was brought back from early retirement to spearhead the hunt for the "Tooth Fairy".[9]

The author appears to have an overactive imagination, but we later learn from the real "star investigator," Robert Ressler, that he assisted Tom Harris and Jonathan Demme in creating a character who uses interviews with convicted killers to help unravel murder investigations.[10] Ressler also advised journalist Ann Rule in her work on the most famous of all serial killers, Ted Bundy, which later became the basis for her best-selling novel. This is why *The Silence of the Lambs* was more than a simple thriller: it touched the intimate bond between American culture and the spectacle of crime.

This is a sign of the connections that have been woven in America between reality, imagination, and interpretation, in which the criminal becomes a model for cultural creation. The success of books and made-for-TV movies on the lives of serial killers proves that there is a mass fascination for monstrous crimes committed in real life. Every aspect of show business is struggling to erase the borderline between fact, fiction, and audience participation. Live-action shows (such as the famous 'America's Most Wanted') involve tens of millions of viewers in crime reenactments, which, although designed to help the justice system, ultimately drag it down toward merciless voyeurism. This trend has accelerated with the new fad of "real-life dramas" that are drawn from the latest events in the news. For instance, just weeks after sect leader David Koresh was killed in the FBI siege on the Branch Davidian complex, his mother sold the rights to her story to Hollywood producer Robert Lee for four million dollars.[11] Lee immediately made *Ambush in Waco* on a movie set built in the middle of the California desert.

This fashion has hit Europe and France as well, where the real people involved in an incident create a considerable draw. The Frenchwoman Laurence Dreyfus, an uncommonly brave school teacher who was taken hostage with her class by Eric Schmitt, refused an offer to play herself in a made-for-TV movie which began production a few weeks after the event, in which Schmitt lost his life.

People have described violence in America as a modern-day echo of a past full of adventure and brawling. But this society's fascination with criminals, whom it watches with a mixture of terror and delight, has not faded over time. Every year, there is a perceptible increase in the amount of horror that is exhibited. The rule for maintaining audience share is to dare to show scenes that are more shocking, and to offer descriptions that are less tolerable, than the last. This trend toward expanding the limits of "artistic license" appears to be unstoppable. And yet, like attitudes toward smoking, it could be turned around at any moment, setting a new trend of phobias that would force people's tenacious taste for hard violence underground.[12]

"Mad warriors," as serious social deviants may be described, do not merely captivate the American audience; they inspire in it a sense of empathetic anger, sympathy, even pity. This is clearly reflected in the film *Falling Down*,[13] in which Michael Douglas plays the role of a businessman who has lost his job and who, in revolt, becomes a killer. On a hot city day, caught in a traffic jam, plagued by flies and a faulty air conditioner, the embittered man goes crazy.

Slowly, his madness sets in. Wearing a white shirt and tie, his pens neatly arranged in a breast pocket and his attaché case in his hand, the man abandons his car in the middle of the bottleneck and "heads home," that is, he goes to see his ex-wife, flouting a restraining order under which he is forbidden from trespassing on her property to visit his daughter. He walks through the city streets, crossing gang territory where whites usually do not dare to tread. As the character makes his way, the film's director manages to show him committing a series of violent acts without making him unlikable. The victim of a cruel fate and a crazed country, he moves forward to meet death as a proud warrior, upholding his principles and confronting all the issues that churn up the American middle class's hatred.

He is careful to pay a Korean drugstore owner, but only after ransacking his shop as "fair" retribution for the exorbitant price of a can of soda. Then, he delivers a (mild) thrashing to two thugs who try to take his briefcase because he has intruded on their territory. In their attempts to fire at him, the thugs end up killing one other instead. He takes their weapons with him to a fast-food restaurant and demands the breakfast menu, threatening the counter people with a machine gun when they refuse to take his order after 11:30. The audience is on the verge of applauding this act of consumer advocacy. He tells the manager of an army surplus store (a misogynous homosexual neo-Nazi who hates gays), who takes a liking to him because of his GI haircut, that he is a good American: a straight, antiracist liberal with no tolerance for Nazi sympathizers (a sine qua non for the character to remain likable). If he killed the man, it would be in self-defense since this "Nazi" is out to rape him. Besides, he has no idea how to use his "borrowed" Stinger bazooka, which he plans to turn on the road work site that is causing the traffic jam: "There's nothing wrong with the road, they're just doing it to raise our taxes," he comments (Schumacher is alluding here to Stephen King's book *Roadwork*, which describes a panic crisis brought on when a neighborhood is destroyed by construction work[14]). In the end, the gun goes off without injuring anyone.

Next, Douglas's character crosses a sprawling country club full of rich old men playing golf; one can only agree with his observation that the park would be better used as a playground for inner-city children. Outraged by this intrusion, a doddering golfer succumbs to a heart attack.

The character treats his ex-wife and daughter gently, so he does not make the audience uneasy. Until the end, he believes that he is a good guy who could not harm a fly. And, by pretending to threaten him with a toy, he "forces" a police officer to kill him, a ridiculous, ironic, and glorious suicide.

Never openly racist or sexist, *Falling Down* is an ambiguous response to the demands of political correctness. The film examines several aspects of the American social crisis and carries a message of anger against outsiders, deviants, and the wealthy. Without actually saying so, it unmistakably suggests that, if nothing is done to stop the situation, it will only degenerate. Subtler than *Rambo* but also more perverse, this film has the potential to become a fetish for any person in the United States and many other industrialized countries who thinks that the time has come to lead a white revolt against the mounting tide of these "dregs of society."

One illustration of such rage was the 19 April 1995 bomb attack on the Alfred Murrah Building in Oklahoma City, which claimed 166 victims, including children in the building's day-care center. Contrary to early accusations that incriminated foreigners, and Muslim fundamentalists in particular, the men who were eventually arrested (and against whom the most evidence seems to weigh) fit the description of "lost soldiers," like the ones often portrayed in Hollywood films. Another new element in this mass murder is that, even if these "soldiers" became mad individually, they are in no way isolated. On the contrary, they are part of a mass culture: that of the paramilitary militias, which, with the freedoms granted to them by the Constitution, are able to mobilize hundreds of thousands of Americans to take part in games the innocence of which is highly relative. It is true that the activities of so-called patriot associations have very rarely led to criminal mishaps, but the imagery that underlies these "survival" groups and their feigned military maneuvers, in which the guns are loaded with paint balls, constantly places them on the brink of uncontrollable disaster. These activities are fueled by hatred and, by listening to militia leaders ranting about threats which have no connection with reality, less solid characters could be made to believe that the President of the United States is an incarnation of Satan and that he is part of an international plot. By extension, federal employees working in a neighboring town can be convincingly portrayed as agents of evil. Militia groups circulated rumors that, for example, these employees were engaged in climatic manipulation that would destroy farmers' crops, or that they were acting to enforce bureaucratic repression against freedom of thought and the right to bear arms. Timothy McVeigh, a Gulf War veteran identified as one of the people who rented the van in which the bomb was discovered, may also have had an impressionable character and was thus encouraged to believe the ideas cultivated by his violent entourage. He is known to have built home-made bombs with the Nicholas brothers, Terry and James (former members of the "militia movement"), on a farm in Decker, Michigan.

Among the current beliefs of these militant groups, there is the conviction that the killing of the Branch Davidian sect followers in Waco two years prior to the bombing in Oklahoma City was entirely the fault of the FBI and the Bureau of Alcohol, Tobacco, and Fire Arms. McVeigh mentioned Waco frequently, and had gone there twice on "pilgrimages" shortly before the bombing. The Oklahoma City attack may therefore have been conceived as a sort of "commemoration," a reaction against the violence of the federal authorities in Waco by people immersed in the cultural context of the militia and who surpassed the violence in Waco with a scheme that was "crazy" but quite in line with their culture, which places individuals in direct competition with organized society.

Are Hollywood and the imaginary violence created by the media to blame for these incidents? We should really be asking ourselves the opposite question: in any culture, who is it that encourages large numbers of people to live in a fantasy world, to such a point that authors, artists, and journalists can describe violent incidents before they happen? For instance, when Joel Schumacher foreshadows Timothy McVeigh in the lead character in *Falling Down*, is he guilty? When Stephen King imagines a pro-life activist crashing an airplane full of explosives into a pro-choice meeting,[15] should he be accused of inciting the Oklahoma City incident? Of course not. In fact, the censorship rules that certain Senators propose to apply to television and movie violence can be seen as a form of denial and a refusal to accept criticism which maintains that the cult of violence is deep-rooted and widespread, even among the most virtuous.

The Myth of the "Mad Warrior"

It would appear, therefore, that we will save a considerable amount of time if we replace the question: "Does the media lead to crime?" with a reflection on why a culture identifies – in emotional, intellectual, and practical terms – with the criminal element, and especially with serial killers.

In a nutshell, the answer is that Anglo-American culture is attracted to uncommon killers because they reflect its own image as an uncommon society. They are a reminder of its legendary tales, which transmit deep-seated values and in which violence has always had a central role as something which is at once desired and feared.

The turbulent settlement of the New World reinstated an age-old condition of constant shifting, from fighter to assassin and from citizen-soldier to outlaw. It brought this condition back on the scale of a continental civilization, whose immense – or imagined – potential was open for all to tap, and to tap aggressively.[16]

This two-centuries-old problem remains current today. By dint of money, science, and technology, the power of this society, which possesses vast logistical, human, and natural resources, has doubled. With the country's unchallenged international political role to prop them up, the people who reap the benefits of this power find it dizzying. For, if they chose to, they could lead a charge on the entire planet and make the world bend to their will. In a sense, the conquest of the New World has been extended directly and almost without interruption by the institution of a new world order, whose governance is left to the discretion of new sovereigns. Who would not find such power inebriating? Who would not be tempted to test his skill in wielding unchallenged aggression, or even in playing cruel games with utter impunity?

It is possible that the constant spectacle of serious crime actually helps Americans (and perhaps the rest of the world) to picture what happens to the mighty when they lose their sense of perspective and of their own place in the human race. It helps to test the limits of one's "freedom" to act and, by default, to prove that all civilizations contain a self-regulating mechanism. In short, we may be engaged in a revival of the mythical initiation passage from savagery to civility.

The Ancient Sources of a Culture of Crime

Of course, violence in America has its own origins, which have been immortalized in countless variations on the theme of colonization and the defeat of the Native American. But stories of the Wild West, which have been criticized to the point of ridicule, have hidden the roots that stem from European tradition. When cowboys inspire nothing more than a smile, the ghosts of secular belief rise again, as terrifying as ever. Their effect is perceptible.[17] In the modern world, savage criminals are a reminder of much more than the violence that went on "West of Los Pecos" or the frenzy in California when it broke away from its European ties. If such characters seem to be (increasingly) central in the ancestral tales of victorious warriors that are handed down through folklore traditions, it is because they raise an ageless anthropological question: that of the choice between civilization and barbarism.

Which of the folk traditions that have been handed down to the present day can put a modern cast on the ancient question of where violence belongs?

This is an important question, because different traditions give different mythical explanations of how the civilization of man came to exist. Some integrate the warrior as a civilian, under certain conditions of loyalty and discipline. Others, on the contrary, assume that combatants cannot be completely civilized or even symbolically "castrated," and that this leads to an irreconcilable conflict between the warrior and the society and, ultimately, to catastrophe.

What is disturbing about American culture in its obsession with violence and fear is that it shows a greater affinity with the message of the latter mythical tradition. The blood-drenched incidents of today waken old demons and gods who were considered to be indomitable in the Celtic, Anglo-Saxon, and Nordic traditions, which are the sources of traditional teaching for the non-Amerindian American population.

If we observe American "crime culture" carefully, one thing quickly springs to light: real crime and horror fiction both draw upon the adventures of mythical warriors. If serial killers and characters in horror fiction have something in common, it is because both the lead characters in modern fiction and those in real crimes reflect the dark heroes of medieval or more ancient sagas. The two modern-day versions of the "mad warrior" – those on television and those in real life – are both inspired by the same figure of a wild Germanic warrior. They share, either in practice or in the imagination, a belief in the intense energy that the human animal experiences in a state of demonic or holy rage. The same compulsive drive toward aggression or pleasure is discharged in good or evil forms of relentless violence.

Tales of Nordic heroes are familiar in the Celtic traditions and Scandinavian poetry from the Viking period, and they have been reinterpreted by the Anglo-Saxons, up to the syncretic creations of the British fiction writer J.R.R. Tolkien.[18] Quite a number of comic books feature Nordic heroes, as suggested by their titles: *The Mighty Thor, Excalibur, The New Warrior*, and *Conan*, published by the famous Marvel Comics, or *New Gods, Viking Glory*, and *Viking Prince*, among others, published by DC Comics. Most of the hundreds of other series that spin out the never-ending battles of the superheroes make some allusion to scenes taken from this mythological tradition.

More than one thousand years later, we find that there is a phantasmatic continuity in the adventure of the raging warrior. There is a similarity between Odin's follower Einhedjar, a lone dragon-slaying warrior, and Rambo as he single-handedly brings down enemy helicopters, just as there is a similarity between the series of violent deaths portrayed in American television dramas and the series of murders perpetrated by real "repeat-offense" criminals (or "avengers"), who are nothing more than killing machines. Repeated acts of carnage, slashing and smashing bodies, appear to be common both to the eternal combat described in sagas of the living dead, who rise each night with the singing of the Valkyries, and to television miniseries, which in each installment replace the dead villains from previous episodes with a new crop, ready for the slaughter. A similar ritual characterizes the real killing sprees, whether they are committed en masse or in a series, which have cropped up from state to state, each time committed by a new kind of killer.

Hardened warriors, whether modern-day or ancient, embody the tragic ambivalence between good and evil, civility and barbarism. Nordic heroes try to establish a balance between benevolent and harmful forces, and between the social order and their personal impulses. Although in some cases this balance is achieved, it remains subject to conflict, uncertain and temporary. In the warrior's fated end we see that, as he shifts slowly but inevitably from good to evil, he is doomed to perish in the massive catastrophe which he has caused by relentlessly attacking those who oppose him, friend or foe. This tradition of cynicism approaches the cynicism that is found among hardened American criminals and which has inspired novelists and film-makers from the "no-future" generation to draw upon their example as if from a dark source. It does not point toward a very peaceful future. America appears to be wavering before a path of no return toward civility, and at the same time dreaming of the road to disaster.

Listening to Murderers

In this book, which is one stage in a body of research on representations of danger in different societies, I will attempt to decipher some of the messages in Anglo-American culture which have been picked up by fiction, myth, and real crime.

The interpretations of motives for multiple murders are themselves multiple, but little has been done in the way of listening to what hardened killers – negative-image "heroes" – have to say about individual or collective acts of barbarism. These human monsters' chromosomes have been picked apart (and of course have proved to be perfectly normal); the courts have berated them for their hunger for public attention; and they have been castigated for their incurable sexual problems or their bloodthirstiness. But people have rarely tried to understand what part these criminals play in the public *mise-en-scène* of their acts. They have rarely been listened to as members (albeit with a peculiar predisposition for solitude and death) of society.

So, in Part One, we will listen to murderers (and the people who observe them) as they talk about what drives them to devour or to make others suffer. It will become apparent that there is truth in the Shakespearean idea that some people have an appetite for misfortune: serial killers are real-life incarnations of the insatiable ogre. At the same time, killers', researchers', novelists', and film-makers' insistence on describing the joys of the criminal act (as a form of repentance or castigation) ultimately raises doubts about how edifying their remarks really are. Creating a setting of horrid pleasures and playing upon people's fascination for them seem to be their way of enjoying a secret indulgence: in other words, condemning a benignly described killing frenzy may be a way of holding on to the object of an – apparently – forbidden thrill.

To this, the intelligentsia of the horror culture will reply, "But of course!" As they see it, the objective is clear: it is more effective to control violence with crude descriptions than with denial through censorship. By showing us atrocities, American culture is in fact reminding us that we all wish for the pain and death of others, and that it is a slim borderline that separates the community of "normal" people who resist this impulse from the blood-thirsty heroes whose acts are a reflection of all people's propensity for evil. This supposed appetite for murder is therefore a manifestation of the death instinct, which destroys social ties and which should be appropriately reprimanded.

Yet one cannot defend an ideology that is based on the pair formed by shocking violence and repression, without some measure of suffering. Even at times when the horror trade seems to be stuck in a routine, it still gives society a thrill to see the death instinct in the savage-warrior theme exposed. The supposed cruelty of dangerous characters is echoed by fictional sado-masochism. The two become caught up in one another until their game of mirrors has played itself out to the end.

What is society's interest in flirting with these dangerous themes? At a time when the world is opening up and traditional signs of identity have been shattered, it would seem that perverse inclinations, even the violent kind, are reassuring, since the object of enjoyment is "getting the other guy." At the risk of frightening ourselves and exposing ourselves to the real terror of extremely violent acts, we have opened ourselves up to a kind of sensual rage. The example of *Falling Down* is typical of the narcissistic comfort of having one's finger on the trigger of a gun.

But real criminals, who are lost in their insanity, take these imaginary pleasures farther: if one considers the atrocity of their acts, it becomes apparent that a human being's regression into such a state of bestiality cannot be fully explained by the fact that he has sadomasochistic tendencies. In their own way, such criminals strike out against conservative or half-hearted interpretations which suggest they have hallucinations of violence, for they experience their acts as a reality.

In Part Two, we will see how, in order to keep from sinking into a total state of bestiality, automation, or soullessness, hardened American criminals often invent new personalities for themselves that are based on the warrior myth. These violent criminals present themselves (and are presented) as soldiers of vengeance, which puts a semblance of a human face on them. They compare themselves to judges or avengers in order to give their acts political legitimacy. In reality, this is a way of trying to make sense of absurdity in order to be able to talk about it.

It is also a metaphor which marks the transition from the criminal to the "good" fighter. For the notion of the "avenger" legitimates wild, reckless behavior that fundamentally has no distinct motives. This means that the superheroes of the screen (Rambo, Chuck Norris, McGuyver, and so on) always react more strongly than their attackers, delivering a hundred times more napalm bombs, grenades, and machine-gun fire. And it works: the pretext – a foe classified as evil – is forgotten, the audience joins in a cry of legitimate rage, and then indulges its need for gore, which is authorized at last.

In fact, the excuse of vengeful justice (which is so frequent in American comic-book plot lines and movies, but also in the explanations that are given for repeated acts of murder) propagates rather than restrains violence. The message conveyed by a hero who authorizes reprisals is not one of equity but one of continued violence. This release of aggression is even more terrifying than the one that precedes it, because it is sanctioned and reveals the potential criminal who lurks behind every avenger. It reminds us that the mask of virtue which we wear in public must never be removed, lest we set off a chain reaction of good to evil, ending in a general state of metamorphosis.

This is the message in comic books such as *Judge Dredd*, *The Punisher*, or *Justice League*, where justice is portrayed with the features of the Grim Reaper. It is also the message in James Ellroy's novels about Los Angeles police detectives who owe their successes to the fact that they bear a close resemblance to the sadistic lunatics whom they track down from one blood-strewn crime scene to the next. It is plainly expressed in the film *Basic Instinct*,[19] in which the archetypal character of a brutish but honest police officer takes a blatantly evil turn.

In some cases, killer heroes make an effort to give a more humane significance to their animal-like violence. The vengeance in such stories harks back to ancient tragic drama and the impassioned debate which it stirred. For, it was the classical authors who showed how private offenses (parricide, incest, etc.) called for the institution of democracy.

We will see that, with multiple murderers who have gone down in history – Edmund Kemper and Charles Manson – as well as with more recent criminals, America has resuscitated the sons of Atreus. But the "American-style" rendition does not end with the pronouncement of a higher judgment. On the contrary, the murderer, an antihero who is associated with madness or monstrosity, is deified or demonized rather than judged as a man. Instead of sending him to meet his inevitable fate, people presume that he is enslaved by an instinct for murder. In the mini-apocalypses that have been created by a number of fundamentalist sects, there may even be a regression toward a prehistoric universe of vengeance-hungry hordes led by an almighty chief who possessed all of the women and reduced all of the men to a state of voluntary slavery.

Put briefly, in the United States scenes of violence are rarely followed by a civilizing process but rather by feelings of uncertainty, and by a state of oscillation between savagery and civility, peacefulness and aggression. The motif of never getting anywhere, of moving in circles and constantly being led back to the start, is so strong in Anglo-American societies that it could even be described as one of this culture's central characteristics. The "werewolf complex" is an essential prototype, perhaps because it provides a natural host for the ambivalent energy that is capable of generating such infinite wealth.

Should Self-Destruction be Eliminated?

The current favor for theories of natural violence (a central belief in Anglo-American culture) seems to coincide with the driving ideal of a worldwide capitalist system. Is there something wrong with this? To begin with, beyond its cult of vitality, one of this theory's hidden aspects is an aspiration to end it all in an orgy of blood. Young people put their finger on this when they started describing themselves as the "no-future" generation. In Part Three, we will see that failure in their dramatizations of themselves as avengers sets the criminally insane on a track of self-destruction. The myth of the werewolf, a manifestation of schizophrenic dissociation, reflects pessimism.[20] As one of the main characters in the Nordic family, the werewolf's appearance marks the beginning of the warrior's irreversible decline. This is only an initial stage, however, for the killer's ultimate fate is not to live as a man-beast, but to wander aimlessly among the living dead, lurching like a broken machine and finally degenerating into a mineral residue like the one that remains after an apocalyptic blast.

What skinhead "warriors," who have gorged themselves (more than the average reader) with hyperviolent magazines and violent racist or nonracist rock music,[21] know is that their fantasies of extermination, blood, and burning are a way of seeking nonexistence. They become weapons, a set of claws, a row of teeth, a system of muscles or clockwork, and are careful to avoid thinking about what kind of person they could be.

When one considers this catastrophic perspective as a whole, an outline rises to the surface, describing a passage between culture and nature, society and wilderness; and, as they walk this line, heinous murderers, who resemble the godforsaken characters in horror fiction, mark the stages of a progression that leads from the most to the least human:[22]

1. *Making a pact with the devil*: Here, there is an attempt to preserve the criminal's human motive (greed, etc.) and the ability to reason. The archetypal character is Dr. Faust, but we will see that this category has been the source of an entire class of American crime (Manson, Berkowitz, Samples, and others), and that it is also one of the richest veins in horror fiction, including many stories by the master of the genre, Stephen King.

2. *Errant souls and revenants*, "who demand that a specific act be performed so that they may have eternal rest."[23] Many criminals commit a cycle of crimes and then stop. They awaken from their state of trance and emerge redeemed and in a sense "rehumanized." This is the case of Kemper, DeSalvo, Berkowitz, and even Manson, who were pacified by incarceration. The series of murders in such cases are attributed to "temporary insanity," which can go into remission.

3. *Ghost-women and vampires*. The face of the murderer's mother often figures in hallucinatory images, and has held and controlled such criminals as Kemper, Mullin, and many others. From Crutchley to Wilder and many other sadistic murderers, serial killers complain of, and in some cases avenge themselves for, something that has been "stolen" from them (and which can be their blood, their energy, or their manhood). Once again, insanity hides behind more or less human motives.

4. *A curse* which causes sickness or death. This is the theme of Stephen King's *Thinner*, and of the apocalyptic events that are caused by scientific sorcerers' apprentices in many "postnuclear" science-fiction novels. Among the criminal class, such fates are sealed when the child is still in his cradle, by a Satanist grandmother (Toole), a slave-driving father (DeSalvo), or something else that triggers the same effects. Here, there is no mention of an involuntary destiny for the criminal; "someone else" is acting through him.

These four initial levels still belong to a world in which human beings remain recognizable as such behind their masks. The next stage is a crucial one, a point of no return. In fiction, it is often symbolized by a physical space – a house, a bedroom, an apartment, or the floor of a building – which is pulled into another dimension. Closed spaces are important in satanic rituals: Bluebeard-like dungeons or Volkswagen buses with their doors jammed shut and transformed into torture chambers. These also symbolize a revolving door between reality and the nonhuman world, a materialization of the stuff of nightmares, or simply an uncertainty about where reality lies. When criminals in this class perceive a flicker of reality, they can sense that they are going insane. They give themselves up to the police to protect themselves from a nonhuman state of being which they have experienced with intimate closeness.

But, once this threshold has been crossed, we can no longer relate to the absolute foreignness of these beings and their acts. There is an overriding theme of *something undefinable* that pressures, tortures, and kills. Since Maupassant wrote "Horla," the Blob and other slime-like monsters have taken on all sorts of shapes and textures – a fog, or a cottony or sticky mass – or even a terrifying absence of definable shape. Among criminals such as Bundy, Berdella, and Joubert, this is the "dark side" of their psyche, their other, purely evil soul, which they never manage to control or explain.

Next, there is the *revenant*, who is condemned to wander along an aimless path (the theme of the wild chase). One recognizes Chase and Mullin in this category, as well as many "random" killers whose human side is reduced to the symptomatic phenomenon that takes over their minds. These criminals are among the living dead: one can no longer attribute an author to the aggressive acts which their bodies commit.

Finally, there are *statues*: dummies, suits of armor, or automatons, who have descended to an even lower level than that of the living dead. Ted Bundy, John Gacy, and Jeffrey Dahmer join the likes of Norbert Wiener's golem, Stephen King's haunted car, Robocop and the living machines in American science fiction. This theme is connected with a sensation that time is repeating itself or standing still, as observed in "mechanical" killers who repeat the same act ad infinitum.

At the end of this descent into hell, the acts of the criminally insane increase the number of their victims, but give no satisfaction. The series of hyperviolent acts, combats, and victims that are common to the three genres – mythical sagas, fantastic tales, and crime – are an indication of despair: the despair of never finding the key to the passageway between the plurality of violent acts and the oneness of an ordinary person, between energy and love, and between things and people.

This taste for the macabre also characterizes the masterful writings of Stephen King and Clive Barker. Latin cultures tend to be more optimistic. French readers consume all of author Daniel Pennac's[24] detective stories with rapt attention, intrigue, and a sense of ironic humor, regardless of whether the plot holds together; and a love scene directed by the Taviani[25] brothers – whose films contain just as much intergenerational venom as Anglo-American cinema – can move a European audience to tears.

But our interest in examining the sinister outlook of criminals and Anglo-American horror-fiction writers is to grasp its secret riddle. For there is a question that appears to thread its way through the myth of an inevitable violent catastrophe, and that is: is the crossover between culture and nature, society and wilderness, and humanity and humus reversible? If there is a path that leads from the most to the least human, and which is taken to various degrees by these messengers of death, could one also follow this same path in the opposite direction, from the least to the most human?

In other words, in its strange determination to bring these terrifying images to life, is American culture unconsciously suggesting that by taking a journey into the midst of these atrocious acts it is possible to stop them and resist them, in the same way as Ulysses' journey allowed the mythical warrior, as he sailed among the islands, to cleanse himself of his thirst for Trojan blood?

On the face of it, the "horror culture" seems to be sending out the opposite message: that is, that the point of the journey – whether it is taken by a serial killer or the director of a "splatter" film – is to imagine increasingly gruesome crimes. Is this culture lacking something that would allow it to "turn around" the serial phenomenon and give it a new direction, from the unpardonable to the benign, from the robotic to the human?

A society enamored of violence may indeed lack a sense of perspective that projects desire not on the thing itself but rather on what all things hide (especially if they appear in series), that is, their irreplaceable value once they are gone. Many venerable societies have assimilated this value through myths of the symbolic castration of a warrior, whether man or woman. America, and especially America as the world imagines it, in a dream where all wishes come true,[26] has not. It may be this limitless dream state (which is now referred to as international postmodernism) that concocts the nightmares which we are about to plunge into.

PART ONE

Living from the Hunt

In order for an act to be perceived as shocking, inhuman and criminal, it must first be given a collective significance. Without this construction, nothing can be construed as evil in and of itself: killing can be a "normal" act in some instances (such as during war, an example frequently given), or it can occur without creating further effects. In some ancient societies, killing a slave or leaving an old person or a young child to die may have been considered as inevitable in some circumstances. Inversely, acts which we consider to be mundane (eating, drinking, and sleeping) can be deemed criminal if they are performed at forbidden times or in forbidden places. In short, no act can be interpreted in and of itself, but only in relation to the social judgment that is applied to it.

Nevertheless, certain acts do not fit into the currently accepted categories of the human culture: they are, by definition, unclassifiable and therefore create intense fear. Serial killings are among such acts. The perpetrator of an uninterrupted series of murders tends to exhaust the legal recourse available against him. In general, one such crime may suffice for the maximum sentence to be delivered, so that a criminal escapes his society's ability to judge him when his repeated offenses become impossible to punish. Sentencing someone to 600 years in prison (like Richard Speck, whose victims were all women) or to eighteen consecutive life terms is, of course, ridiculous. Moreover, as they are judged separately for each crime, multiple killers have some hope that, from one extradition to the next and from one courtroom to the next, they will escape the ultimate punishment. In other words, and taking the problem to the absurd, the more murders they commit, the less they risk the death sentence.

The impossibility of passing judgment occurs at a "level" of atrocity that exceeds the limits of condemnable actions. Whether the murderer hacks his victims into nine pieces or prefers to mince them up, the law has no provisions for such additional offenses. And yet this gruesome attention to detail in the excessive behavior of certain murderers leaves us aghast by the horror of their extreme acts.

Whatever the courts are unable to judge, fiction writers incorporate in their work. Legends, novels, films, biographies, televised debates, and other genres all work together, spinning a web of words, interpretations, and images around unspeakable acts and gradually alleviating our deepest fears. This type of collective effort is being applied to the area of violent crime in America. The category of serial killing is as much a new concept in scientific police work as it is a sign of cultural maturation or evolution,[1] which casts the moral debate upon other phenomena.

An outline of the deviant criminal, whose once blurry profile is slowly coming into focus, emerges from this collective construction, bringing with it an implicit discourse on private and public violence. This societal molding of the serial killer offers observers a series of profiles and incarnations that differ slightly from each other but which appear as if they were superimposed. Images of hunters, warriors, wild animals, or instruments of death fade in and out of view. Is it merely a coincidence that, as the collective portrait of the hardened killer wavers between different forms, children around the world are playing with toys that imitate the same transformations: robots with animal faces, helmeted like ancient warriors and wielding futuristic rocket launchers and medieval daggers with equal ease?

To understand "how these things work" – that is, how and why the social debate conceals and reveals these images of barbaric killers, slanting them first in one direction, then in another – we should follow the example of these children with their toys: let us therefore start by examining incarnation number one, the manhunter.

CHAPTER ONE

The Adventure

In the legends of the American serial killer, Henry Lee Lucas and Ottis Toole are two characters who stand apart, not only for their psychological profiles but also for the enormous number of people they slew, first singly and then together, between 1979 and 1983.

As horrifying as the two- or three-figure number of the murders they committed may be, the most alarming figure is that of the freakish or dangerous characteristics they had between them: patricidal tendencies, sadism, cannibalism, alcohol and drug abuse, an inveterate gambling habit, a nomad lifestyle, prostitution, incest, felony and theft, desecration of graves and mutilation of corpses, all of which were the least serious of the offenses they committed. If one were to imagine a "full-strength" version of the antihero, these two would surely fit it.

But our reason allows us to believe only so much before we begin to suspect that something is simply not possible. Consequently, these real human beings who engage in excessive acts begin to appear instead as imaginary figures who symbolize evil.

If the stories of Henry Lucas and Ottis Toole (and of many other notorious murderers) have created this problem, it is because they were pieced together in part by society's imagination and bear the combined effects of the murderers' own boasting, local police tales, and sensationalism in the media. But it is also because there is a prevalence of syncretic allusions to Nordic warriors in American culture, even if no explicit reference is made to them, as in extreme right-wing politics in Europe.[1] Hence, before our disbelieving eyes, an uncanny resemblance emerges between Henry Lucas and Ottis Toole and the nearly homonymic Loki and Odin, extremely wicked and yet central divinities in the Germanic and Viking cultures from the fourth to the twelfth centuries.

Holy Rage

Warriors find their inspiration mainly with the help of stimulants. One has only to look around the commuter railways that serve the Parisian suburbs to see groups of young people in castoff military clothing and punk haircuts, seeking courage from a copious consumption of beer (in some cases sweetened with hashish) before hitting the city streets to "tag" as many buildings as they can or cover their rivals' tags. But this is still just a war of signs and signatures, not of murders. At a higher level of delinquency, heavy drinking is also part of the preparation for assaults on immigrant populations in France, Germany, and elsewhere.

But, in the battle royal between society and the totally marginal groups embodied by certain American murderers, a stronger source of inspiration is needed to put aggressive energy into action. Ottis Toole, the son of an unreformed alcoholic, began drinking very young and never stopped. He took hallucinogenic drugs for the first time at the age of eight, and his mother stuffed him with barbiturates to try to calm his uncontrollable aggressiveness. He has consistently maintained to anyone who would listen that, if he killed people, it was always under the influence of alcohol or drugs. When asked to talk about the acts of dismembering or cannibalism which he allegedly confessed to, Ottis states that he perpetrated them in a state of alcoholic semiconsciousness or under the influence of LSD or speed. He has created a character for himself who is excited or "turned on" by killing and who is reminiscent of the warrior gods that followed Odin (arguably, another coincidence): Ottis seems to live for all forms of drunkenness, just like Odin, who sustained himself on wine and blood, leaving solid foods to the other gods.

It should be pointed out that in Old Icelandic, *odin* is the past participle (*od*) of the verb *vada*, which, like the Latin *vadere*, means to go. Odin therefore means "gone," a word which could be used to describe someone who has had too much to drink or who is taking a mental trip induced by hallucinogenic drugs.[2] The Old English *wod* ("the possessed"), the Latin *uates* ("the divine," "the vaticinator"), and the words *woids*, meaning anger in Gothic, and *woth*, meaning poetic inspiration in Saxon, all derive from a closely related Indo-European root, as do the correspondingly named divinities Wothan and Woden (Old English),[3] otherwise known as Odin. In the Nordic cosmology, Odin also represents action, by contrast with his brothers (who were sired by the same universal genitor) Vili ("will") and Vé ("sight"). The god of fury and action, Odin is placed (owing to the wealth of stories about him) in the center of the Nordic pantheon,[4] by contrast with the Greek and Latin cultures, in which the symbol of diurnal light

(Zeus) reigns as the sovereign, while Orion, the nocturnal hunter (whose name resembles "Odin"), is slowly driven back into the wilderness that lies on the fringes of the civilized world. For Orion to return to civilization, he must first be initiated, that is, he must die a barbarian and be reborn as Dionysos ("the twice-born").[5]

Henry Lee Lucas (the son of a drunkard and an alcoholic prostitute, whom he murdered) also sank deep into drink and acts of rage. During his several periods of internment in hospitals for the criminally insane in Michigan and Virginia, he tried to warn the psychiatrists that his psychotic "needs" were real: "I tell them my problems, and they don't want to do nothing about it, but there is a hundred, oh, about a hundred women out there that says different."[6]

Like a mystic reading the future, he warned the courts that as soon as he was released from prison he would start killing again, relentlessly. Nor would he give up drinking; and, if one believes the story his friend Toole has told of how Lucas initiated him to cannibalism, Lucas would not take just any drink: "Lucas gave me bits to eat but I never believed him until I saw him cut someone's throat, collect the blood that was spilling out in a jar and drink it. Then he said how good it was . . . that it was much better than drinking champagne or wine."[7]

This statement makes us somewhat less incredulous. These words, which were propelled worldwide by the media, explain how Toole and Lucas came to be seen as monsters that were beneath the human race, and why (with their assent) they were accused of hundreds of unsolved murders in several states across the United States. It is a rare occasion when such demons – or gods, drinkers of nectar and kvasir, the libation of blood drunk by Nordic heroes[8] – are available to take the rap for their own actions.

Readers may still remain skeptical, since only a corner of the veil has been lifted. But let us accept, at least for the time being, the thesis that commentators, police officers, journalists, and novelists all treat this type of hardened criminal as a demonic god, and that it fills them with a holy dread to imagine characters who have crossed the borderline separating them from the world of common mortals. Acceptance of this thesis elucidates many mysteries, for what interests us here is the collective effort to construct a myth and to give it social depth in all of its components, variants, and details.

This argument is puzzling to anthropologists. Indeed, how can one posit that our contemporaries, members of a highly evolved scientific culture, would seek to reconstruct a myth that even resembles those of the hunter-soldier societies of two thousand years ago?

Wandering, Hunting, Possibly Dying

Like many other serial killers, Toole and Lucas were vagrants, "road runners." But they did not travel on foot. Like the knights-errant of old on their trusty steeds, or lonesome cowboys on their mounts, these killers had their cars to provide them with both the means to stray and their main weapon for battle. If, as one of Toole's former employers is quoted as saying, "Toole was interested in one thing: his old car" (although he did not have a driver's license), it is likely that this was somehow related to his first murder, which he committed when he was fourteen years old. Toole had been present at a murder and the killer, wanting to get rid of the witness, had then turned on him. Toole climbed into the man's car, took the wheel, and attempted to run him over. Without the car, he would have died.

After this spectacular getaway, Toole wandered by pickup truck through the western United States, where he is alleged to have killed at least four persons during a six-month period in 1974. He had no qualms about making these violent assaults, one of which consisted in bursting into a massage parlor in Colorado Springs and raping and killing two young women. But his favorite indulgence, like that of the Viking god Logi, meaning "fire," was arson and he set hundreds of fires in many different states.

Lucas, who killed his mother in 1960, was released from prison ten years later and lived by his wits and petty theft. He drove a series of used cars across the United States, killing women, men, and children by the dozen and occasionally raping his dead victims.[9] He probably did not commit the 360 crimes he confessed to, but we are encouraged to believe that a probable one hundred criminal counts could be upheld against him, and that he committed the dozen murders for which he was actually tried, as if killing were a casual pastime, in the same way as other people go rabbit hunting or blueberry picking.

He then crossed paths with Toole and became his lover. Starting in 1979, the two bloodthirsty vagrants wandered together like Hengest and Horsa ("Stallion" and "Charger"), the two mythical leaders of the Anglo-Saxon invasion of Great Britain. They preferred to loiter around route I-35, picking up hitchhikers and broken-down drivers and luring them onto side roads, where they raped, killed, mutilated, and even ate them. They claimed to have committed 108 murders together.

Toole and Lucas are the absolute opposites of the classic American tramp portrayed by Jack London or Kerouac, but despite their monstrous acts they had a love for the road and wide open spaces, and were it not for these they would quickly have been apprehended.[10]

The metaphor of the bloodthirsty vagrant is ancient. We should recall that, in the Nordic countries, Odin "the horseman" or "the attacker" is also the god of dangerous marauders and he travels accompanied by his dogs Greed and Dread. Helmeted like a Hell's Angel, Odin steals mead and is hence the god of looters. Also called "road-wise" (*Vegtamr*), he wanders his path in search of people to cast spells on, animals to hunt, misfortunes to inflict on others, wars to wage, or women to abduct. Odin (who can appear in several places at the same time and change shape – *fjölnir*) is also the god of the secret paths that lead to hell. Route I-35 is such a path, and, since Toole and Lucas traveled it, it could be renamed *Helvegr*, "the road to hell" in the Ancient Germanic language, or *Hent an Anaon*, "the way of departed souls" in Old Celtic.

These two monsters conjure up metaphors of the "wild hunt." It has become current in the United States to use hunting images to describe multiple killers, whether their technique is one of random kidnapping or of ambushing victims, like the "mass" murderers who have committed multiple shootings before being arrested or turning the gun on themselves.

In the first category, we discover a scenario that has been common in the United States for more than one hundred years: a Bonnie-and-Clyde-type chase in which the pursued become the pursuers. New cases crop up regularly. In 1975, for example, J.P. Knowles killed thirty-five people he encountered during a run from the police who had been sent to track him.

Rarer and perhaps more significant are cases in which ordinary Americans suddenly take to the road, seeking both freedom and death. The forerunners (and a relatively tame example) of this trend were the young Paul Krueger, seventeen, and John Angles, sixteen, the proud offspring of two extremely wealthy families, who shared a love for horses and lawless hunting. One day in 1965, they took off on a reckless adventure to "join the Mexican Revolution." On their way, they killed three fishermen and then stole their boat.

In the same period, there is another relatively mild case, which set the paradigm for the category of ambushers: a boy named Michael Clark parked his car on the side of the highway and, using passing drivers as his targets, wounded eleven persons and killed three. This well-mannered youngster and "mother's boy",[11] an excellent student and boy scout, so shocked the innocent American public of the 1960s that he became the inspiration for Stephen King's short story "Apt Pupil," in which the author gives the main character all of the diabolical traits his real-life model lacked by portraying him as the spiritual son of an aging Nazi, in hiding since the war. This example suggests that in order for the character to be believable he must have an explicit link with an inherited ideology of war, which is easily provided by creating a connection with Nazi Germany.

It should be pointed out that the symbolic borderline between a hunting party and a punitive or purge-like attack is very slim, as reflected by the cases of the Canadian Corporal Lortie, who went on a shooting binge, spraying the Quebec Parliament building with machine-gun fire, or Marc Lépine, who summarily executed fourteen students at the Ecole Polytechnique of Montreal in 1989.[12] In a madman's mind and in the minds of the general public, the possibility of an oscillation between the states of hunter and avenger, and, as regards the victims, between animal and guilty human, is ever present.

A famous case involving one such "hunter on the run" is that of James Oliver Huberty, who burst into a McDonald's in San Ysidro, California, and fired 245 rounds on a crowd of customers, claiming forty victims (21 of whom were killed). Huberty, who worked as a welder (but who also had an embalmer's license), had just been fired from his job. On the morning of the shooting, he visited the San Diego zoo with his family. When he left to collect his weapons, he told his wife: "I'm going hunting . . . hunting humans." This phrase had such an effect on the sociologist Elliott Leyton that he used it as the title of his remarkable work on serial killers.[13]

Huberty was also described by his wife during a number of interviews as a "Nazi," to summarize his privately professed opinions about society. Our attention is drawn here to a phenomenon which we will come across repeatedly: American culture's propensity to connect atrocious murders of all kinds with an image of Nazism, which has become the paradigm for political Satanism in the Northern Hemisphere.

It is possible that Huberty knew that Saint Hubert is the patron of hunters. But he may not have known that a number of scholars of mythology consider Saint Hubert and Odin to be one and the same: a dangerous hunter gripped by a fever for the chase (*jagdfieber*) but ultimately excluded from the group before his sacred reincarnation.[14]

The danger of the hunter has been feared since earliest antiquity: if he becomes carried away by his blood lust, he may confuse licit prey and domestic animals, enemies and friends. Of course, there is a difference between assaulting one's loved ones and attacking the enemy, but this taboo is not so explicit in all societies, or for all individuals. Once again, it is this possibility that an armed citizen may succumb to a sudden mental slip that is reflected in the criminally insane. When Lucas, who had already killed his mother, confessed to killing and dismembering his fifteen-year-old mistress, Becky, Ottis's niece (and who may even have been sired by Ottis with his own sister), Ottis instantly forgave him. It was as if he were acknowledging that the irresistible force which acts upon the criminal mind cannot be deterred by any form of love or family loyalty.

Naturally, "going berserk," a state of being possessed that leads to savage recklessness, is not peculiar to Western or Nordic cultures. Among Native Americans, paranoid psychosis was ritualized. Among the Ojibwa, *Windigos* killed their families and then fled, attacking others and eating human flesh before finally being apprehended. Other known forms of such possession include "Arctic hysteria" among the Inuit, in which sufferers find themselves naked in the frozen wild after a desperate chase, and the murderous flight of the *latah* of Malaysia or the *amok* of Polynesia, in which the victims run far and wide, killing everything in their path before committing suicide.[15]

But it is probably the theme of the wild soldier/hunter that developed in the West and in the Celto-Germanic Nordic countries which maintains the greatest ambiguity between its different aspects. Insanity versus bellicose energy, marauding versus the noble hunt, looting versus taking "legitimate" booty, or vengeance versus a taste for death is never clearly distinguished, and the wily Odin (also known as Merlin the wizard, who is sometimes possessed by madness) perfectly symbolizes the continued presence of this ambivalence in warrior figures, whom modern-day serial killers seem to bring back to life. But why does this passion for ambiguity persist?

CHAPTER TWO

Capture

The Catch

As soon as he spots his prey, a murderer who is on the hunt will try to capture it in flight. The sight of his victim awakens his desire to seize it and to impose his will upon it. When the victim is sacrificed, it is not to Odin's incarnation as *Vegamtr* (the Errant) but rather as *Haptagud* (the god of bondage), who has the power to freeze enemy warriors, whom he then leaves to his thugs. One of Odin's contemporary incarnations is Count Zaroff,[1] who invites people to visit his island, shares a meal with them, and then explains the rules of his game: he will give them a running start to reach the end of the property before being captured and killed. This is a common theme in Anglo-Saxon epic literature. In his *Tschaï* series, science-fiction writer Jack Vance imagines a race of superior beings whose favorite pastime is to hunt humans who are on their way to gather gem-bearing plants. This is the theme of the "born victim": people trapped by their own greed and tormented by the nonchalant cruelty of a manhunter.

But does the theme of hunting human game exist only in mythology? Certainly not. When he was arrested in 1984 in Alaska, Robert Hansen had killed seventeen prostitutes in the following way: he piloted his victims by plane to isolated areas, explained the rules, gave them a head start and then began to chase them, ultimately shooting them down like deer. Another example dates from 1979, when a young San Franciscan was stabbed by a masked man in paramilitary clothing and forced to witness his girlfriend being bound and disemboweled. The murder weapon was "the exact replica of the one which the Count [Zaroff] carried when he wore his black hunting suit."[2]

If these killers had read the works of historian Pierre Vidal-Naquet,[3] they would have known that they were reenacting the three-thousand-year-old myth of the immature hunter whose cowardly, treacherous, nocturnal methods prevent him from attaining the status of full manhood as an honorable member of society.

This indicates the prevalence of the theme of an adolescent who is confined by his aggressive fantasies. In role-playing games (which have become even more sophisticated in their computer versions), scenes are created depicting hunts to track human prey under the lead of a grand master. In a case of patricide which occurred in North Carolina, the fiction took over reality: a group of teenagers became so caught up in a game of "Dungeons and Dragons"[4] that they convinced themselves their parents were a gang of evil kings who killed knights in order to steal their treasures.

John Joubert, a teenage murderer in the early 1980s, was also an avid "Dungeons and Dragons" player. He wrote these words in his boy-scout notebook: "Life is a road with many paths; don't get lost." For anyone who is familiar with the terminology of "magic" culture, this is a sign: the players, who imagine they wield limitless power, conceive of life's path as a continuous series of actions and deviations, where breaks in the road cause them to be teleported (one of the basic special effects in computer games), but this does not make them abandon their quest. These "grown-up children" simply cannot find their way out of the enchanted forest.

Imprisonment

Predators immobilize their human subjects in a special place to torture or kill them later. Inside such prisons, time is drawn out so that the hunter can fully enjoy every form of torture he inflicts on the victim. The imprisonment techniques used by multiple killers are effective, but hardly display any refined skill. The acts are perpetrated in the victim's or the killer's home, in a car or a pickup truck, or in the woods. Reproductions of medieval horror chambers rarely exist, and the instruments of torture are unsophisticated: kitchen knives, rope, stockings, etc. Indeed, the practical requirements of the job are in contradiction with the décor. But, if the mundane backdrop does not diminish the atrocity, it does not add to it either; and, in fact, the sense of terror felt during confinement is created by verbal and imaginary innuendo. Thus, criminal "jailers" (such as Mudgett, Heidnik, Kraft, or the "Mourmelon killer" in France[5]) acquire a sort of narrative voice, believing that the prisons or desolate forests they create in their minds really exist.

Stephen King is without a doubt the master of the sadistic fictional narrative, and for our purposes he reflects the emergence in Anglo-American culture as a whole of a relish for criminal fiction. King first gained notoriety as a young writer in the 1970s, a time when the student protest movement and the war in Vietnam were forcibly bringing the American public down from a high point and when the wish for magical power, which had been disappointed in reality, could only come true in fantasy. Hollywood was in a crisis and popular fiction had grown stale, but a wealth of imagination was there, in teenage literature.[6] An avid reader of *Creepshow* magazine and other comic books, King was also a regular moviegoer. Films such as *Dawn of the Dead, Invasion of the Body Snatchers, The Amityville Horror, I Was a Teenage Werewolf* and *The Texas Chainsaw Massacre* left a strong impression on him. Although it had become standard fare, this culture was still considered somewhat disreputable, in the same way as intellectuals today prefer not to know what their children read or watch on television or at the movies.

King made a double-or-nothing wager. His ambition was to give fantastic literature values that were acceptable to the general public by sending the message to a humiliated America (which had not even begun to dream that Russian communism would one day spontaneously collapse) that, although a winner's life may be a chain of hardships, at the end of the road lies the promise of success. King's happy endings fill only a few pages. On the other hand, his descriptions of pain and suffering take time. He was a voracious reader of Alexandre Dumas, so he knew that readers could be kept hanging on for hundreds of pages while the author describes, for example, the oubliette from which the Count of Montecristo would attempt to escape. The longer these trials and tribulations, the greater the promised revenge.

Closed or linear spaces are places for racking up vendettas: they draw a path that leads through a succession of ordeals, like the Stations of the Cross, and one by one these raise the promise of redemption at the end of the road. King creates such places in many of his books: in *The Shining*,[7] it is the isolated hotel; in *Misery*,[8] the locked room where the hero is held prisoner. In his story "Shawshank,"[9] it is the prison cell from which Dufresne, a model prisoner in an American penitentiary, digs a tunnel with a tiny pick. In other settings, it is a little raft[10] that carries along a group of youngsters until they are sucked into an evil lake, or a supermarket which is descended upon by a diabolical mist.[11] It is the home of an aging Nazi where the evil teenager of "Apt Pupil"[12] takes refuge, initially to hear his stories of the Jewish extermination, and, once he has turned the tables on his host, to put his new-found knowledge to the test. In "The Boogeyman,"[13] it is the closet from which the imaginary monster emerges to come and kill the children. In *Thinner*,[14] it is the bathroom where the dieting hero incessantly goes to weigh himself. It is the classroom where the young hero of *Rage*[15] takes his classmates hostage and even kills some of them. And it is the abandoned well in which a husband, mortally wounded by his darling wife Dolores Clairborne, lies trapped.[16]

There are also linear spaces along which certain characters must move in order to progress from one stage to the next. A number of King's books use this type of unwinding technique: in *The Dark Tower*,[17] a worn-out, wounded gunslinger makes his way along a narrow, imaginary beach, stuck between a sea of monsters and a bluff filled with scenes of horror. The dangers materialize one by one, some in the form of giant lobsters with razor-sharp claws. In *Run or Die*,[18] the road race in which the organizers kill all of the competitors except the winner is run along a country road which no one can escape from. *Running Man*[19] takes readers panting along a New Yorker's jog through hell with inner-city ruffians at his heels. Many stories take place around a confined linear space: in "The Body,"[20] a group of youngsters playing on a railroad track become surrounded by a deadly swamp, which they will fall into if they step off the tracks, and in "Night Surf"[21] a group of children who have survived an apocalypse are forced to live on a beach. In "The Ledge,"[22] the hero must edge his way around a building, with the pavement three hundred feet below, in order to win a bet.

Trains and roads are symbols of doom. The only way to escape is through an accident, which brings death to some and survival to others. In "The Breathing Method,"[23] a pregnant woman who is decapitated in an accident continues to breathe and gives birth to a healthy baby.

King created this type of role playing, in which the entire environment is transformed into an obstacle course strewn with dead ends, cages, and paths that go around in circles, making his characters' lives resemble a game of shutes and ladders. The computer has since perfected a similar kind of mobile captivity in a highly visual version. A little man composed of high- or low-definition pixels, must make his way through a succession of obstacles over a course that rolls out like a conveyor belt. If he becomes skewered, snipped to bits, dismembered, swallowed, or drowned, he is immediately resuscitated at the starting point. In their obsession with winning this game, teenagers can become trapped for nights on end, shut up in a sensory prison and an endless cycle that constantly leads them back to "square one." What could be a more fitting image of eternal damnation?

The third and last sort of closed space in King's writing is that of a small isolated village in the forest or in the mountains. Such spaces include the haunted village in "Jerusalem's Lot"[24] or the lost town in Nebraska where a group of abandoned children form a cult to worship the corn, in "Children of the Corn."[25] Others include Little Tall Island, the middle-class island town in *Dolores Clairborne*. Variations on deadly dull northeastern American suburbs appear in *Pet Sematary, It,* and *The Tommyknockers*. The most terrifying that I have come across is the tiny village depicted in *Needful Things*, which becomes plagued by a seemingly friendly shopkeeper's rumors and which I can picture in my mind's eye: a community of middle-class Americans (many of whom could be the parents of a serial killer) living in a morass of boredom and repressed feelings of spite for their neighbors.

The terrifying thing about these places is the circular bond which connects their reassuring ordinariness with a propensity to isolate oneself from the civic and cultural world and thus to create a community of savages. Here, King's work is reminiscent of the nightmare portrayed by John Boorman in *Deliverance*. People who have seen this 1972 film will remember that it is the story of four friends who decide to go kayaking in a wooded region somewhere in North America, where they encounter a group of virtually mute hillbillies, who bear all the signs of generations of incest. The natural paradise is transformed into a living hell when one of the group is raped by the inhabitants. When the hero of the story kills the rapists, the local population mysteriously finds out and gangs up against the terrified men in order to kill them. Two of the "good guys" manage to survive the trip down the river, on which they are in open view of their hidden pursuers. But only one of them comes through the ordeal with his mind intact: the one with the wild streak, naturally.

What we have here is an explanation of the Anglo-American world's fascination with power; for criminal violence and the violence that leads to freedom are inextricably linked. The anxiety which we experience by living in a world where we enjoy so much freedom seems to sustain an aggressive, vengeful energy in people, which prevents them from becoming prisoners of their free will.

In 1974, Boorman produced another excellent film, called *Zardoz*, which was once again related to his obsession with isolated places, although this time he used a socially symmetrical setting: a futuristic camp for the elite, which is cut off from civilization. In this perhaps premonitory science-fiction film, he paints a picture of post-World War III bourgeois society, shut off in an ecological microparadise that is like a country club separated from the rest of the world. Around it, humanity has returned to a state of nature and is kept this way by a secret military group (led by Sean Connery). The unity between the outside world and civilization is restored when the mercenaries understand that they have been manipulated and invade the paradise to take power.

Zardoz (a title derived from *The Wizard of Oz*, a hundred-year-old fantasy inspired by Celtic legends) is a transposition of the Odinic myth of the fall of Asgard, the city of the Nordic gods, which is sacked by demons. Unlike the myth, which was popularized by Wagner in *Götterdämmerung*, the demons as Boorman portrays them are a group of powerful leaders who lock themselves up in an Edenic city.

The fact that this film-maker's career never really took off (his two relative commercial successes being *Excalibur* in 1981 and *The Emerald Forest* in 1985) may perhaps be explained by the fact that he is too frank in affirming the heroic and apocalyptic meaning of a theme that is central in Nordic literature and simultaneously in approaching the dangerous zone of extreme right-wing fantasy.

By contrast, Stephen King, who writes about far-off lonely places, hardly appears to pose a threat to the tranquillity of America's collective conscience. He does not allow any symbolic inversions between the small closed system (where people are tortured) and the large open system (where one would always enjoy the benefits of freedom) to occur in his works. When reading King, one often thinks: "These out-of-the-way places are full of lunatics!" but one seldom thinks: "Our dreams of a machine-operated society are going to get the better of us in the end." Boorman, on the other hand, clearly suggests this, as have a number of other authors who are on the other end of the ideological spectrum, including British and Americans from the beatnik generation, who in some cases (Stanley Kubrick, for example) were censured in their own countries. Yet what is the crime in recalling something which Anglo-American culture already has a strong intuition about, i.e. that civilization is precarious?

The more it fills the immense space that houses its "system," its networks, its market, and its technology, the more civilization resembles a thin residue floating on the surface of a savage reality. The slightest commotion could cause this bubble to burst, reducing even erudite Harvard graduates to a state of flesh-eating brutes: fundamentally, the dinosaur theme in *Jurassic Park* carries exactly the same message.

Shock and Terrify

Frightening people is a literary and cinematographic art form that is harmless as long as no real risk is incurred. Criminal terrorism, however, is intolerable. The difference between the two is fundamental, and yet in both cases the actors work in the same way: they push their targets (whether real victims or an audience) into a place where they lose their footing.

In a collection of essays on his work,[26] Stephen King describes ten basic fears, which he refers to jokingly as "fear-bears": the fear of closed places, of the dark, of sticky things, of deformity, of snakes, of rats, of insects, of death, fear of others, and fear for others. He gives an interpretation of a George Langlahan story, which appeared in *Playboy* and later became the basis for the film *The Fly*, as a combination of the fear of deformity and the fear of insects. King himself combined the fear of the dark and fear for other people when he wrote "The Boogeyman."

This methodical listing of psychological weaknesses reveals that, behind the more romantic character of the novelist, King is also a cataloguer. It exposes a sadistic tendency in authors who attempt to control others through the fear they inflict on them, reminiscent of psychotics who cannot stand other people's presence unless they themselves have "the last word." If they do not, they have the sensation they are disappearing. This is a way of trapping others to avoid being trapped oneself, a strange fantasy that totally destroys self-confidence.

In order to sustain feelings of disorientation, horror, and terror in their victims and prevent them from finding sources of reassurance, sadists need to be inventive. They do this by setting the tone for their actions, like a concert pianist who captures the audience (with feelings of joy, as opposed to terror) by leading them from one unexpected sensation to another. Agatha Christie perfected this now classic plot-setting technique in *And Then There Were None*, which has been emulated in detective fiction ever since.

Tom Harris is another good example. He forces the reader to "become" the sadistic subject of the book and therefore to enjoy the horrifying surprises he holds in store for the victims. For instance, when a policeman reconstructs a double murder committed by Francis Dolarhyde, alias "The Red Dragon," he accuses Dolarhyde of having taken pleasure in terrorizing the woman (by forcing her to witness another murder) before killing her: "Mrs Leeds was lovely, wasn't she? You turned on the light after you cut his throat, so Mrs Leeds could watch him flop, didn't you?"[27] The reader is projected into the murderer's mind, and thereby into the thoughts of a woman who watches helplessly as her husband is killed, knowing that she also is doomed.

Creating alternating feelings of hope and fear in the victim augments the killer's sense of control. Later in the novel, Dolarhyde attacks a reporter who once described him as insane, kidnaps him, and plays cat-and-mouse games with him until the last minute, first making him believe that he is saved and then drenching him with gasoline and setting him on fire, bound to a wheelchair that he sends hurtling down a hill. This is one sadist who also has a taste for showmanship!

Harris subtly intertwines the killer's sadistic relationship with the victim with the relation between author and reader, but King had already perfected this method for putting his readers into a state of shock. The first pages of King's *Carrie*[28] open with a description of the girl's menstrual blood flowing into the shower drain in a school-gym locker room. This "nonviolent" blood is just a foreshadowing of the real massacres to come, and is all the more frightening in retrospect.

King often uses bodily secretions to shock the reader: saliva, vomit, diarrhea, sweat, bloody noses, razor nicks, ejaculation, urine, and so on. All are part of everyday life, but the puritanical rules of etiquette require silence on such matters. Like a perennial teenager (who also writes for teenagers), King has a liking for scatological turns of phrase. "Oh shit, it's shit!" yells the guard when he discovers that Dufresne has escaped through the sewer system in "Shawshank." But, under this cover of crude language, King delivers moral messages: "He went up to his room and masturbated." Who would be guilty of this type of offense? The evil neo-Nazi boy in "Apt Pupil," of course, who suddenly yells "Suck my cock!" at his mentor, a former SS officer named Dussander. When Dussander calmly describes sending people to the gas chambers in *Zyklon. B*, he explains: "They then began to vomit and defecate involuntarily." The elderly man adds that he personally has to rely on suppositories to move his bowels.

King is not the only author to tap this scatological vein. British author Clive Barker speaks elegantly in his novel *Cabal* (written in a rather bombastic style) of the taste of "shit rising up in the mouth." This is a commonly used method, which transports the reader to a world where things are less reliable than they seem and awakens his sense of terror by activating his phobias.

Another method consists in speaking about atrocities and death in derisive terms, as if to indicate that anything can happen in a book because the destruction of a (fictional) human being is meaningless. One such example is that of a furiously jealous husband explaining to the reporter whom he is trying to force out onto the ledge of a building that, if he falls from the forty-seventh floor, when he hits the pavement his body will make a sound like an overripe watermelon exploding.[29]

Deceive and Mislead

Unsettling one's victims or readers is a way of "keeping a grip on them." The tactic is to give them false hopes, to manipulate what they believe is true, and to lead them into error.

Trickery is the art of the gods of the professional trades – a real group of con men: Mercury, with his twisted caduceus, is the god of thieves, criminals, physicians, and merchants. His Nordic alter ego Odin is referred to as the "craftsman of woe," because, with his talent for cunning, he is able to lay traps and provoke people to kill each other. He works incognito, disguised with a mask or a hat, a wolf skin (*ulfhed*) or a bearskin (*berserk*).[30] He is an excellent artificer, both in warfare and in love.

Deception is accepted in fiction in the same way that it is at a circus, because readers, like an audience of "rubbernecks" at the big top, know that there are no lasting consequences in this game. But deception is also a prelude to murder, and it facilitates repetition of the crime. John E. List killed his wife, his son, and his daughter by calling them home one by one from their outside activities (a job, a friend's house, school) and shooting them in the head, and none of them ever knew what had happened to the others.[31] In general, the "tricks" that serial killers use to deceive their victims, such as hiding their real intentions, breaking into the victims' homes, or luring them outside, are improvised with incredible sang-froid. Like Odin, Ottis Toole never showed his feelings: he was a calm, quiet factory worker (a welder, to be precise). He only went hunting at night. Lucas was both a beast and a con man, and had the ability to deceive and persuade. In the film *Henry: Portrait of a Serial Killer*,[32] it is suggested that the murderer pretended to be in love with Becky, a girl who had witnessed his slaying of her brother, and that he lured her away and killed her in a motel.

In the real story of Henry Lee Lucas's life, deception is also at work. He killed a woman who in complete confidence hired him to work as a handyman. He also killed Becky Powell, probably in a surprise attack, and then strewed the nine pieces of her dismembered body in a field.

But, if trickery lets the killer mislead his victims for the pleasure of seeing them panic (perhaps in so doing the killer feels less lost himself), it is not without risk, for nothing can more easily be turned against him; there is no situation more ambiguous.

One of Odin's incarnations is *Vidolfr*, the "red-eyed" wolf who lives in the forest, an ancestor of modern-day hunters and wearers of infrared glasses, who are able to spot their prey in the dark; but he paid a heavy price for this ability. He might love to make people lose their way in the woods (like Stephen King, who makes his character Mrs Todd lose her way along a shortcut through the Vermont forest[33]), but in order to earn his manipulative powers he had to sacrifice an eye to memory (*Mimir*), leaving him half blind or even sightless (*Blindi*).

CHAPTER THREE

Cruelty

Kill or Torture?

Once his victim has been captured, imprisoned, and filled with terror, a hunter has two possibilities: either he will make a quick meal of it, or go slowly and have some enjoyment. Here, the more refined pleasure of inflicting pain before killing or devouring becomes the antithesis (in appearance) of voracious animal energy. Killing in great numbers or causing suffering thus becomes a choice between opposites.

Of course, in some exceptional cases, the two are combined. Between 1972 and 1983, Randy Kraft, a computer genius and cracker of military codes, killed sixty-seven persons, all described with care in a book that was recovered after his death. He was also a sadist, and dismembered his victims while they were still alive, burned, and sodomized them.[1] He was judged guilty of *a mere* sixteen murders. Another unusual case is that of Dean Corll, David Brooks, and Elmer Henley, who killed and tortured twenty-seven young boys in Houston between 1972 and 1973. Yet another is that of antique dealer Robert Berdella, who between 1984 and 1988 tortured six teenagers with electrical wires and then killed them.

But, with the exception of such rare examples, hardened serial killers are only vaguely interested in torture and become much more engrossed in post-mortem dismemberment, somehow memorializing their victims by cutting them into pieces.

It is, however, undeniable that a few criminals manifest real pleasure in leading people slowly down a path of fear and suffering and in placing their victims in a state of vulnerable inferiority.

What are they searching for when they indulge in these sadomasochistic acts? An author of books on vampires – imaginary serial killers – offers the following explanation: "What a dream come true for the hateful, the weak and the repressed to become wild beasts and to possess strength, violence and irresistible sadistic tendencies; to no longer feel pain but to inflict it voluptuously; nor pity, but to take their vengeance continuously; to no longer tremble but to horrify; a fine prospect!"[2]

Certain motives – hatred, vengeance, and especially the desire to exercise an influence over others – thus become comprehensible; one might even sympathize with them. And, indeed, killers who describe themselves as sadists also subscribe to this social commentary. For example, one of the serial killers who often used the media as a mirror to inflate his own ego, the so-called zodiac killer, sent a letter to the San Francisco press in which, like a homespun Marquis de Sade, he described in vivid (and apparently humorous) detail various outlandish forms of torture whose sole purpose was to demonstrate the torturer's supremacy over the victim: tying his sex slaves to an anthill and observing them as they writhed in pain; force-feeding them salt-preserved meat and refusing to give them anything to drink; skinning them alive to enjoy the sound of their screams; or locking them in a dungeon and forcing them to play pool in shoes that didn't fit.

This childish message (which may have been nothing more than a prank) is ironic to the point of parodying Gilbert and Sullivan's *Mikado*.[3] But this does not mean that he never acted out his literary descriptions in reality. In any case, if the letter writer did not do so, his alter ego Gary Heidnik, who struck several years later in Philadelphia, may well have done: Heidnik's satanic practices were the model for Tom Harris's character James Gumb, who trapped his prisoners in a pit and starved them. In 1986, he transformed the basement of his house into a harem, where he kept sexual slaves. He kidnapped a number of young women and brutalized and tortured them with electrical shocks or by plunging a screwdriver into their ears. He killed two and fed their bodies to his dogs. He was sentenced to death in 1988.

Another case is that of Herman Webster Mudgett (also known as Holmes), who commissioned a veritable house of horrors to be built in Chicago, with fireproof rooms, oubliettes, gas chambers, torture chambers, and various accessories. Despite the discovery of the remains of twenty-seven skeletons on the premises, he was only convicted of one murder. But that murder was enough to sentence him to death by hanging, in May 1986.

In reality, true sadists are uncommon even among serial killers, and they rarely externalize the sick jubilation that they are rumored to experience. People who have commented on heinous crimes tend to amplify, or even to invent, a sadistic side to these acts, as if to cover the banal (and hence even more atrocious) reality of the crime with cries of horror. The crime is thus smothered with exaggeration, the purpose of which seems to be to hide the even more intolerable, absurd meaninglessness of the murder.

The media provided an example of such exaggeration when it spread the idea that Roman Polanski's wife Sharon Tate, who was murdered by the Charles Manson "girls," had had her breasts cut off and had been tortured sexually; and this was how the crime went down in the entire world's memory. However, the horror of the act was both more "humane" and more insane than this. In reality, Sharon Tate was stabbed to death by a mystical madman when she was eight months pregnant. The murderer aimed for the chest in order not to harm the baby, who would not have died had the mother's body been discovered sooner. But the media preferred to condense the crime into a satanic image of the perverse desire to mutilate.

In another example of fictive satanic practices, when Bret Easton Ellis published his *American Psycho*,[4] the story of an imaginary killer who subjects some twenty female victims to horrifying forms of torture, he raised a storm of protest from feminist groups, who accused him of creating "new recipes for torturing women."[5] But these reactions reinforce the credibility of the perverse pattern, used by the author to intentionally distort real paranoid schizophrenic practices, of which we will examine some striking examples later. For, by placing a piece of cheese in a woman's vagina and releasing a starving rat to go after it, or by making another of his victim's breasts explode, Ellis's imaginary criminal adopts a socialized sadistic behavior that plays to the gallery. His one desire is to wring cries of horror from his audience. Real psychotic killers do not respond to fictional blueprints in this way.

What interests truly sadistic killers, and what is more unbearable than scenes of wrenching pain or obscenity, is to chase down their victims, to catch them, and to draw out their suffering in order constantly to reanimate something that ultimately escapes the killer: the very essence of human life. The criminally insane bear only a fleeting resemblance to the sado-masochists portrayed in novels and film. At a certain point, and without warning, the killer's slightly perverse pleasure exceeds "normal" limits and a cloak of silence shrouds the scene. The awful truth then becomes clear: there is no secret horror lurking beyond this silence; all are silent because, before a pure act of life and death, there is nothing left to say. There is a hush: human beings cease speaking to each other. They become animals, or less than animals: they are stumps, worn and tattered by the wind (which, according to Scandinavian lore, is what humans were before the Word).

Sadism as Part of "Human" Nature

Therefore, people take literary depictions of sadistic fantasy too seriously. Moreover, there are many noncriminal sadomasochists, who, despite their leather clothing, chains, rubber, and the assortment of rings in their ears, lips, and nipples, never indulge in blood crimes and certainly not in murder. They navigate in a passive–aggressive orbit of fantasies based on social inequality, reliving the relationship between baby and mother: a tiny, tender, and passive being that wants to become the pleasure toy of an active giant.

Even in cases where the criminal actually believes that a sadistic scenario which drives his compulsion to repeat a criminal act is real, sadism is still a fiction, a backdrop, a display of symbols. Modern fiction incorporates the idea of sadism to a certain extent, because it tries to connect the nonsensical nature of crime with an "evil" intention, whereas real criminals, as I have found consistently throughout my research, exhibit only nondesire and a mechanical, nonhuman compulsion. Tales of perverted passion are therefore an attempt (by the police or by novelists) to humanize the criminally insane or to make them subject to a debate in which a desire can be used to explain the basis for the motivation of their crimes. And it is only once this desire has been established that they can be condemned as degenerates.

American fiction was born from the myth of a mad hunter, a hunter who possesses intolerable characteristics. But, when real criminals reveal their base candor, fiction attempts to bias the brutal truths they expose. Stories attempt to blunt the sharp edges of reality and make it fit into a category of reprehensible pleasure, but they do not deny that all forms of unprovoked brutality exist.

There is some ambiguity in the wall that has been built up against a kind of unspeakable atrocity that indulges evil pleasures, and criminals are not always wrong when they refute such interpretations. Moreover, when murderers try to make themselves appear more human, they often use the opposite tack, i.e., they argue that they are engaged in an aggressive, paranoid battle to ward off their enemies. They present themselves as combatants. This, as we shall see later, makes them the most faithful – but also the least credible – embodiment of the warrior myth.

Making the Pain Last

This has become a common technique in movie making. Instead of the ritualistic sadomasochistic orgies depicted in Clive Barker's films, where the heroes are poked with safety pins,[6] this genre includes the horrifying *Reservoir Dogs*,[7] in which the audience watches two police officers in the throes of death, bleeding profusely, and being tortured for over an hour. One of them is tied to a chair, and a smiling criminal calmly removes one of his ears as rock music plays in the background. Severed ears as a prelude to a series of sick pleasures have in fact become a very popular motif, both in fiction (*Koko, The Red Dragon*) and on the screen, including the discovery of an ear by the inhabitants of a small American town in David Lynch's 1986 film *Blue Velvet*.

Stephen King must also be mentioned here, because most of his texts are constructed around a long-lasting scene of pain, which is broken down into smaller time sequences that unfold like so many additional forms of torture. One of King's favorite techniques is to introduce a measurer of time, a modern variation on Edgar Allan Poe's pendulum.[8] Many chapters or sections of his books have a specific date and time as their title. Official documents are also used to mark time: a dated contract, a death certificate, newspaper articles relating bizarre happenings, coroners' reports, and so on. King takes great care to mark the progression of his stories with such pieces of objective evidence, thereby giving the horrors that his characters suffer, minute by minute, a tone of authenticity.

The brutal portrayal of atrocities that occur just outside the realm of normal life is a classic construction. Years ago, Roger Caillois remarked that it was this that set "fantastic" fiction apart from fairy tales. King has a subtle way of applying this principle, which harks back to philosophical roots. To the question: what mundane occurrence could lend itself to a horror story? King's answer would be: anything that is regularly repeated in the human body, anything that links time with biology.

In *Carrie*, he uses the female body's built-in reference to the irreversible cycle of life: menstruation. This takes him back to the ancient taboo that links menstrual flow to the lunar phases and associates it with the existence of uncontrollable female powers. It is the horror of discovering her natural sexuality that triggers Carrie's "abilities" (telekinesis, or the ability to move objects, in parascientific language). Her tragic end is brought on because of the connection she establishes between the transition into adulthood and an unbearable feeling of dirtiness, which drives her to "displace" increasingly dangerous objects.

But King's specialty is to draw out the most excruciating moments of pain. Commenting on King's work, McDowell[9] points out that what makes his narrative so effective is the perfect balance he achieves between moments of mounting tension and moments of relief. This sadistic technique encourages us to believe that the scenes of torture will lead to something else. Just when we think they are finally over, he springs a new, more abominable scene on us, although we cannot imagine a higher summit of horror than the last.

One of King's preoccupations is imagining how a victim who has been prepared for the slaughter (by being bound, locked up, wounded, etc.) can find a way to keep going on, despite the fact that everything is in league to immobilize, shatter, and defeat him, and to make him wild with fear. He creates the most terrible effect in *The Long Walk*, not by making the reader realize that almost all of the characters will be killed, but rather by describing their growing state of exhaustion, which is only exacerbated by their hostility toward each other. In *Misery*, the wounded hero's misadventures following his escape from a car accident, after which he is immobilized and later maimed by a demented nurse, are recounted in detail on every page, repeated and heightened by anxiety. "The Last Rung on the Ladder" is a story about a girl who amuses herself by jumping from high places until she finally kills herself, very much like the masochistic roommate in Polanski's *Single White Female*.

Drawing out time by elaborating on details is not reserved exclusively for torturing the characters in a novel. It is a general technique that is applied to things and to words: when Charlie, another "gifted" child character, sets the three cars of his pursuers on fire by means of mental telepathy, the author provides a second-by-second account of what happens in each car, describing in "slow motion" how they smolder, and minutely recounting the explosion, combustion, and resulting spray of molten metal.

King also puts readers to the test by force-feeding them long literary passages, endless digressions, biographical recapitulations, and vaguely philosophical observations, which only intensify the anticipation of the horror to come. It was King who said (surprisingly) that the best way to keep the reader's attention is to bore him. His precursors are also unrestrained practitioners of dogmatic writing: contemporary American horror fiction has a rather dull "science-lesson" side to it, which is supposed to amplify the atrocities that it foreshadows or prefigures. In the books *Le Jeu du chien-loup* or *The Red Dragon*, readers must plow through the discussion of a group of coroners (a technique one also finds in detective fiction). In *The Silence of the Lambs*, we are given a lesson on moths (the killer's emblem being a skull-headed bombycid). In *The Mask of Loki*,[10] readers are subjected to a course on the war methods of the Templars in the Middle East. In many books, American institutions, including the police, the justice system, or the university, and in some cases geopolitical projects, etc. are described in detail. Despite their trivial or even entertaining and interesting aspects, these scholarly diversions add to the cold rationality that is characteristic of many such books.

King attempts to understand why he received so many letters from readers claiming to have enjoyed every line of *The Shining*:

I think that the key to this may lie in a line of movie criticism from *Newsweek* magazine. The review was of a horror film, not a very good one, and it went something like this: "A wonderful movie for people who like to slow down and look at car accidents." It's a good snappy line, but when you stop to think about it, it applies to all horror films and stories.[11]

I would add that this is true insofar as reveling in horror is one of the basic components of sadism; for fiction writers are at pains to equal or surpass with their imaginations the real acts of the most depraved criminals, or to attain a level of professionalism which even approaches that of police interrogation officers. But what form of "confession" are they trying to obtain from the public, which is an avid consumer of these depictions of horror? Perhaps they hope to coax out of its shell of silence and nebulous meaning the confession that people have a fear of being alive, and to make this a matter of public concern in order to bring it under control.

Memories

After laying the traps that place the victim at their mercy and then destabilizing him with fear and making him wild with pain, sadists relive the most significant moments of the experience in their imagination, to such a point that it is not clear whether their pleasure comes from actually causing pain or from representing it after the fact in their mind's eye or through the eye of a camera.

Harvey Murray Glattman was arrested in 1954. He killed young women whom he had recruited through the personal columns ("Seeking young lady who likes to dance"), but he first raped and carefully photographed them. A collection of photographs which he had taken just before his victims' deaths was discovered among his belongings.

Jerome Brudos had the same love of photography, as well as a fetish for shoes and garter belts, which were the subjects of his photography. Their captive models were all murdered, of course. *Peeping Tom*, by Michael Powell, gives a powerful cinematographic interpretation of Brudos's fantasy. Carl Boehm plays the part of the assassin who filmed his victims and killed them, using the camera tripod as a sword. Distributed in 1960, this work drew severe criticism from the establishment, but it was considered to be a masterpiece of British film making.

Toole and Lucas are also supposed to have filmed the slaying of their victims. This, at least, is the legend that was introduced by the movie *Henry, Portrait of a Serial Killer*, in which the audience witnesses the slaughter of an entire family via a video camera, which the criminals are said to have brought to the scene of the crime.

It is difficult to say whether the rumors about "snuff movies" were created by the existence of real video footage of murders filmed on the scene and distributed clandestinely, or whether this is a sick publicity stunt by the horror-film industry. It is certain, however, that a number of serial killers (such as Berdella, Kemper, and Dahmer) were indeed amateur video-film makers and that they preserved their crimes on film so as to have a lasting image of the bodies in various stages of dismemberment. It cannot be denied that certain killers have a true fascination for death: a sort of hungry surprise that is reproduced every time they discover that life does not exist "in the body." The worst sadists are often in search of something they have lost. They are just one step above schizophrenic criminals, whom we will discuss later.

One of the most illustrative cases is that of police officer Gerard John Schaefer,[12] who struck in Florida in the 1970s. He is alleged to have killed thirty-four women, twenty of whom have been proved to have been his victims. He used his authority to apprehend them, then took them into the woods, where he conducted sessions of rape and suspension with ropes, which he attached to his car. He took his time, occasionally leaving to return to work. He killed his victims by hanging, sacrificing them ritually (which harkens back to Odin, also known as *Hangagaud*, the god of the hanged). He spoke to them, played on their fears and hopes, drew pictures of them, photographed them, and seemed to be particularly interested in the involuntary defecation which occurs during hanging. He was captured thanks to one of his victims, who escaped during his absence, and a wealth of clues were discovered in his home: women's clothing and jewelry, piles of sadistic magazines, and a collection of drawings and collages showing scenes of himself hanging women. In some cases, he had added "captions" exhorting readers to come watch these victims as they dangled from the end of a rope.

But why are sadistic killers so fascinated by the way life "dangles" at the moment of death that they totally ignore the person from whom they are taking it?

Why Sadism?

Real sadists appear to be less fascinated by physical pain (like the sharp pain of a tooth being drilled, as portrayed in spy films from the 1960s) than by the suspension of time, which allows them to savor the "best" moments, when the victim displays his human nature as he loses his human dignity: in sudden transitions from assurance to surprise, from dignity to supplication, from consciousness to unconsciousness, and from life to death.

One might think that this careful attention is directed toward a person who is not present and for whom the victim is a substitute. It is as if the sadist were making the victim suffer before slaying him in order to create the illusion that he is killing someone else. The victim is made to play the role of a living person who, in death, forsakes himself. But the sadist does not want to forsake or lose anything. He will not deny himself the enjoyment of his violent behavior or his love–hate pleasures. On the contrary, he preserves these through his nonconfrontation with the symbolic presence. By assuring himself that there is no one – that is, no real human being – behind the person who is made to suffer and die, the sadist is in turn assured that he is free to live and take his pleasure when and how he wishes. In Freudian terms, sadistic murderers seek to create a situation in which the absence of the human element, i.e. the father in his societal role, leaves them free to usurp the power and supposed strength of the father without having to symbolically murder him.

By removing themselves from the situation in which they place others, however, and by destroying their victims, sadists find themselves faced with the absurdity of an empty world and their doubts return. They are compelled to repeat their acts, because, once the victim's cries have been silenced, the world of pleasure and the world of death are once again separated, and the specter of the father figure rises again. If he were to face the absurdity of his acts, a sadist would be annihilated, and he therefore must plunge back in, by either watching films of past crimes or reliving them in his mind.

We should recall the story of the nomad Ilk hunters, who were studied by Colin Turnbull.[13] This Ugandan ethnic group, who were removed from their territory when it became a national park, are only able to survive through acts of cruelty, which seem to be their way of denying their unhappy fate by ridiculing the weak: tripping an elderly man, making a stranger lose his way, beating a child with a stick, and so on. But, if cruelty helps them to survive, it also seems to have doomed the group to live in the same abject conditions that they ridicule in other societies. By laughing at the pain they inflict on others, the Ilks appear to be saying that it is they who take the beating, lose their way, fall, and suffer violence, and that, in a sense, they like it; for, ultimately, they prefer pain to annihilation.

Masochism: the "Wrong Way Out"

This leads us to the pleasures of sustaining pain as opposed to inflicting it. Masochism is common among aggressive criminals (such as Albert Fish, who had a predilection for self-inflicted burns, and Edmund Kemper, who played "chicken" in the road). It can also be detected in the outbursts of combative rage that are described in novellas and sagas. It may take the form of a ruse, or of a test of strength. The patience of a tortured hero only legitimates his revolt and his urge to counterattack. This is a classic story line in American film, for example in *Rambo*, whom we see being battered on the screen, pectoral muscles a-quivering, glistening with sweat and blood, with his eyes turned skyward like a grotesque Christ figure, before he takes his revenge on the evil enemy.[14]

Masochism exists as a variant of courage in societies that celebrate heroes (it is recalled that, in a number of Amerindian ethnic groups, symbolic status is raised by voluntary submission to torture). Self-inflicted suffering thus acquires value, as, for example, when Odin hangs himself from a tree for nine days and puts out one of his own eyes in order to attain knowledge.

Masochism also has a derivative function: to avoid having to make a confession of cowardice, or to gain acceptance among a warrior community despite one's cowardice. Warriors – who are "big babies" – have no choice but to admit that they are cowardly. If they were not, they would find the wherewithal to reform and to strengthen their moral fiber through a form of virility that corresponds to contemporary cultural development. It is in this area that they lack courage, preferring to boast and brag rather than to acquire the true virtues of a "real man." This is one of the most familiar themes in mythology. According to the saga, Sigurd, slayer of the dragon Fafnir, is not as heroic as he appears. For, it is in fact Reginn who shows him how to spear the dragon as it passes by the hiding place where Sigurd is safely out of sight. Nor does Sigurd die a hero's death: in one version of the story, he is slain ignominiously in the forest by his half brother; in another, he is stabbed to death as he sleeps beside his wife. His only claim to being a hero is that he is a man of his word. Because he preserves this bond of honor, everything that has dishonored him is forgiven and, because of his faults and weaknesses, he is allowed to seek redemption.

This is where masochism comes in. As a paradigm of penitence through small doses of pain, masochism takes the form of a series of propitiatory or initiatory tests. People believe themselves to be better and stronger because they have been subject to terrible and countless tortures. One frequently observes eroticism in self-imposed violence, experienced as punishment from the mother or a maternal figure. The boar, for example, in the myth of Adonis is Aphrodite's pet. Orpheus is torn apart by female assailants.[15] Similarly, one recalls the young girls who flagellate Artemis Orthia, Thessalos, who is battered by his mother, Ulysses transformed into a horse by the witch Hals, Diomedes devoured by the mares of Heracles, Aura, who eats the sons of Dionysos, the Lemnien women with their foul breath, who murder their wayward husbands, and so on. By suffering instead of challenging their leader, masochistic warriors create a link between their fear and their imaginary pleasures. Unable to control their mothers, they take pleasure in making themselves objects of the mother. They change from agents to "patients." This is often true of multiple killers, such as Chase, Mullin, Kemper, Bundy, and others, whose retreat into a world of pain is modeled after their dysfunctional relationship with their mothers, as we shall see.

However, the effects of masochism and the historical fact that masochism helped to bring our civilization's heroic, barbarian past to an end should not be misinterpreted: masochism is closely related to constantly relived fantasies of assault, aggression, and premeditated murder. The act of turning masochistic violence against oneself may reveal certain inadequacies in the "combatant" model, but it also reinforces this model.

The combination of sadism and masochism locks people up in a cycle of distress. The criminally insane who kill are therefore not only a symbol of resistance against a repressive society, they are also symptomatic of people's fear of not fitting the norm.

Often, murderers are portrayed as the casualties of other people's abuse. The victims of solitude, they also display a total inability to live autonomously or to enjoy their privacy. By slicing the bodies of the men he picked up and whom he suspected would later abandon him, Jeffrey Dahmer showed that a civilization of mutual manipulation and broken communication offers no reprieve, either from within or from without. The grim fate of being reduced to a mere "data byte" awaits anyone who plays this game. But Dahmer also reminds us that those who dare to break the code of work and money are condemned to a solitude in which meaning is annihilated and words cease to exist.

As mute about their crimes as the officers who ran the concentration camps and who treated as trite acts that were beyond description, multiple murderers are like a reincarnation of the Viking convicts banished into the forest to suffer the "sensory deprivation" of human contact (called *skoggangr*), which made them revert to a state of speechless, grunting beasts. But their exile also reminds us that eternal silence awaits anyone who seeks a community based on unconventional values. By giving this silence a material form through their appalling acts, serial killers, our modern-day werewolves, express a solidarity with the collective will to punish defection. They agree to play the role of the outcast, to endure the inevitable effects on their existence, and thus to reassure a purely repressive society, which acts as their guardian and their judge.

Cruelty: a Fear of Becoming Civilized

In concluding this chapter on cruelty, I am reminded of the title of a lecture given by the astrophysicist Hubert Reeves: "Is nature cruel?" This is one of the main questions that arose in relation to Darwinism, and it continues to haunt society today as we confront the daily reality of crime. One wonders if murderers are fundamentally impervious to the veneer of civilization, or if they are the result of the "forces of nature" and have remained in a savage state owing to some genetic or cultural aberration.

If one observes the debate between criminals and society, however, it seems more appropriate to ask whether it is not culture that has a monopoly on cruelty. For, if one defines cruelty not as making others suffer, but as taking an analytical approach to the effects of suffering and echoing them in representations of the self and of others, then cruelty is indeed a matter of culture. As a game in which one consciously sets oneself apart and does so calculatingly to achieve intense enjoyment, cruelty is the work of criminals and fiction writers, who could almost exchange roles: criminals inflict real suffering, but rarely pay attention to the details; writers deal only with imaginary suffering, but their boundaries are limitless.[16] Criminals destroy the setups they have created by killing, whereas writers are artists of the fantasy of killing.

Admittedly, killers have to work quickly for fear of being discovered, while authors have the time to construct a detailed plot. This may also be a question of talent: the delicate art of terror necessitates learning and practice, which are inaccessible to the murderer, who is incapable of waiting to act on his impulses or of forestalling a sudden urge. Criminals who try to be cruel are rarely able to go beyond games of cat and mouse, which are soon over, either because the victim has lost consciousness or because he has died. Fiction writers are more apt to take a languorous pleasure in imagined atrocities, in some cases filling thousands of pages. They can create characters who relish such perverse pleasures and through whom criminals are depicted as evil lovers of human flesh.

Sadomasochism as it is portrayed in American novels and films therefore begs the question of art's role in inciting violence. The provocative sadism in fiction or film writing derives from the elaborate care with which objects are prepared for destruction. So careful is this preparation that one forgets that its final outcome is death, and no amount of foreshadowing can change the total absence of meaning of death in fiction or film.

The fact that authors and film makers are so intrigued by the details of spectacular crime may be based on a shared desire to eliminate the moment when death must be stared in the face: i.e., when the sign of one's virility is a relinquishment of pleasure. This would mean that the art of sadism consists in a mute observation of horror rather than in an adventure beyond the norms of society. Sadists would rather be perversely humanized as killers than acknowledge their insanity. Hollywood's progressive subtle development of perversion in its no longer truly pure heroes seems to have reintroduced a pleasure principle into scenes that were once intended to depict the phobic dualism between violence and purity.

If novelists use the idea that there can be pleasure in atrocity to trigger their readers' indignation at the intentions of another human being, they also use it to solicit indulgence. In sadomasochistic tales, "bad-to-the-bone" villains who enjoy the pain of others still remain captivating figures, and their punishment by the forces of good can itself become sadistic, because of the pleasure involved in hunting the forces of evil.[17]

By maintaining that criminals are perverse, a violent culture may become caught up in a maze of twisted meanings. On the one hand, it expresses its distress over vicious acts, but, on the other hand, it admits that it no longer knows how to stop them.

Perhaps it does not want to stop them. After all, confronting the reality of the adult world, in which ideals cease to exist, is at times so difficult that it is better to imagine an enchanted realm where intentions, even if perverse, reign.

We have to hold on to this thread tightly, for it will lead us to the heart of the werewolf myth: hesitation, the fear of choosing, and the need to maintain two states that alternate between animal and human, insane and perverse, hunter and hunted, in constant motion.

CHAPTER FOUR

Ogres

Modern legends of savage "hunters" attempt to attribute a strong sexual desire to these criminals/gods. Their wild abandon is explained in terms of an urge or a passion: a love of hunting, a weakness for drink, a thrill in reckless speed, the cruel excitement of playing with terrorized and wounded prey, sadomasochistic practices, etc.

As we have seen, however, within this general scheme of explanation, opinions are divided into two groups: there are those who attribute destructive energy to an indiscriminate hunting instinct and those who see it instead as cruelty directed against one person. And, once the victim has been slain, this alternative reappears. In some cases, the victim is devoured with gusto, whereas, in others, phobia prevents direct consumption and instead perversely turns these feelings against the self or transforms them into a fantasy of purity.

We shall begin with the first interpretation, in which the murderer is seen as having a bulimic appetite for activity and a gluttony for violence.

The Paradoxical Taste for Murder

The very word ogre evokes images of Gargantuan gluttony. In fact, it is simply another variant of the name Odin (*Odr*), the central god in Celtic and Germanic legend. Commentators and novelists who deal with multiple crime, therefore, adopt an Odinesque interpretation when they describe murderers as being driven wild with burning desire and a hunger for pleasure. They can thus explain the sick urge to kill as a form of greed, and fuel the reader's hatred for those who actually indulge such reprehensible impulses.

Even without the introduction of sadism, such acts become surrounded with an aura of gourmet pleasure. Movies have suggested that, like Thor, who broke the necks of the giants' daughters, Ottis Toole and Henry Lucas broke the necks of prostitutes with a single sharp twist, and especially loved the snapping noise of cracking vertebrae. The noise of the neck vertebra snapping under a knife when the head detaches from the body was equally pleasing to Edmund Kemper, the Californian killer of well-to-do young girls. He explained this, seemingly without pretense: "You hear that little 'pop' when the head [is] separated from the body and you pull their heads off and hold their heads up by the hair. Whipping their heads off, their body sitting there. That'd get me off."[1]

Another – fictional – example is a scene in *The Silence of the Lambs* in which the young officer Clarice Starling goes in search of James Gumb, who is watching her from his basement through infrared glasses. He takes his time aiming a weapon at her, fantasizing (you can feel him salivating) about what he plans to do: first scalp her, then place the scalp on his own head to frighten the woman he is holding prisoner, and who hopes that Starling will come to her rescue:

> He played his infrared lamp up and down her. She was too slender to be of great utility to him. He remembered her hair, though, from the kitchen, and it was glorious, and that would only take a minute. He could slip it right off. Put it on himself. He could lean over the well wearing it and tell that thing, "Surprise". It was fun to watch her trying to sneak along. [. . .] It would have been fun to hunt her for a long time – he'd never hunted one armed before. He would have thoroughly enjoyed it. No time for that. Pity.[2]

The current trend of increasingly hard violence has led from the taste for killing, maiming, and dismembering, to cannibalism. Again, fiction tends to assume that this implies enjoyment. Tom Harris, for example, establishes a logical connection between his psychopathic killer's custom of devouring his victims' faces and his taste for fine cuisine: "Dr. Hannibal Lecter lay on his cot asleep, his head propped on a pillow against the wall. Alexandre Dumas's *Le Grand Dictionnaire de Cuisine* was open on his chest."[3]

Real cannibals seem to confirm this inclination: Ottis claimed he ate humans because "people taste good." When he was being tried for the murder of a child whose head was recovered from a canal in 1981, he admitted to killing the "delicious" boy.[4] According to a rumor, which he never denied, he cooked human flesh on a barbecue grill and ate it with his own special sauce. His friend Lucas bit his victims before killing them, then hacked them to pieces (the original meaning of the word "harrowing" comes to mind), removed their genitals, and eviscerated them. Although these self-proclaimed deeds may only be true in part, their effect is to spin out the myth that there is pleasure in crime, which is essential to arguments in favor of more severe sentencing.

Even the rarely established cases of criminals who kill "for pleasure" are portrayed as caricatures, such as the Albert Fish case, which dates from the 1930s in New York. Fish was an elderly excessive polymorphous pervert who took just as much enjoyment in cutting adolescents' or children's bodies into slices and cooking them as in indulging in coprophagia. His self-inflicted tortures ranged from jabbing needles in his skin to placing cotton wool in his anus and setting it on fire. He also enjoyed torturing his young sexual partners and sending pornographic letters to respectable married women. Fish claimed to have spared one of his "partners" when he saw that the pain he was causing him by attempting to cut off his penis had become too great. Does this mean that, at least occasionally, he had a "conscience"? Whatever the answer may be, Fish, a glutton for this type of stimulation, is quoted as having said: "Pain is so wonderful, if only it didn't hurt!"[5] This outrageous statement suggests that there were limits to his perversion, contrary to what the authors of serial-killer novels assume.

Fiction's Fascination with Hunger

As in its treatment of sadism, fiction is too expansive in its treatment of hunger. It embroiders and expands on it, mixes it up with other things, and gives it too much ornamentation. The real "cooks" here are not the killers, but the writers and the movie makers. In *The Silence of the Lambs,* a connection is made between intelligence (the insane psychiatrist Hannibal Lecter's extraordinary insight into others), the compulsion to devour (Lecter likes to eat his victims raw, starting with their faces[6]), and sick experiments (there is an example of another murderer who starves women to death so that he can remove their skin and wear it as clothing).

To create their monster, Tom Harris and Jonathan Demme[7] melded together the characteristics of several real criminals. The pit in which James Gumb leaves his prisoners to starve appears to be taken from the case of Gary Heidnik, who was sentenced to death in 1988. Heidnik founded a satanic cult (the United Church of the Ministers of God), in which he tortured women, but he was not interested in removing their skin or in making clothing out of it. This was the favorite indulgence of another criminal, Ed Gein, a famous psychiatric prisoner, who was interviewed by several film makers. He dug up female corpses and used their skin (like his imaginary emulator James Gumb[8]) to make jackets and face masks. He killed several times, but basically he was a necrophiliac (with memories of a possessive mother) and a fetishist. Using him as a model for the killer in

The Texas Chainsaw Massacre (who wore a mask made of skin) was therefore inaccurate. Hitchcock strayed from the original when he used Gein as the model for the killer in *Psycho,* who stuffs his dead mother's body. (This left Anthony Perkins with a lifelong phobia.)

Another inaccurate composite character is that of an anonymous letter writer who sends coded messages and Chinese ideograms to the newspapers (Tom Harris's character Jaws) and shares some traits with the zodiac killer.[9] However, the murders which have been most convincingly linked to the zodiac killer are more indicative of criminal insanity than of sadism. The mad psychiatrist in *The Silence of the Lambs* may in some ways suggest serial killer Ted Bundy, who also studied psychology, but Bundy neither dismembered nor ate his victims; however, he was truly sadistic and he practiced neck breaking on an industrial scale.

The truly insane do not have an equally bulimic appetite for a vast number of different perversions. Their personalities do not multiply in the same way as Americans multiply their debts, their homes, their divorces, and their cars, but are instead fixated on a precise, deep-rooted question. This is why, when they have worn out every possible combination in order to give their eager public the overinflated product it expects, writers always come back to the real models, which are at once simpler, more enigmatic, and all the more terrifying because of this. For, although fiction hesitates to show criminals as they really are and offers only an embellished portrayal of them, it cannot escape the question criminals inevitably raise: beyond perverse games, what really constitutes atrocity?

An Undifferentiated Sexual Appetite

Repeat-offense killers might say that the answer to this question is: total confusion and hybridizing of the sexes. These antiheroes, whether mythical or real, are characterized by their indifference to their sexual persona. Henry Lee Lucas is a case of confusion between the sexes, the species, and the generations. According to Ottis Toole, he had intercourse with dogs, cows, and goats, and, although he had a vague preference for murdering women, he was bisexual and equally comfortable in sexual relations with young girls or adult men. Toole was initiated at a very young age by his sister Drusilla, aged twelve at the time, who dressed him up as a girl and prostituted him on the streets of Jacksonville. He continued to cross-dress, even after his marriage to a woman named Novella, twenty-four years his senior, and his sexual relations with men led him to meet Lucas on a one-night stand.

There has been considerable mythologizing of Toole's life, which has echoes in Norse myth. For example, Loki is a male god who transforms himself into a mare to be mounted by the stallion Svadilfari, and it is difficult to tell whether he is the father or the mother of Odin's eight-legged charger Sleipnir. Such confusion also exists in Greek mythology. Heracles disguises himself as a woman to escape being killed by Antagoras at Cos, and Hermaphroditus is feminized by fusing with Salmacis, who becomes his female genitals. Many mortals are transformed into animals, including Harpalyce, who becomes an owl, Lycaon, who becomes a wolf, and so on. But the polymorphism among the Nordic gods is phenomenal.[10] Starting with the mother of the Scandinavian giants, who gives birth to animals, humans, and chimeras, these gods without a doubt surpass Zeus and Apollo in this area, despite the constant disguises which the Greek gods wore to seduce their lovers or trap sinners. Their inclination toward sexual license indicates a lack of interest in differentiation: everything is reduced to gesticulation and organic functions. There is no real pleasure except in affirming the gratuitous quality and the freedom of the most natural acts through which life and death continuously flow, with no particular significance.

From Tasting to Phobia

From this description of the voracious appetites of several of the most notorious criminals and characters from horror film and fiction, we can compile a list of attributes that they share with Odin *Harilo* (the Ripper), an ogre who hunts aimlessly in the woods and byways, catching what he can, having his way with it, torturing, killing, mangling, and in some cases devouring it.

This theme is not limited to the Nordic world. Hesiod reminds us that, in ancient Greece, Dionysus was also a "tearer of human flesh, taking pleasure in bondage and bloodshed."[11] Like any good hunter-warrior, Dionysus tore apart his prey with his bare hands and, in a reversal of fortune of the type that appears in all mythologies, he was also hunted down and dismembered at the hands of his pursuer. Greek cooks preserve a trace of this distant past by testing lamb for doneness by tearing it with their hands. This somewhat primitive pleasure recalls what was once a practical ability: the strength to dismember an animal manually may have been the mark of a physically able warrior, who could survive without mechanical or domestic assistance.

By contrast, many people in the United States are nauseated at the sight of a whole dead chicken. Thus, from the poultry counter to the horror-fiction shelves, stores must keep their consumers' stomachs from turning: the raw truth must be remodeled so that the living being is forgotten, and the wrapping must be clean, plasticized, hygienic, and embellished with soothing colors. Once these requirements are fulfilled, death becomes marketable. Similarly, if they are protected by a deluxe cover and fancy design, novels can contain the most gruesome atrocities without disturbing the reader.

Displays of repulsion are a cliché in horror films and novels. Their purpose seems to be to exculpate a forbidden desire. By vomiting after having witnessed an abominable deed, American heroes "prove" their sensitivity; thereafter, they are forgiven for committing atrocious acts . . . for a good cause. Like all phobias, feelings of revulsion at the thought or sight of dismemberment are ambiguous. They reflect a desire that is always present in repulsion. They awaken our connection with a time before civilization and a yearning that is made licit by an outward appearance of disgust.

How does one make the crossover from a direct desire to consume to a phobia, which is perhaps typical of what is, no doubt reductively, referred to as "Northern culture" as compared with other classic heroic tales? Desire appears to be replaced by disgust in cases where a confession of desire would be radically dangerous; for, if the mere acknowledgment of craving a pleasure places a person outside the realm of humanity, he would rather deny it to himself and to others. The threat of death can therefore trigger substitutions of phobia for desire. Criminals, whether real or fictional, live in danger of their own acts being turned against them. Their wish to kill and devour is immediately followed by nightmarish fears of being killed and devoured themselves. The idea of the act is associated with an image of a man-eater being eaten or a killer being killed, not only among real murderers but among all people who experience desires of this sort. The thought that one could take pleasure in ingesting human flesh means that one is already dead in the eyes of humanity: people scream in fear when they see images of a vampire, because they know that a desire to draw blood from their fellow man could also be awakened in them. But, by the time a person actually becomes aware of sharing this vampire desire, his phobia has already created a barrier, eliminating the intolerable idea that he is, in fact, already "one of them."

Reactions of denial are also found in our culture. For example, when the vampire-movie craze was flourishing in the 1970s, there was a plethora of stories about serial killers who bit their victims as a sort of entree to a cannibalistic meal. Simultaneously, a phobia for animal meat developed in Anglo-American youth culture, giving rise to a trend of vegetarianism. No direct causal relationship can be established between trends in fiction and behavior,[12] but the coincidence is too remarkable to be ignored. One could assume that, by becoming current, real, and human in the form of a serial killer, the blood-drinking vampire emerged from his macabre but hardly credible habitat to become a plausible alter ego, and that this sparked a reaction of total denial. Suddenly, culture caught a glimpse of itself in the mirror. By becoming vegetarians, did people think that they could categorically place themselves above the suspicion that they, too, were "one of them"?

In the 1950s, characters as grotesque as Albert Fish (who boasted that he prepared the thighs of his young victims on a bed of fresh vegetables) seemed to be so exceptional that there was no need for the phobia mechanism to be activated. Similarly, Ed Gein, in his desperate attempts to "get under" the skin of the mother figure (sometimes having to dismember several women in order to obtain enough skin), is seen as a sort of supernatural anomaly. But, starting in the late 1970s with Lucas and Toole, two necrophiliac anthropophagic freaks, unimaginable horror came dangerously close to home. It came even closer with the trend toward realism in American films such as *Alive*, whose director got the story from an article about an airplane that had crashed in the Andes, leaving the survivors with no other food than the bodies of the dead victims.[13]

In this context, it is hardly surprising that a disgust for meat emerged and masked the potential aggressiveness of the wild-warrior culture, especially if one considers the hidden feelings of guilt that are associated not only with individual or social violence, but also with much deeper issues, which have remained in limbo since the Nazi regime but which may reappear at any time. For example, isn't there, looming somewhere on the fringes of the collective conscience, a secret fantasy of exterminating "excess" populations (the "other" ethnic group, the "other" religious group, third-world populations, etc.), whose land and goods could then be put to use, like the fortunes inherited from landowners who died of the plague during the fourteenth century? People who claim to be repulsed by such ideas generally tend to acknowledge their own complicity.

Others prefer to cross the fine line that separates phobia from hysteria: New Age gurus and other sect leaders encourage this when they tell their clientele of religious "ideal shoppers" to awaken the monster inside them, which has been stifled by its own forgotten victims. The ability of a repressed desire or memory and its symbolic exhumation to "ease the conscience" and "open the mind" is a very popular theme in the United States today and has been cultivated by self-proclaimed shamans who specialize in "psychoanalyzing" such repressed memories. Sherill Mulhern[14] has shown that these analysts attempt to dig up memories of real traumatic experiences from their patients' recollection of things that happened to them in early childhood (in exact opposition to Freudian psychoanalysis, which is only interested in the memory's symbolic value). Generally, such episodes involve incestuous rape or, oddly, acts of pedophilia inflicted by Catholic priests, some of whom have been prosecuted, thirty years after the alleged facts. In such cases, the memories, which may be just retrospective hallucinations, similar to the hysterical confessions of Loudun's "witches," have been used in a cultural battle to reduce the presence in the United States of everything that is associated with Latin cultures and their forms of religion. With the demographic rise of Latino Americans, these religious practices are perceived as a challenge to Anglo-Germanic and Protestant hegemony.

But the active mechanism in hysteria is always a phobic pleasure. In a country where sexuality is both overstated and repressed, the presentation of forbidden pleasures in the form of a virtuous and "horrified" denial allows for imaginary satisfaction without guilt, as guilt is deflected onto the "criminal." Death comes out of the closet, only to don the horns of a scapegoat. The American public's perverse titillation with salacious rumormongering is clearly unrelated to the inevitable presence of pedophiles in the population.

From Hunger to Pragmatics

If hunger (something "vile") quickly leads to the emergence of its counterpart, phobia (which is "socially acceptable"), the same is not true of other, more practical supposed motives. Criminals who ingest human flesh or use it for reasons other than their own enjoyment no longer awaken repulsion but instead curiosity and an "ethnographic" interest. It is this type of interest that Ottis Toole is trying to awaken when he explains: "Sometimes my grandmother tried to get us a fresh body, and she would cut off the head . . . She would hold the head in her hands and wait for the skin to dry, or else she would remove the skin from the head and stretch it over her body. She said it made her skin stay young."[15]

It is possible that traditions of the occult have some connection with the rites of antiquity (chronicled in Hellenistic literature), which are largely composed of antiaging rituals, such as the story of Medea opening Aeson's throat to purge the old blood and replace it with an elixir of youth. The selection of "choice" parts (the head, sexual organs, or heart) is another theme that echoes the most ancient myths, whose symbolic value is invoked, unconsciously no doubt, but not innocently, by criminal commentators. For example, when Stéphane Bourgoin asked: "Did Henry [Lucas] eat people too?" Ottis placidly answered: "Oh, sure. He says he didn't, but he's a liar. He loved all parts of the body . . . like the heart."[16] Why the heart, one might wonder? Lucas's tastes will remain an eternal mystery, but it is known that the heart had a crucial role in anthropophagic rites in which guests were lied to about what they were eating.

Ottis Toole added this about Henry Lucas: "He told me: 'you just ate a person!' and I said 'What?' I didn't know. The taste isn't very different from other kinds of meat. Sometimes I was so out of it I didn't even know I was eating a person. I drank blood, too."[17] Ottis was probably also lying, but he did so with genius, for, although he never had any schooling, he reconstructed the rites of Mount Lyceum and the sites consecrated to Zeus in ancient Greece, which often revolved around mixing the heart of a child with animal entrails to trick those who took part in the ritual meal and to test their reaction and the extent of their horror when they found out what they had eaten.

The theme of cannibalism, which recurs among serial killers and in the literature about them, remains a mystery. The subject of hunger has been raised, only to be buried in phobia. A greed for possession has been mentioned, only to invoke the awful social marginalization that has always been the fate of those who indulge in it.

It is likely that this is a cultural reflex. The society which thought that it was possible to discuss violence ad infinitum may be encountering one of violence's most natural effects: the shift from conscious pleasure to unconscious repulsion. It seems that the prediction made in *A Clockwork Orange* – that an overdose of atrocity eventually disgusts even the most hardened delinquents – is coming true and taking over an entire population.[18]

If this is indeed the case, we must not congratulate ourselves too soon, because a fear of violence can in fact lead to worse forms of violence. It is time we finally listened to the terrifying message that real killers are sending out, in actions that echo the romantic and perverse model of the greedy and cruel hunter, strengthened by an army of fiction writers who ride under the banner of Stephen King.

PART TWO

Heroes or Villains?

CHAPTER FIVE

Enforcers

Criminals and heroes have always been placed in the category of hunter, sadist, or ogre; but one senses some resistance on their part to these labels. For, although novelists, film makers, and the police prefer to call them "sadistic monsters" or "psychotic killers," murderers have a clear preference for another name and, indeed, for another calling: that of "warrior."

In Part II, we will examine the efforts of the worst and sickest of these warriors to survive, by examining a number of their different personas: the avenger, the lost soldier, and, finally, the servant of the devil. One can already guess the logical conclusion of this investigation: the criminal is dehumanized and reduced to an animal – the very principles of the werewolf metamorphosis.

Vengeance and Hatred

Hatred is recognized by human beings living in society, as is one of its possible causes: injustice. Vengeance is one of its potential consequences, although vengeance that falls outside the framework of the law is condemned.

In this context, repeat-offense murderers pose a problem, for it is hard to believe that there is any form of hatred that would not dissipate after a killing. Yet the motif of hatred is the one that appears most frequently in fiction and in reality, probably because it is so "easy to relate to." Even a disoriented vagrant like Ottis Toole consistently answers the question of why he killed by saying that he was reacting to an attack or to someone else's evil designs on him:

Q: "What made you commit these crimes?"
A: "Well, because someone had hit me or tried to cheat me, so one way or another, I got even."[1]

In fiction writing, vengeance is a hackneyed cause. In Peter Straub's *Koko*,[2] the theme of the warrior is crossbred with the story of a childhood shattered by sadistic adults. A young American soldier becomes insane after he is forced to kill a group of Vietnamese children hiding in a cave. Years later, he kills his old war buddies, one by one. Through the probing investigation of a pediatrician, we understand that the person hiding behind the nickname "Koko" witnessed his mother being killed by his father and had also been the victim of repeated rape. In this story of "repressed memory," the lead character takes his revenge by avenging the Vietnamese children, with whom he identifies.

This novel is a paradigm of psychosis. The dominant idea is one of predestination from childhood, but this is then translated into an endless battle, which is sustained by legitimate (or at least understandable) vengeance, resulting in a blood bath and the sacrifice of the hero. Beyond the devices it uses to express this excessive desire for warrior-like vengeance (i.e., the complicated hypothesis of childhood psychosis), *Koko* is only one of hundreds of stories with the same plot, from *Rambo*, to the latest movies, to geopolitical fiction demonizing Middle Eastern groups (or potential traitors within the country).

The motif of vengeance also allows murderers and the people who study them to give broader social significance to their acts, for instance by interpreting them as a form of political revolt. This happened in the case of Mark Essex, a young African American, who, following a long ordeal with racism in the United States Navy, became a Black Panther and finally ended up isolated and deranged. He launched an ambush from the roof of a building and killed or wounded dozens of police officers and passers-by before being killed himself.

Charles Starkweather's social revolt consisted in a ten-day-long killing spree. The murders, which he perpetrated in succession on sociologically stereotyped victims, can be read as an accelerated climb up the social ladder. The nineteen-year-old youth, humiliated by his job as a street cleaner in a small Nebraska town, began his crimes at the bottom of the social scale by killing a gas-station attendant, and then went to the home of his fourteen-year-old girlfriend and (with her assistance) killed her blue-collar parents and younger sister. The pair took off in a car, killing along the way a farmer, two students, a shop owner, and, finally, a well-to-do local family.

Starkweather explains most of the eleven murders as acts of legitimate self-defense: he killed his girlfriend's blue-collar father because he was armed, the farmer because he was about to get his gun, the little sister because she was screaming with fear, the student because he wanted Charles to hand himself over so that he could take all the credit, and so on. He has less to say about what caused him to mutilate a female student or accept the wealthy family's hospitality before killing them.

In prison, Starkweather spoke. He explained his insane acts as revenge on the society that had ruined his childhood. He had been a stuttering, bowlegged, red-haired boy and everyone had poked fun at him, causing him to fight and to become increasingly isolated. Forced to live in squalor, he experienced the "hidden injuries" of his class.[3] He described the act of killing as a way of taking hold of his destiny, a violent impulse to bring distant dreams into immediate reality (like James Dean, who was one of his idols, in the film *Rebel without a Cause*). "How long do you think I'd have lived? Forty years? too long. Ten years? too long. Better a week with the one who loved me for what I was."[4]

Essex and Starkweather therefore display motives that can be "socially" interpreted. The sociologist Elliott Leyton assembles a large number of such cases to demonstrate that crime is the enactment of a war between the classes and follows a behavioral pattern that is etched in the imaginary competition between social groups.

But I think this explanation is too hasty. In the Mark Essex case, it is clear that the young activist had none of the discipline of a military combatant. He placed himself above the revolt, and when he was confronted with racism he saw it as more than an intolerable offense, but indeed as a logical impossibility, which led him to an act of heroic suicide. Behind an outward appearance of political protest, what he was truly unable to stand was not racism but the simple fact of being "different" in society, which he discovered when he left the sheltered surroundings of his middle-class black community.

Starkweather was certainly a rebel à la James Dean and had reason to complain about society, but he also had a dark side. His writing includes poetry and praise of nature, and yet he describes nature as a series of motionless, lifeless images. As a child, like many future serial killers, he killed everything he could hunt – rats, squirrels, and small house pets – and had dreams of the Lady of Darkness coming to take him away from this world.

If there is a social element that must be considered here, it is the category constituted by these criminally insane "warriors" and the strange community of pessimists that they form. Catastrophe is their real love object, in the same way as passive reflection is the indulgence of melancholy souls. They cause catastrophe to occur, drawing it carefully toward them, re-creating their world in the form of a gaping hole (the *Ginnungagap*, or primordial abyss, of Nordic tales), which they will gratefully allow to swallow them up in the end. "Shoot me" were the words of Ted Bundy when he was finally apprehended by a police officer after an orgy of killings.

Sociologists such as Leyton have in my opinion been taken in by the social or political protest that is invoked as the real motive for criminal insanity: the demand for social recognition, for consideration and love, revenge for past injustices, a purifying mission, a rebellion, etc.[5]

In the same way as psychotics are encouraged to connect their sickness with an identifiable cause (anger, a feeling of persecution, etc.), repeat-offense killers are led to explain their acts as vindication: recovering a debt, remedying injustice, criticizing the system, committing altruistic murders for the good of the family, and so on.

Two frequent indicators suggest, however, that there is something else behind these "psychosociological" motives:

1. The fact that serial killers have a penchant for taking their revenge, not on rival or power figures, as is assumed in violent fiction, but on women, children, or adolescents, who are easily manipulated victims and therefore implausible objects of revenge.
2. The fact that, when they attack men or couples, they often speak of a diabolic mission, ordered directly by the "forces of evil."

These are two indications that insanity is present. Although it cannot escape the social nature of the symbolic, this type of insanity occupies a particular place, which sets it radically apart, in such a way that naive sociological theories fail to grasp it.

Avenging a Humiliated Father

People who have seen the film will remember that, in *Conan the Barbarian*, actor Arnold Schwarzenegger ("the black sword" in German) plays the role of a muscle-bound quasi-paleolithic Nordic warrior, whose mother is decapitated while the hero is still a child. This severed head triggers an entire process of revenge, which underpins the plot. For the California killer Edmund Kemper, on the contrary, rage against his mother was what triggered a hunt – real in his case – for young girls to decapitate: he beheaded thirteen women before finally giving himself up to the police in 1978.

Edmund Kemper was certainly the most famous of these "haruspices," searching for a hidden meaning inside the body and in its different parts. Reporters and writers still line up for interviews with "professor" Kemper in his California prison cell, hoping to obtain a threatening or coldly analytical quote.

His case is familiar and allows us to define at least two new facets that differentiate him from "ogres," such as Lucas, Toole, and others:

1. Not all serial killers are reckless hunters or disoriented beings who confuse human flesh with meat or dead baby's skulls with their own skull, deformed in childhood.[6] They are on a crusade of bloodthirsty violence. In Kemper's case, the crusade was directed against his mother, in other words against a hated mirror image of himself.
2. These crusades are planned far in advance and carried out with the methodical care of a professional. This reveals the multiple killer's military side. It is not enough just to fight: he must have a plan of battle as well.

After he beheaded the young girls, Kemper transported the heads like an ancient warrior bearing his enemy's head on a stake to display his victory.

He later specifically targeted his own family. By killing his mother, whom he accused of betraying his father, he fell into the category of Orestes-like avengers and ushered America into a new arena of classic drama. He tore out his mother's larynx, attacking and rebelling against the organ of speech and the law. The Kemper case offers an explosive lesson: abusive and dominating mothers beware, for you are the cause of the warrior's imbalance. This message is incessantly repeated by the countless researchers and visitors who have seen Kemper, a model prisoner, who has now been sanctified and grown famous.

But to turn the American dream into the American drama requires an enormous cultural effort, and current use of the Kemper case in no way indicates that internalization produces a vast collective "catharsis," as in Aeschylus' *Choëphori* or *Eumenides*. On the contrary, there is not a single female figure in the "Kemper lesson" who comes to terms with paternal legitimacy. There is only overwhelming isolation in a society devoid of human contact, with the exception of violent contact between men and women.

Finding Soul Mates

When he was still very young, Kemper associated eroticism with hatred and death. Orgasm, hatred, and killing were one and the same in his mind, and were brought together in a medieval-type fantasy:

> We lived in Montana, in a house with a huge basement: it was like a dungeon. I was eight and my imagination was working at full speed. There was an enormous

furnace that was hooked up to the radiators, and the pipes made a lot of noise. I was fascinated with that furnace. I thought the devil lived inside it.[7]

The boy slept in the basement. His youngest sister remembers that he used to act out his own execution there. She would lead him to a chair, blindfold him, and smother him, as if he were in a gas chamber (this was around the time when Caryl Chessman was sentenced to death). Fascinated by the "decapitation concept," he also played with a miniature guillotine.[8]

Edmund lived in a world of hate for his two sisters and his mother: "My mother treated me as if I was her third daughter [. . .] She used to whisper in my ear that my father was a bastard."[9] He took punishments for one of his sisters, and was jealous of her "because she had everything." Enraged when his mother took away a toy pistol, he decapitated his sister's Barbie doll and cut off its hands, which would become the ritual of his future killings. He then severed her cat's skull, exposing the brain, and killed the animal with a knife. Later, when he was about fourteen, he fired shots at a neighbor's dog.

He said that he wanted to kiss his teacher, but that he would have to kill her first, using his father's bayonet. This is one of the most significant objects in the life of Edmund Kemper III, the third in line to bear the martial emblems of his name.[10] His mother used to remind him that the only things his father (Edmund Kemper II) had left him in his will were "his medals and his war stories." Imagining his father as a combat machine, whose battles were invalidated by his mother, he assimilated the paternal function with pure, sterile destruction. From that point on, he believed that in armed violence he had found an outlet for his own identity, which was trapped in a mirror of female faces (his mother's and sisters'), and that he could thus make these reflections disappear.

It clearly appears that Kemper identified with a paternal warrior: his hero was John Wayne, who reminded him of his father, also tall with small feet, like himself.[11] But the paternal hero, who was always involved in some crusade of vengeance, had a strong contender: he could not compete with the mother's voice, which was devastatingly effective:

My mother was over six feet tall and weighed close to two hundred pounds, but she wasn't fat. That woman terrifies me. She has a set of vocal chords like you can't imagine. She beats men at arm-wrestling. [. . .] She always dominates her husbands. It wasn't any different with my father. One day, he had enough [. . .] My father couldn't take it any more and he left us. I used to cry a lot at night when I would hear them yelling at one another.

In the end, the warrior is defeated by his female adversary: "My mother was very strong and she wanted a man who was very strong. My father was very big and very loud, but he was very weak and she wanted the opposite."[12]

A rapid acceleration of events occurred when Kemper's mother (more abusive than the mother in the Pierre Rivière case, in France[13]) threw his father out of the house. The enormous, violent "Valkyrie" later went through a string of husbands, emasculating them and "using them up and tossing them out" at a speedy pace.[14] The Kemper legend suggests that he made a final weak attempt to resist insanity when one of his "stepfathers" treated him kindly, bringing an end to his daydreams of execution. But the kind stepfather was also ousted, and Kemper's criminal fate became inescapable.

At sixteen, Edmund threatened one of his substitute fathers with a hammer, with the intention of stealing the family car and going to look for his natural father. Worried, his mother sent him to her parents' ranch. He took revenge by killing birds and squirrels. The grandfather confiscated his rifle, but he stole it back, killed his grandmother with a shot in the back, and killed his grandfather "so that he wouldn't see her body." Then he called his mother.

He was institutionalized at Atascadero until 1969 and the psychiatric staff released him (against his will) into his mother's care when his symptoms of mental disassociation had disappeared. This was the start of a mortal showdown: "My mother and I started right in on horrendous battles, just horrible battles, violent and vicious. I've never been in such a vicious verbal battle with anyone." But their fights were not limited to verbal abuse: "One day, she hit me so hard in the mouth with her belt that it broke [. . .] She told me to shut up, or the neighbors would think she was beating me up."[15]

Edmund made a few feeble and ultimately abortive attempts to find a job and a place to live. He showered his mother, who often appeared unannounced at his lodgings, with presents. Faced with the certitude that she would live forever, like an antagonistic second self, Kemper's mental condition shook like a sail in the wind. At one point, he was tempted to commit suicide:

> One of my favorite pastimes is to lie down in the middle of the road, as if someone had hit me, and to wait for a car to drive by. I hope that one of the drivers will be drunk enough to run me over, but they all hit the brakes and stop before. It makes them furious when I get up and run away.[16]

It would take two more years for Kemper's hatred to explode into a saga of eroticism and death. The explosion was planned: he picked up dozens of hitchhiking coeds around Stanford University in order to practice and work on his "gentlemanly" image. He fixed the passenger door so that he could lock it from the driver's side (a technique also used by Ted Bundy, Kenneth Bianchi, and Angelo Buono). He committed his first acts on two eighteen-year-old girls. On an isolated dead-end street, he forced one of them to lock herself in the trunk of the car, asphyxiated the other with a plastic bag, slit her throat, and then stabbed the first girl. He brought the bodies back to his apartment, raped them, took polaroid pictures of them, cut them up, and buried them with the plastic bag. He kept the heads awhile and then disposed of them in a ravine.

In September 1972, he strangled and raped a young Asian-American hitchhiker and kept her head in the trunk of his car. He buried the body and severed hands near a religious retreat in the mountains. In January 1973, he forced a Cabrillo College student to climb into the trunk of his car, and then killed her with a .22 hunting rifle. He hid the body in a closet in his mother's house, engaged in the usual acts and dismembering, and buried the head in his mother's garden. Starting in February 1973, the connection between murdering young girls and his hatred for his mother became clearer: he began to pick up hitchhikers after having arguments with his mother. He killed them while he was driving and took their bodies back to his mother's house. At night, he decapitated them and had intercourse with the bodies, hid the heads under his bed after meticulously removing the bullet, and finally disposed of the bodies. The next eight murders he committed took place in the same way, but he kidnapped his victims closer and closer to the Santa Cruz University campus, where his mother worked in the administrative offices. Kemper's penchant for preppy girls is probably best interpreted as a logical "progression toward the mother." He questioned them in detail about their families, their studies, and where they lived, before killing them, and is said to have freed a number of girls who did not fit the ideal profile.

By choosing his victims for their social resemblance to his mother, their immense psychological distance from her became more intense. If he killed them it was because it would be unthinkable for him to establish a relationship with girls who would reject him. As he explains in a description of his crimes:

> These girls weren't much more than children, I suppose, but I felt . . . that they were old enough to know better than to do the things they were doing . . . out there hitch-hiking, when they had no reason or need to. They were flaunting in my face the fact that they could do any damn thing they wanted, and that society is as screwed up as it is.[17]

They were both eighteen at the time, I think, and I was twenty-three, which isn't that much of a gap, but it was just like a million years.[18]

There is a paradox between this infinite distance and the proximity which Kemper sought with the mother figure. Perhaps he thought that he was a girl, but that he was in radical conflict with other girls or women. During his crimes and during fights with his sisters or mother, he was looking for something to manipulate, a "living human doll."[19] He seemed to be acting out his old jealousy for his sisters and their dolls. When he consumed the various forms of "bait" which these girls possessed, he always finished with the heads, which he liked to "talk to." There is a strange dissociation between "talking" with these heads and eroticism. Did Kemper see himself as one of his sisters and, by extension, a mirror of his victims? The words he used to describe his enjoyment in severing and removing heads were about "getting off." In any case, when Kemper was asked what he thought when he saw a pretty girl in the street, he answered: "One side of me says, 'wow, what an attractive chick. I'd like to talk to her, date her.' The other side of me says, 'I wonder how her head would look on a stick.'"[20] He certainly appears to be reacting to an enemy warrior and hence an alter ego, a female alter ego.

In May 1973, he became seized with the idea of ending his mission by attacking someone from his own world. In the early morning, he went into his mother's bedroom and struck a blow to her temple with a hammer. Then, he turned her on her back and slit her throat. He decapitated her, cut out her larynx and threw it in the garbage. He placed the head on a shelf and raped the body. He was surprised that his mother, so easy to kill, had turned out to be as fragile as the other women he had murdered, although he had always believed that she was invulnerable. He felt a sense of triumph over the dead mother, whose left hand he also severed. Kemper had read the Bible: was his intention to signify the biblical punishment that is prescribed for women who steal a man's virility? One is reminded of Schreber, a paranoiac studied by Freud, who referred to the demonized figure of his father as a "stealer of souls."

But Kemper was not yet totally satisfied. He still had to kill the alter ego closest to his mother, or possibly someone who recalled the image of his sisters. He invited his mother's closest friend to dinner, punched her in the stomach, and then strangled and beheaded her. Very shortly after this last murder, he gave himself up to the police, with the feeling that he had finally finished his mission and with the self-confessed fear that he was losing control of himself and beginning to hallucinate.

Kemper: Orestes, or Perseus and the Gorgon?

What is the reason for this journey, which ends with the symmetrical murder of the mother and her best friend? The Kemper case wavers between two contradictory interpretations: on the one hand, Kemper is an Orestes figure, a quasi-legitimate avenger of the paternal order demeaned by an abusive mother; but, on the other hand, he is the negation of any form of masculinity that is civicly or socially acceptable.

By carefully separating the head from the body, Kemper transformed the female love object into a trunk, an object bearing precious things (he did not dare touch the breasts, for example) that is cleanly separated from the power of speech and from the face, which he is unable to eroticize. By throwing away his mother's larynx, Kemper performed a symbolic castration of the male hidden in her throat.

In psychological terms, Kemper is not able to make the symbolic separation that gives the father the ability to restrain his warrior power. He is totally unaware that such a form of paternity exists. He uses real pieces of flesh to distinguish the desired female body from the castrating conduit for speech, which he in turn emasculates.

Nothing in his own accounts or in the copious commentary produced by dozens of journalists and psychiatrists has been able to elucidate his fatal error. Kemper does not talk about a dominating mother, but rather about a nonexistent father, reduced to the form of a bayonet. Incapable of ending his self-proliferation as a mirror image of the mother (or, rather, of the nonfather), his only way of exorcising this phenomenon was physically to isolate it in "sisterly" forms.

The terrible legend of Kemper the "champion" conjures up images of a painting by Hieronymus Bosch: in a detail, a child in swaddling clothes is held by a father with a hag's face and a fish tail, whose body is the bark of a hollow tree and who is mounted on the back of a giant rat. This representation of the hollow and more or less androgynous father also recalls the tree of the Celtic, Nordic, or Germanic worlds (*Yggdrasill* or *Irminsul*), a gigantic hollow phallus gnawed upon by all sorts of vermin, elves, and dragons. Perhaps this is the miserable fate of a manhood that is unwilling – and unable – to forgo the pleasures of an imagined all-powerfulness. When British skinheads proudly brandish a replica of the Arthurian sword Excalibur before marching off to terrorize a Pakistani community in a Birmingham suburb, or when their German (or Swedish) counterparts make a ritual sacrifice on Jul (the pagan Christmas) before setting fire to an apartment building where foreign families are lodged, they are unaware that the equivalent of these purely aggressive phallic symbols is a huge hollow tree, where men are hanged, like Odin, and lose their sight.

The Mortal Mother

It is no coincidence that the theme of vengeance leads to a discussion of conflict with the wife or mother. Nor is this due to a bias toward psycho-analysis or a psychological approach. It is because present-day murders and myths persistently lead us there. Kemper, for example, forces us to solve a puzzle that is distressingly common among repeat-offense criminals, as well as in many horror stories: why is vengeance more often directed against mothers than against men, when it is the father's status that appears to be the target of violence? And why must the murderer kill a series of women in order to be avenged of his mother?

There is an overwhelming predominance of women among the victims of murderers who are seeking revenge. This can, of course, be explained by the ease with which a man can apprehend women, who are physically weaker and culturally less aggressive, and by the eroticism that is associated with murders by heterosexual criminals. For a number of American feminists, there is no mystery in this propensity to hunt women: in their view, it is second nature to man.

The very idea of vengeance is, however, not clear, especially when it is repeated. Lucas's reproach against his mother for having prostituted herself seems too inconsequential, but the theme has been picked up by many murderers, as well as in film, by Hitchcock. In fact, the "bad mother" character seems to have claimed a place for itself on the screen. Arthur Shawcross, who murdered black prostitutes in Rochester, New York, between 1988 and 1990, after having killed and mutilated women in Vietnam, said that his mother had sodomized him with a broomstick, tearing his anus. The hatred that Shawcross "displayed" in this way was probably mixed in with erotic fantasy.

The same is true of Samples. A Vietnam veteran, Samples had a curious experience as a child. One night, while he was sleeping, lying between his mother and a pregnant aunt, the aunt had a miscarriage and the boy was splattered with the blood. Later in life, he developed the fantasy of being killed by an Amazon who stirred his insides with her spear. At thirteen, he "accidentally" shot himself in the stomach. He enjoyed hurting himself with knives and pins, and elaborated on this fantasy until it included the Amazon's death. Many years later, he eviscerated a woman with whom he was sleeping, and one of her friends. Police officer Robert Ressler, who has reported on the case, did everything he could to prevent Samples from being released from prison, sure that this was a typical multiple murderer and the product of a real childhood trauma (perhaps a victim of "repressed memory"). The episode was a sign of the obsessive connection which Samples made between orgasm, masochism, bisexuality, and a longing for death. The only conclusion one can draw is that vengeance, when present, is only one ingredient among others for the murderer.

The answers to this riddle are also best sought in fiction and mythology, although we should point out that these each lead in a different direction: fiction, which is more "expressive," tends to put the blame on mother, whereas epic myth brings something very different to bear.

Before the wave of political correctness, which has generated stories of superwomen who are just as bloodthirsty as their male counterparts, the misogyny in the theme of vengeance was more obvious in fiction. For example, as Stephen King sees it, a man can be a killer or a sadist, but true horror is something female. If King is convinced that he can frighten any audience with his set of "fear-bears", he himself is most frightened by a peculiar figure: that of the mother as a paralyzing man-eating machine.

There is no doubt as to the sex of *Christine*, the killer car, and the sex of the underground monster is also clear (despite the fact that its name – *It* – is neuter). There is also the crazy female nurse in *Misery* and, most recently, Dolores Clairborne, a criminal who is on the warpath against abusive men. Incidentally, the author dedicated this last book to his mother.

King establishes a link between the monster's female nature and the mechanical progression of horror. An industrial dry-cleaning machine switches itself on without warning, tearing off a worker's arm. Over-stimulated by its consumption of blood, this female presence cannot be stopped from swallowing everything that comes within its reach. Likewise, once they start, adolescents with supernatural powers, such as Carrie and Charlie, will never stop killing. There is also a relationship between the female, maternal type and all-powerfulness: the shapeless thing in *It*, which gives birth to a series of various secondary forms (zombies, evil spirits, storms, fires, etc.) from its own substance, can exercise control over its offspring from a distance.

The overbearing mother is not only represented as a machine or a thing, but also as an environment, in which a series of tortures are inflicted in progression. For example, in *Charlie*, the "Box," a secret laboratory in Longmont, Virginia, is a place where gifted children are sent, and manipulated. This deadly smothering characteristic is also found in *Mist*, which devours all forms of life outside the safe haven of a supermarket. In order to escape, the characters have to flee from the closed space and its ill effects.

The escape is doubly beneficial, as it also distances them from the mother figure (as with the child character in *The Talisman*, by Peter Straub and Stephen King).

The Woman in the Room is a short story about a son who administers euthanasia to his mother, who is in the final throes of a terminal cancer, and it echoes the death of King's own mother from a painful cancer. In the same story, the mother asks her son to raise her legs, a theme which is reversed in *Misery*, where the nurse breaks the legs of a writer who has fallen into her hands following a car accident.

King explains that some mothers are fully supportive of their children's literary careers. Could such women be the model for the overly maternal nurse in *Misery*, who loves the writer's books and forces him to write one for her? King chose this "novelist-maker" character from the cases of nurses who kill children and who in the real world make up the majority of female serial killers. Clearly, this is offered as an explanation of vengeance: because abusive mothers commit a sort of infanticide, they engender adults who are obsessed with destruction and vengeance against women.

Beyond these horror specialists, the theme of the domineering mother is recurrent in Anglo-American films. In addition to *Braindead*, with its grossly exaggerated "antimaternal" message, *The World According to Garp*[21] comes to mind. The novel tells the story of a man who was conceived by a nurse with one of her dying patients and who remains emotionally dependent on his mother all his life. The David Lynch film *Wild at Heart*[22] deals with the pure love of a young couple, who are relentlessly pursued by the girl's mother.

What is the Point in Killing "All Women"?

Anglo-American fiction affirms the culture's fear of mothers who smother their children, but it does not explain why all women become the targets of multiple crime. The possible origins of this must be sought in the distant past, and in the essence of what the Kemper case so clearly expresses.

Once again, there are two distinct traditions. Nordic mythology does not allow for direct competition between a man who is on the warpath and the feminized figure of a "nonfather." However, Greco-Roman mythology shows in plain terms the unbearable mirror-like relation between female and male warriors when the male is emasculated by his failure to ascend to the father position.[23]

Hence, among the many female warriors in Nordic poetry, few actually fight. They are therefore generally not subject to the violence of others, but instead serve as emblems for a weapon's power of devastation (Herja), (such as Gertrud, who represents the strength of the lance; Gerirdavör, a goddess and lance-bearer; Brunhild, who represents the chain-mail coat; Skjaldmaër, the shield-bearing virgin, etc.). They can also take the form of angels (a cross between a woman and a swan or a Vedic *aspara*) who support the fighters. This allegorical aspect precludes any real participation or chance of physical retaliation: in the closest example, Brunhild is sent into a spell-induced sleep for having disobeyed Odin and can only be released by Siegfried.

On the other hand, women are suspected of corrupting virile men with their beauty, their love potions (Freyja), and their jewels (Güllveig). They weave combat between men, predicting death (like Göndull, Odin's magic wand) or paralyzing the warriors by casting a spell on them. They share the male combatants' wily qualities, as well as their less "virile" aspects, similar to the way that, in ancient Greece, nocturnal hunting with a net and trap was performed by youths who had yet to prove their manhood with a courageous deed.

It should be noted that Nordic goddesses who incarnate wife, sister, or daughter roles often bear a stigma of dishonesty. These women are more independent than the women of Greek mythology, and they may even be disobedient and fickle; their liaisons are frequent, and their marital relations unstable. Skadi, Gerd, and Freyja do not truly accept their husbands. Generally speaking, beauty is associated with the "Vanes" side of the great warriors' nature (i.e., it is wealthy, incestuous, and corrupting). Many warriors are polygamous. Siegfried is married to Brunhild, but he soon forgets her and marries Gudrun. When he is reminded of his domestic duties, he sends his second wife's brother to consummate his marriage to Brunhild. When she learns of this, she takes her revenge by having Siegfried killed by one of Gunnar's brothers who is not bound by fraternal oath. There is a large variety of such stories of unconsummated marriages and betrayals that ultimately end in murder.

Women as a Degraded Second Self

An explanation of the vengeance that is directed against women in repeated murders may lie within these complex mythical dramas. The theme of the unfaithful woman, when considered as a reflection of the warrior's cunning (and therefore weak) side, legitimates revenge that appears outwardly to be base (cunning is associated with weakness, because a "real" warrior can draw upon his physical prowess). It reflects rage against the self but turned against the opposite sex, owing to a failure to prove one's manhood, which has become inaccessible (as in the Kemper case). In this imaginary setup, being cheated on by a woman is not only humiliating for the man who is attracted by extreme forms of violence, but it also forces him to acknowledge that, like cheating, his violent tendencies lie outside the male code of honor. By choosing an unfaithful woman, a violent man coaxes the truth of the situation to the surface – that is, that he has got what he deserves for having betrayed his own manhood. Through her actions, a woman "of easy virtue" reflects on him as an unmanly and "nonvirilized" person. Betrayal (or allegations of betrayal) in a sexual relationship is therefore a signal that triggers vengeful rage in the criminally insane.

In mythology, the remedy for betrayal in a normal marriage is brutal sequestering or kidnapping, for the purpose of immediate consummation, but not for the propagation of a legitimate lineage. If a warrior's failure to keep his word is punished by his expulsion into the bloodthirsty, barbarian horde, a woman's unfaithfulness in marriage is grounds for acts of atrocity. The different versions and inversions of this symmetrical relationship are countless in Nordic mythology.

One finds similar accounts dating from the Middle Ages. The *Wunderer* or errant hunter is a late Tyrolean interpretation of the Odin myth, which develops into stories of ogres and the villain Bluebeard.[24] Orkise the giant hunts the virginal Lady Luck with his dogs, in order to devour her as revenge for her refusal to marry him. A connection with modern-day criminal vagrants is made in L.Q. Jones and Alvy Moore's strange film *A Boy and his Dog*,[25] in which the hero, a knight-errant in a desertified postnuclear world, offers his dog "Blood" as food to a girl, who, in an reverse interpretation of the Orkise story, forces him to marry her and thus to increase the stock of fertile males, which her degenerate subterranean society is lacking.

All of this would be rather unremarkable if it were not for the fact that, once again, the structure of the myth is reproduced among real multiple murderers, who are like mythical warriors brought to life. Christopher Wilder, a multimillionaire racing-car driver and "save the whales" advocate, raped and tortured women whom he asked to pose as models for his photographs, and then killed them (there are eleven established counts of murder against him and hundreds of counts of rape). His hunt began on the day a girl turned down his proposal of marriage.[26] The most famous repeat-offense murderer, Ted Bundy, also began his criminal career after being dropped by his girlfriend.

The Vampire's Secret Femininity

The case of the "vampire" John Brennan Crutchley runs along similar lines. Crutchley, a highly skilled computer programmer, kidnapped numerous women. He then bound them and drained their blood, using an intravenous tube, slowly weakening them, filming them, and in all likelihood drinking their blood. Supercop Robert Ressler is convinced that Crutchley killed more than a dozen victims this way (women who disappeared from all of the neighborhoods in which he lived), but few pieces of material evidence have been gathered, excepting the evidence of rape, puncture marks, and wounds, and the accounts of his few surviving victims.

His fascination with women's blood reminds us that, in stories of ritual cannibalism, flesh is often that of a male child, while blood is that of a girl. Throat cutting is most often connected with the immolation of a girl (Iphigenia, the sister of Orestes, for example), whereas the preparation of cooked flesh revolves around male sacrifice. This is tied in with the opposition (still prevalent in modern Greece) that is drawn between the wolf, which is said to drink lamb's blood, and the lion, which eats the flesh of cattle.[27] These examples of dualism are also comparable with ancient conceptions of genetics, in which man is said to provide the seed, which constitutes mettle, while woman provides the nourishing sac, which is largely made up of blood (the same blood that is shed during menstruation). In Nordic mythology, the symbol of embryonic fluid derives from Kvasir, who, although he is male, is defined only by his effusive poetry. Kvasir's fermented blood is placed in an immense "maternal womb" in the mountains, where Odin comes to drink it by creeping in through an orifice atop the cave.

The theme of a man drinking a woman's blood is symmetrical with that of a man's strength being sucked out by a woman. According to Chinese Tao philosophy, a man will try to reverse the phenomenon by soaking up the female secretions and absorbing them during sexual intercourse, in order to replenish his strength. The man who is worn out and weakened by sexual relations, emptied of his energy and his manly will, is a repeated theme in the heroic legends from which fantasies of seductive, inveigling, corruptive, and vampire-like women are derived. There appears to be a transition from the legitimate ingestion of the mother's blood by the fetus or her milk by the child, to an illegitimate and dangerous "extortion" from the male, for, as he is composed mainly of muscle and bone, he does not have excess blood to shed like women do, and therefore quickly becomes empty.

This myth is reconstituted in "vampire" killers' minds, but in a confused way. For Samples or Chase,[28] the question of whether blood is drawn from the mother or the father appears to be unresolved. On the other hand, in the Crutchley case, one has the impression that he was attempting to recover blood that was stolen from him by a woman. As a child, Crutchley, who came from a well-to-do family, was also dressed up as a girl, like Toole, but by his mother. One might imagine that he wanted to demand of the women he killed: "Give me back my female side," which his officially male existence had stolen from him, or inversely: "Give me back my male blood," which had been stolen from him when he was a child.

On the same topic, the vampire theme, of which the American and British (and even Mexican) movie industries offer us a steady diet, elucidates the myth of the demented combatant, with which Anglo-Saxon literature has been obsessed for centuries. Unlike the werewolf, which is a "raw" image of the mad warrior, at once human and animal as well as carnivorous, the vampire is more effeminate and "devirilized." In the most flattering portrayals (which include most of the Terrence Fisher films and Francis Ford Coppola's recent *Dracula*), he is an affected aristocrat, born to a life of luxury. In Werner Herzog's *Nosferatu*,[29] starring Isabelle Adjani and Klaus Kinski, Kinski creates the character of a sickly sweet hermaphrodite, a romantic bloodsucking character, whose languorous manners surpass even Murnau's dandyish Count Dracula. Moreover, all of the Dracula characters are surrounded by a bevy of female vampires, who are both sisters and wives, and vampires can even become female themselves, in order to lure their male victims.

Everyone knows that the vampire meets his fate by being impaled on a stake, which bears an uncanny resemblance to a phallic symbol. The vampire's "soft" assault, which is characterized by ingestion, and his death by impalement on a sharp stick, like Saint Theresa, his mystical mirror image, make him highly evocative of the female nature.

As real-life avengers, contemporary serial killers are therefore reminiscent of what is veiled (and suggested) in the vampire myth: an anger that is directed against a supposedly "unfaithful" female. They consider their mothers to be guilty of pumping the life out of them, of stealing their virility or "corrupting their blood." And it is their mothers (or maternal figures) whom they kill, like Kemper, who had no "real" father figure and who dreaded the prospect of an eternal confrontation with his own image reflected in his mother's face.

But beyond these "charges of theft," which are in a sense substantiated by the vampire myth and provide an opportunity for the murderer to assert himself in the social debate, by maintaining that he acted in order to execute an impure or unfaithful woman, we now know that this is not the heart of the matter (Kemper's blatant insanity is proof enough of this); for, beyond vengeance, there lies the terror of an infinitely redoubled mirror or sister image of the self.

CHAPTER SIX

Taking Orders from the Devil

Murderers and Religion

With Herbert Mullin, we shall encounter "criminal values" and the way in which these have created the circumstances for a series of "missionaries of the devil," including Berkowitz, Manson, and others, to emerge. These murderers are not seeking revenge on a mother figure, but rather are doing the bidding of an evil father. They are the weapon of a missing father, and they try to convince themselves (and us) that they are guided by a sovereign who must work clandestinely, because he is pursued by the official forces of "good."

Act one, scene one, of the Herbert Mullin tragedy begins in 1972. The former A student and star athlete (voted best sportsman in his class) has changed. Traumatized by the death of one of his best friends, he has had a sudden breakdown. He begins to take LSD and to practice self-mutilation, including burning his penis. His begins to behave outrageously in public, asking women in the street for their hands in marriage. Rebuffed, he attempts to join the homosexual community, which also rejects him. He tries out different personas: hippie, yuppie, pacifist, Marine, leftist, and finally member of a religious sect. Each failure leads him back to the psychiatric ward, which does not want him either.

Were this a play, the voices of the chorus would be raised in alarm: "What happens next?" Herbert Mullin leaves his room, where, like Antigone after her brother's death, he has erected an altar to the memory of his friend. His father's voice has ordered him to make human sacrifices in order to prevent an apocalyptic earthquake that the voice predicts will result from the US withdrawal from Vietnam. The feared earthquake is both a consequence of the pollution of American values and the cause of a literal state of pollution created by an explosion of a subterranean miasma.

Mullin drives off in his car and picks up and kills an old tramp. Two weeks later, again following orders from his father, he picks up a hitchhiker, stabs her in the car, and pulls over to the side of the road, where he eviscerates the girl and hangs her intestines from the branches of a tree, in order to observe the process of decomposition.

Casting entrails (animal and occasionally human) to predict the future was a common ancient ritual, in which a material form was given to the nonhuman element and to the missing animal or person. Mullin's ritual recalls the Viking "blood eagle" (blodörn), which consisted in making an incision in the victim's back, between the ribs, through which the lungs and thorax were extracted and arranged like a pair of wings.[1] Both vengeful and derisive, this exposure of the "organs of glory" was a manifestation of the warrior's fate.

Mullin's twelve successive killings were attempts to personalize his victims according to the one form of logic he possessed: religion and morals.[2] He confessed his crimes to a priest, but stabbed him immediately afterward, claiming that he had volunteered to be the next victim, as ordered by the father. He then went in search of the drug dealer who had sold him his first marijuana cigarette, killed him, and, to be prudent, massacred the man's entire family and the people who had given him the man's address. His reasoning seems to have been that, since they had known his evil former classmate, they had to die as well. Moreover, he believed that they had offered themselves voluntarily as an act of atonement.

One month later, Mullin scolded four young campers for "corrupting nature," but, when he realized that they were not interested in what he had to say, he killed them. The last victim described to him by the voice of his father was a Mexican man, who was mowing his lawn when Mullin killed him, in plain sight.

Mullin was a "father seeker," although federal agent Robert Ressler sees him merely as a random killer.[3] As in the Kemper case, Mullin's mother demeaned his father, but Mullin also had an advantage (if one can call it that) over the type of schizophrenic who becomes reduced to a zombie-like state: he heard voices; to be precise, he heard the voice of his father ordering him to kill. His world was therefore not totally reduced to a mass of "poisoned" organs, for his mother, a devout Catholic, had apparently managed to communicate respect for some semblance of order to her son. It was on this basis that he built up his hatred and his motives for seeking justice. The death of a close friend, which he associated with a plot against himself, was hence the justification for his insane quest.

But was Mullin a believer? Certainly, the "pollution" which he wanted to examine in his victim's intestines was not really a form of moral impurity but more the verbal figure of a physical world and a threatened earth: it did not represent ethical breakdown but rather (and especially in California) geological catastrophe. Despite his attempts to defend various dubious arguments, Mullin – although he was perhaps not as "random" a killer as the police believed him to be – was incapable of sustaining his claim of paranoid vengeful aggression. Even this proved too much for him to handle. But in the end he revealed the key to his mystery: inexplicably, his father, and hence his own identity as distinct from his mother, could only exist in a bowel movement, a shuddering deep within the organs that are the vectors of life and pollution. For someone like Mullin, a figure of looming death, there are therefore no real actions or real vengeance. Thus, throughout the long chain of assumed roles in which he attempted and failed to humanize himself (by playing the all-American boy, the rebellious hippie, the soldier, or the Bible-thumper) and the string of victims he chose in the name of the father, he was fleeing this awful, annihilating truth.

Mullin is much farther removed from the category of sadistic killers than from necrophiliacs like Ed Gein, who was so uncomfortable in his own skin that he sewed together the skins of dead women to shield himself in their protective lining. He is yet another reminder that murder is primarily an attempt to reconstruct a whole person who does not seem to exist, and only secondarily an act of aggression. But he also reminds us that, if such killers exist, it is a father who made them.

From the Son of a Bear to Son of Man

Multiple killers have revealed that their degree of insanity increases with the proximity of an object that represents the father, and wanes when the father is associated with something vague or missing, which leads to a mythical substitution. If the father is a bayonet for Kemper or a voice for Mullin, we find that for Sam Berkowitz or Charles Manson he is humanized in the form of malevolent intent. In these two cases, the satanic figure, which was only a sketchy idea for Mullin, takes on a greater presence, which is at once more credible and more mystical.

There is also a change in the choice of the victims. Not only are wife and mother attacked, but so are images of happiness, togetherness, and a healthy family. In an effort to understand the incomprehensible, people will often attribute mystical powers or satanic impulses to serial killers, and this is frequently reinforced by serial killers themselves, who may truly believe they have a social mission. Distorted perceptions may help witnesses to explain the killer's strongest motivations to commit crime. This extra-ordinary observation, made by District Attorney Bugliosi after the Manson trial, is an example: "Midway through the arraignment I looked at my watch. It had stopped. Odd. It was the first time I could remember that happening.

Then I noticed that Manson was staring at me, a slight grin on his face. It was, I told myself, simply a coincidence."[4] What Bugliosi is trying to suggest here is simply that Manson was truly invested with magical powers. It is incredible for an officer of the court to manifest such irrationality, but this only serves to underscore the superstitious climate that had formed around serial killings in California in the late 1970s.

New Yorker Sam Berkowitz, a.k.a. "Son of Sam," shrouded himself in an equally thick haze of satanic lore. Criminal sociologists, such as Elliott Leyton, have tried to dismiss his nonsensical discourse as the mere defensive tactics of a criminal attempting to pass himself off as crazy. I think that this gives too little importance to certain elements that can help us understand the American cultural context. On the other hand, journalists, such as Maury Terry, claim that the police covered up Berkowitz's affiliation with a satanic cult, and that they also covered up Manson's cult connections, Fred Cowann's neo-Nazi activities, and the fact that other gunmen had been present at the scene of the murders. These are probably hysterical rumors, but they and Berkowitz's testimony must be taken into account. By the same token, in a case such as the witch trials of Loudun, which took place in the seventeenth century and in which all persons involved were devoutly religious, it would be impossible to consider the inquisitors' remarks separately from the statements of the accused. Moreover, 1979 was a year in which the American movie industry launched several of its biggest "satanic" hits: from *The Exorcist* to *Salem's Lot*, the United States was confronted with some of its oldest fears. Like the film industry, the criminals must have seen the trend coming. Shawcross, for example, claimed to be the reincarnation of Ariemes, a thirteenth-century cannibalistic fiend, and many other hardened killers affected demonic behavior.

We should point out that there is an affinity, as found in the Mullin case, between the voice of a diabolical father and the order to purify the world with fire. Berkowitz,[5] like the Satanist Toole, was fascinated with fire, and there are an alleged 1,400 counts of arson against him, dating from before 1976, when he began to kill young couples in their cars by shooting them in the face.

Hide-and-seek with Father

Berkowitz was an adopted child from a lower-middle-class Brooklyn neighborhood. He was separated from his mother at an early age and, like that of other serial killers, his future was foreshadowed by a precocious career as a vicious child, who loved to torture family pets: at seven, he poured ammonia into his adoptive mother's fish tank, poisoned her pet canaries, and gleefully tortured moths and mice. The experts say that this was a way of testing his power over living beings. An unstable and aggressive child, he never was able to accept the fact that he had been given up and, after his adoptive mother's death, when he was fourteen, this second loss set him off on a feverish hunt to find his natural mother. He volunteered to "fight the communists" in Vietnam, and was then sent to Korea, where paradoxically he refused to engage in active combat. He contracted a venereal disease and – once bitten, twice shy – remained chaste from then on. His beliefs, which were highly virtuous and even puritanical, wavered between patriotic values and pacifism, but were always tinged with an apocalyptic urgency. He felt a sense of responsibility with regard to society, public morals, and the future of humanity. In some ways like Ted Bundy, he devoted himself to acting as a savior, a policeman, or a vigilante. Later, he said that what he most enjoyed about his crimes was to watch the police investigation taking place around the victims' cars.

Berkowitz's career as an arsonist lasted until he found his biological mother, and the murders began when she revealed who his real father was. She admitted that her married name was not the same as his natural father's, who had died several years earlier. Berkowitz's fragile mental picture of this imaginary father and of his reunion with an ideal family was shattered, confirming his fear that he was born from "nothing"; that he had somehow been spit out or accidentally produced, the result of fornication (clandestine sexual relations, which the ancients depicted in the old baking rooms, or *forni*, which have been replaced in modern-day imagery by the back seat of a car) and hence a child of the state and the system: a son of Uncle Sam. This discovery was his justification for considering the murders he committed as the acts of a virtuous moralist. He told his psychiatrist, a Dr. Abrahamsen, that extramarital sex was a heinous sin and that the fact that he had been conceived in a car plunged him into the depths of illegitimacy.

He discovered an emptiness inside himself because of his missing father, and he filled the void with a rage he disguised as "black" mysticism:

> the demons have an amazing way of leaving you feeling like an empty vacuum, leaving your life void of many things. However, the unclean spirits will fit the very same void which they so subtly created with evil light and evil knowledge. "The void has been filled," I told Mr. Breslin; however, it was replaced with a dark foul substance, that resulted in death and destruction.[6]

The demons who create the void are also "castrating," and they envy his penis in the same way as he envied the adoptive father, who sent him out of the bedroom where he had surprised his parents making love. This transposed primitive scene is contradictory because, since his real father has been annihilated, it is feelings of jealously toward the adoptive father that mask his own absence of desire.

The delusions which he drew upon in his crimes consisted in a sensation both of emptiness and of being filled with another person's will, which he later used as justification in his own defense. "After having read the book *Hostage to the Devil* by Malachi Martin, I now have no doubt that I am a person who has been visited by an alien force or being."[7]

He attributes his desire to kill to his father and demon master, who "filled the void." This three-hundred-year-old demon, "Sam Carr," also possessed the neighbor's dog or spoke with the voice of the imagined father. He drove Berkowitz into the streets and ordered him to commit the murders one by one, designating his victims, who came from Queens, where the girls were "prettier." These acts of substitution/filling a void – murders that replaced male sexuality – were therefore dictated by an ambivalent father figure, which was both patriotic and demonic. Berkowitz thus became "Son of Sam" (SOS) and the missions he was assigned brought about powerful apocalyptic warnings: "I am the demon from the bottomless pit on earth to create havoc and terror. I am War, I am Death, I am Destruction."[8]

The demon by which he was possessed gave him a young girl to "sacrifice," but she escaped after the first blow from the knife, and Berkowitz, perhaps just as terrified as she was, also ran away. From then on, the demon preferred to send him after young women who met their lovers secretly in parked cars. Berkowitz played the virtuous "divider," springing upon the couples and aiming for the mouth with a .44 Magnum he purchased in Texas. He committed six such assaults, which were mainly directed against the girls in the couples, in most cases killing them while their partners generally escaped, either wounded or disabled for life. Berkowitz derived sexual excitement from assaulting these couples, but it occurred either while he was anticipating the murder or while he was observing the police investigation and reconstituting the crime in his mind.

Something else lies behind these episodes of imagined possession by demons, but what? I do not think that they are simply attempts to attract attention. Satanic tendencies probably hide more simple forms of the death instinct, as reflected in this poem, which was found on Berkowitz's person when the police arrested him:

> And huge drops of lead
> Poured down upon her head
> Until she was dead
> Yet, the cats still come out
> At night to mate
> And the sparrows still
> Sing in the morning

This text warrants comparison with a poem attributed to the zodiac killer (an unidentified murderer who also attacked young couples, killing the girls), which was found carved on a table at the San Francisco Public Library.[9] In the bizarre single verse, drops of red blood drip onto the red dress of a woman, who is in mortal fear of death, while death is described as nothing more than life vanishing into the unknown. In both cases, one finds an idea of death as something inconsequential, a negation of the victim's humanity, and descriptions of an eternal cycle of death and sex as vital necessities linked in the inevitable fate of living creatures and of things.[10]

In the Berkowitz case, this unjustifiable connection between sex and death is revealed in two ways:

1. The period of latency and the very long suspension of time before the first act (during which he "kept busy" by committing acts of arson, until the "void" filled by the father was revealed to him).
2. The diabolical figures, which lend a moral, albeit negative, undertone to the murders.

These disguises were not pure illusion, but a means for Berkowitz to communicate and to communicate through his crimes. Without them, researchers would have nothing to cling to but the inhuman silence that surrounds the most industrious mass murderers, such as Bundy, DeSalvo, and Dahmer. These murderers do not deal with medieval devils, or with anything else, for that matter, except a mechanical compulsion, in which human life and its illusions all disappear.

Charles Manson

If Berkowitz wanted to create a sort of pseudosocial father by inventing the son of Uncle Sam (and of the system and an anonymous society), Charles Manson identified with Christ, and had to find a name that would suit his divine origins.

Born in 1934 in Cincinnati,[11] in 1998 the self-named Manson ("son of man") has now been in prison for nearly forty years. His mother, Kathleen Maddox, was concerned that he should have a father, and in 1936 she sued a certain "Colonel Scott" for having sired her illegitimate child. The court decided in her favor and ordered Scott to pay child support. During one of Manson's hearings, an examiner deduced that Manson's father might have been black, because, when asked whether he hated blacks, Manson replied that he liked blacks like his father. But the allegation's only effect was to suggest that a love–hate relationship lay at the root of Manson's insane mystical fantasy connecting African Americans with the end of the world. Whatever the truth of the matter, the paternity question comes up in all discussions of the Manson case, because he has also stated that prison was like a "father" to him.

His mother, a streetwise prostitute, held up a gas station when Manson was only eleven. The child was sent to live with a stern, religious aunt (similar to the alternating images that Toole had of a witch-like grandmother and a devout Christian mother). At thirteen, he followed his mother's example and consequently was made a ward of the court. Unluckily for him, the appointed guardian was an equally corrupt uncle, who gave him his training as a professional burglar.

Violent and unpredictable, the boy made a series of attempts to run away from home, but was brought back and grounded every time. Nevertheless, he was occasionally capable of exemplary conduct and joined various religious groups, including the Church of Scientology. But he seemed to be seeking a much stronger form of punishment than these could offer, and finally received a fifteen-year prison conviction for car theft, simply because, by moving between different states, his crime was considered a federal offense and was hence punishable with a much heavier sentence than if it had been a local offense.

His masochistic side materialized during drug-induced hallucinations, in which he felt nails being driven into his hands and feet and his bed turning into a cross. His relationship with Rosalie Jean Willis gave him the inspiration for his own assumed name (Charles Willis Manson) and its psychotic meaning: Charles's Will is Man's son.

In the 1960s, now safely in prison, Manson learnt how to play the guitar and impressed his psychological counselors, who believed that he could become a professional musician. He discovered the Beatles and played their hit songs, with a visible twinge of jealousy. He interpreted "Helter Skelter" and "Revolution Number 9" as subliminal messages of the apocalypse, addressed personally to him.

Released in 1966 at the height of the West Coast student movement, he soon found that he could surround himself with young girls who were caught up in the vast and shapeless hippie movement, using his guitar, his Beatles songs, and his strange magnetism. As one of his early groupies, Sandy, put it, "The first time I heard him, it was like an angel singing," and Lynette Fromme (who made a failed assassination attempt on former President Gerald Ford) described how he radiated a sort of magic. In a few years, he had become the guru of a veritable eschatological sect, which he called "the Family." Living from hand to mouth, the Family, which grew at its largest to 100 members, functioned in the original sense of the word, i.e., as a group of slaves or servants around a master (as in the "familia Herlethingi," Odin's followers). The men were rarely authorized to have sexual relationships with the women, since Manson always had priority.

In his anticipation of the end of the world, Manson led his followers into the desert. He settled in an abandoned former movie set near Los Angeles. As his sense of himself as the chief of a disorganized horde increased, he committed or commanded a number of exactions. He ordered the murder of a cowboy, named "Shorty," who was struck on the head with a pipe, stabbed by the members of the group, and then decapitated and cut into nine pieces, as in a Dionysian ritual. It was from this desert ranch that Manson organized his 1969 punitive expeditions against the inhabitants of two Beverly Hills mansions, and it was during one of these that Roman Polanski's wife, Sharon Tate, and four of her friends were killed.

Manson was not present during these acts. He operated "long-distance," playing upon the state of dependency to which he had reduced his followers, whom he sent to commit the murders for him. Maxwell Keith, the lawyer who argued the defense of the "Manson girls," emphasized their mental submission to Manson, who ordered them to "kill for him":

> Mr Bugliosi read to you at the close of his argument on the guilt phase, the roll call of the dead. Let me read to you now, ladies and gentlemen, the roll call of the living dead: Leslie, Katie, Squeaky, Brenda, Ouisch, Sandy, Cathy, Gypsy, Tex, Clem, Mary, Snake, and no doubt many more. These lives, and the lives of these three young girls in particular, have been so damaged that it is possible, in some cases, their destruction is beyond repair.[12]

As District Attorney Bugliosi (quite convincingly) demonstrated, the purpose of these criminal expeditions to Beverly Hills was to provoke the white population and to pit it against the African-American community at a time when the Black Panther movement was very active, thus setting off an irreversible civil war, which Manson referred to as helter-skelter. Most people will remember the Beatles' song of the same name, recorded on their *White Album*.

To prove his allegations were true, Bugliosi had to put together the pieces of a puzzle: the letters written in blood ("PIGS") on the walls of the mansion (supposedly written in reference to the police by black activists) and the other components of Manson's eschatological delirium:

Q: Did Charlie oftentimes use the word "pig"?
A: Yes.
Q: How about "helter skelter"?
A: Yes.
Q: Did he use the words "pig" and "helter skelter" very, very frequently?
A: Well, Charlie talks a lot . . . In some of the songs he wrote, "helter skelter" was in them and he'd talk about helter skelter. We all talked about helter skelter.
Q: You say "we"; are you speaking of the Family?
A: Yes.[13]

Manson predicted that the victory of the blacks would bring an end to helter-skelter, but that, when they realized that they were incapable of leading the world, they would have to accept the leadership of his sect, which at that point would come forth in triumph from the desert. As Bugliosi put it:

Judgment Day, Armageddon, Helter Skelter – to Manson they were one and the same, a racial holocaust which would see the black man emerge triumphant [. . .] That Manson foresaw a war between the blacks and the whites was not fantastic. Many people believe that such a war may some day occur. What *was* fantastic was that he was convinced he could personally start that war himself – that by making it look as if blacks had murdered the seven Caucasian victims he could turn the white community against the black community.[14]

Eschatology and Satanism

Manson's eschatological beliefs were not solely derived from his active imagination. It appears that he was inspired by the credos of various syncretic sects, which believed in rather ill-defined combinations of God and the devil.[15] At the time of the Manson crimes, a satanic church, founded by Anton Sandor (a name which contains an anagram of "Satan"), had sprung up in Los Angeles and was demanding (via the press) that acts of abomination be committed. Over a number of years, Manson is said to have made contact several times with sects that were spinoffs of the Church of Scientology. He also was acquainted with followers of the Church of the

Last Judgment, a group of former Scientologists who worshipped both Christ and Satan, led by Robert de Grimston, alias Robert Moore. They predicted that a violent Armageddon was imminent and that only a chosen few would escape. They also believed that the Hell's Angels, who sported Nazi symbols, including swastikas and German war helmets, were the horsemen of the Apocalypse. Jehovah, Lucifer, and Satan were three equivalent divinities, and they were unified through Christ. Satan and Christ would return at the end of the world: Christ as judge and Satan as enforcer. According to the precepts of the sect, people must love their enemies; thus, if Satan is Christ's enemy, we must all love Satan. Hence, the lamb and the goat go together.

Literary Sources of Obsession

We should point out that, although it was carried out collectively, this psychotic nightmare was hardly more vehement than the ramblings of the Romantic English poet and painter William Blake, who, two centuries ago, sought to reconcile heaven and earth and the lamb with the tiger. It is this same dark romanticism that continues to flourish in contemporary Anglo-Saxon culture. American culture itself believes that its foundations were laid during the witch hunts, especially those that took place in Salem. This small legendary East Coast town became a site for collective hysteria in the eighteenth century, leading to the condemnation of dozens of persons accused of practicing witchcraft. The theme has been used often, most memorably by Arthur Miller in *The Crucible*, a play that draws a parallel between the witch hunts and the trials of the McCarthy era.

In one of his short stories, H.P. Lovecraft situates the den of the monstrous beast Cthuhlu under the Salem church house, an idea used by Stephen King in *Salem's Lot*, which is about a town haunted by vampires. The same theme is found in a number of movies made in the 1980s, which depict whole communities of vampires or zombies, guided by wicked ministers or priests. The recent satanizing of pedophile priests in the United States is echoed in many other aspects of this culture.

Moreover, in the European and Latin cultures, the devil tends to be portrayed as the loser: in making his 1987 adaptation of the Georges Bernanos novel *Sous le soleil de Satan*, starring Gerard Depardieu and Sandrine Bonnaire (the first French film to win the Palme d'Or at the Cannes film festival since 1966), French film maker Maurice Pialat was certainly bowing to an international trend, but he did so by delivering the traditional Catholic message that damnation (that of a country priest who is able to raise the dead) will be forgiven by divine grace. The forces of darkness only appear on the face of the earth for an instant before being sent away again, chased back by the illuminating power of love.

To return to the Manson case, the most fascinating aspect is therefore not the guru's mystical, satanic ravings, but rather the wavering reaction of the justice system (and, consequently, of American society) to his mythological delusion. As at the witch trials of the Middle Ages, people believed that Manson was possessed: even the "superhuman" leap he made over the defense attorney's desk to attack the judge was interpreted as virtual proof of this, considering his unhealthy appearance.

This propensity to confuse fiction, superstition, and reality touched the life of Roman Polanski, who was then married to Sharon Tate. Tate had just finished making the David Ransohoff film *Eye of the Devil*, in which her costar David Niven was the victim of a sect who practiced ritual sacrifice, dressed in hooded costumes. Suspected by the press of partaking in sexual orgies and possibly of worse, Polanski, the director of *Rosemary's Baby* (after the novel by Ira Levin, which portrays scenes of a satanic sect), was later found guilty of statutory rape. After a self-imposed exile in France, he returned to a career of making films with psychological and masochistic undertones. The strange circumstances of the murder are thus characterized by false appearances, which may have been too bold – especially given the North American culture's tendency to confuse make-believe and reality – and which are reminiscent of how, in the Middle Ages, actors who played the part of the devil ran the risk of being stoned.

After the Manson episode, the satanic current subsided neither in the United States nor in international culture. It enjoyed a heyday in 1970s films, with such works as Italo-American director Dario Argento's *Inferno* (1979), in which he suggests that Rome, London, and New York were consecrated to the three main goddesses of hell: Suspiria, Tenebrarum, and Lachrymarium. Argento has explained that his films are conceived as Dionysian pagan ceremonies: ceremonies of fear, laughter, and blood.[16]

Since the late 1970s, the Satanism theory has been used in interpretations of serious crime – whether real or in literature – and has also directly encouraged real crime. Several years before Mexican director Jodorowski made *Santa Sangre*, there was a spate of multiple crimes that were said to have been committed "under the influence of the devil." From 1968 to 1980, the Zanis, who engaged in witchcraft, terrified the state of Texas with a string of armed robberies and murders. In 1985, charges were pressed against the heavy-metal group Judas Priest for encouraging adolescent suicides with its subliminal messages.

In the 1980s, Mike Ryan became famous as the high priest of a murderous cult. In 1989, Richard Ramirez, the "Night Stalker," was sentenced to death for murdering fourteen people in Los Angeles. During the trial, he raved about his "worship for Satan" and screamed: "I loved all that blood."[17]

Other criminals have come from religious cults in the American South and Mexico. For example, in April 1989, while conducting a search for a student named Mark Kilroy, the police discovered a mass grave on a Santa Helena ranch near Matamoros, in Mexico. The presumed authors of the crime were a group of mystic drug smugglers, whose leaders, Adolfo de Jesus Constanzo and Sara Aldrete, were obsessed with the *Santeria*[18] rituals. On their journey toward the United States border, Constanzo would offer to perform purification rituals for between $8,000 and $40,000. He and his small group soon entered the world of ritualistic murder. They tortured their victims, skinned them alive, and tore out their hearts. As the established *mayombero* (black witch), Constanzo promised his followers that he would make them invulnerable to bullets. He did this by brewing the blood, hands, and tibias of a human sacrifice in a "cauldron," which also contained the victim's skull and brain. He had wanted the brain of another criminal or madman, but finally settled upon a white victim, who would be easier to terrify. The victim was bound and eviscerated alive. As he watched, his killers tore out his heart and bit into it, so that his brain would be filled with dread when he died.

The group was also partial to American horror films, and Aldrete projected John Schlesinger's *The Possessed* for her initiates, which stars Martin Sheen in the role of a police psychiatrist who is persuaded to sacrifice his own son in a magical ritual.

Without implicating religions (or assuming a priori that any one of them has a connection with crime), one does notice that contemporary commentary from all groups in the American melting pot tends to refer to "signs" of a diabolical presence, imagining that "satanic" fiction and reality have a mutual power of determination over one another. In his *Histoire générale du Diable*,[19] Gérald Messadié warns against this phenomenon and suspects that a vast cultural regression is occurring in the United States, through the growing number of sects and the obsessions reflected in popular fiction. He may not be wrong, except that this tendency does not concern only a subculture but Anglo-American culture virtually in its entirety, and the phenomenon is not new; on the contrary, it is a constant, unchanging, and uninterrupted reality.

Cosmological Pessimism

One finds a deep-rooted source of the eschatological pessimism for which Manson became such a familiar symbol, not in the satanic undercurrents of fundamentalist Christian groups but in what these undercurrents hide, or in some cases point to explicitly, with their strange syncretic beliefs: that source is the combat between Odinic warriors, which is at once fatal and resurrectional.

It should be recalled that Odin's warriors aspired to a hero's death even more ardently than the Greeks.[20] Admittedly, they did not run a great risk of being killed during battle, for every night their strength was fully replenished at a grand banquet held for them in Valhalla, where they dined on the flesh of Saehrimnir the boar.

But their divine existence could not shelter them from collective death. While Greek mythology presents a stable universe under diurnal sovereignty, the deeply unstable dark cosmology of the Nordic tradition tends toward general destruction, which occurs when the forces of hell rise. Well before the introduction of Christian eschatology, there was Midgard, the world of man, which was encircled by a cosmic snake perched in the tree of the universe and where the fundamental abyss could open up at any moment, causing a fatal rift that would swallow the mountains and the sea.

The giants and demons were said to emerge from this abyss, borne on ships made from the unnaturally long fingernails of corpses, while the living dead rose with legion force to assault the divine fortress. Eight hundred phalanxes would fall upon each of the 500 gates of the city of the gods during this "clash of powers" that brought on the day of reckoning, before Muspell the giant set fire to the earth and sky.[21] The attack would then be launched from all sides, as the giant wolf Fenrir, who symbolizes the untamable errant warrior, prepared to swallow the heavenly city, the giants destroyed the cosmos, and the sun disappeared, only to rise again above a new earth where a few straggling heroes (including Odin's son) survived.

Of course, life and vitality always emerge again after the world has been reduced to ashes, but the heavenly city's encirclement by hostile powers never ends, and little "gremlins," such as Loki, who bring beauty and harmony back to civilization, also give rise to a hungry evil force, which grows stronger and stronger and less and less obedient.[22]

This constant uprising of the forces of darkness and the cyclical return of beings from hell, for whom some hardened criminals have claimed to be the prophets, do not belong exclusively to Nordic symbolism (they in fact contain traces of Indo-European lore), but it is within this symbolism

that they are especially important. By contrast, in Greek and Roman mythology, the pact that divides control of the earth between Zeus and Hecate
(or Hades) is much more stable. Even if the spirits of the underworld
sometimes haunt the earth or assault its dwellers, the cosmological balance
is not threatened.

Inversely, in the Nordic world, a "hero's death" is doubled by a collective
combat, which necessarily ends in extinction, followed by a new beginning.
This setup has been handed down to modern lore via more or less marginal
forms of religion, escaping accusations of heresy (Gothic Aryanism) and
the judgment of Scandinavian or Anglo-Saxon puritanical churches, and
predicting the return of the Antichrist.

When the FBI made its assault on the Branch Davidian compound on
19 April 1993, there were 100 deaths, most of them voluntary or forced
"suicides." The total devotion that cult leader David Koresh required from
his followers was similar in its conception to the loyalty that Charles Manson
demanded from the Family. But it also is reminiscent of the abnegation of
the young Goth warriors in their devotion to king Theodoric (*thiuda-rik*,
"king of the people") or, going even further back in time, of the sacrifice
of the servants and companions of ancient chiefs, who accompanied them
to the tomb (such as Attila's companions, who were buried in the nearby
tumulus of Etzelburg when Attila died).

In *The Stand*, Stephen King gives a good description of the irresistible
force of personal destiny, in scenes that portray the world ending in pain
and suffering. King imagines the survivors of a deadly flu epidemic, which
leaves the United States devastated, going on a long, mystically planned
journey. They experience a magnetic attraction for their final destinations
– a new holy city or a new hell – which are reflections of their deep nature
– good or evil, saints or devils. There is a similar setting in *It*, in which the
heroes who want to destroy the evil force feel an impulse to come together
from faraway places and, once they have formed a "critical mass," to join
their spiritual powers in the final crisis to hunt the monstrous being.[23]

What is the significance of this conjunction between themes of demonic
possession and the end of the world? By introducing an intention to kill
and a will to destroy the world, it resolves the tension created by attempts
to humanize harmful acts. Myths, which are revisited by criminals, criminal
researchers, and fiction writers, thereby tell us that an evil will is only the
localized manifestation of a desire for massive, cosmic destruction.

The act of demonizing a specific person is therefore a delicate symbolic
operation: as in *Needful Things*, even Satan ultimately walks off into the
horizon or dissolves, leaving behind the type of void that Berkowitz
described. But the threat he poses is thereby generalized, menacing the

entire planet and becoming synonymous with pollution, overpopulation, and clandestine or "North–South" immigration, which contribute to the destruction of the ozone layer. The generalization of horror fiction and young Americans' insatiable bulimia for the terrorizing thrills they get from "Jurassic" monsters, which are more like demons than animals, are thus combined, metamorphosing the devil into a physical, climatic, or even environmental phenomenon.

Meanwhile, with regard to real criminals, the problem remains entirely unsolved: how can one argue that notorious assassins are still human enough (even if they are damned or condemned) for their acts to have any exemplary value?

PART THREE

Wild Animals, Death, and Robots

Up to this point, we have dealt with the spectacular aspect of crime, as if it were a sign of the criminal's will to communicate but also of his self-affirmation in an opinion debate. There is, however, every indication that we must look beyond this mask to discover what it is that actually drives these human monsters to kill, regardless of their own will and whether or not commentators consider them responsible for their actions.

We will therefore examine why multiple killers appear to be set on a path of destruction from the start: no one can influence their fate. Once it is in motion, the machine cannot be stopped, and this fact seals the doom of such people, who are prevented from discovering love by their obsessive quest for literal truth.

Are these relentless hunters even capable of entertaining illusions of happiness? It is not very likely.

We will then consider the crucial role in criminal development of myths of animal mutation, and more specifically the werewolf myth. And, finally, we will consider how the themes of technology and machines have transformed the idea of animal metamorphosis into images of cosmic death and a veritable "mineralization" of the soul, both in society and in the most appalling cases of serial killings.

CHAPTER SEVEN

A Special Calling

The Inexorable Fall of the House of Usher

In the minds of many real killers and in works by a number of authors, time is locked with two keys. The first is inexorability, both in terms of what awaits the victim and in the criminal's transformation into a ravenous monster. The second is that, in all of this, we are informed of the outcome in advance, and thus trapped in our prior knowledge of the looming catastrophe.

We shall start with inexorability: any device can be used to symbolize it, such as the strange importance of names in a preordained fate.

No one is indifferent to the emblem of a name, which is given (or denied) at birth. It is a word that has an effect on others but which also can be used against its owner in the form of teasing or snide remarks. Of course, like the other factors that make up a multiple killer's real and symbolic world, the problems which may stem from a patronym have existed for masses of other people, without producing the same disastrous effects. Yet it is difficult not to think of family names as one of society's ways of testing its members, the point being that people should not take themselves too seriously.

One of the differences between the vast majority of people and the criminally insane is that the latter take even the tiniest clues as to their calling most seriously indeed. If we accept that they have a consuming fascination with their own destinies, believing that words have an absolute power of determination and are a guarantee of physical contact with "the father," we are nevertheless stunned to discover the tragic signs that can be read into the most ordinary names. I have already discussed the coincidence between the military meaning of Kemper's name and the importance of his identification with the father as warrior. But did Richard Speck think about the English meaning of his name (spot, particle), and did he know what it meant in German (bacon)? Could Gary Heidnik not have known that his name meant "impious" in German (*Heidnich*)?

Can one really assume that Charles Starkweather was not influenced by his name? (Incidentally, Stephen King gives us a fictional character, the "evil twin," whom he names Stark (grim, stiff).) It is also interesting to note that the most bloodthirsty errant killers include a Chase and a Wilder. And, of course, there is Samples, who eviscerated his victims and whose name conjures up images of tasting choice morsels.

By taking the name Manson ("son of man"), Charles Manson distanced himself from his mother (Maddox), whose name might sound like "mad dog" or "mad ox" to a self-condemning mind. Ted Bundy's mother's family name was Cowell, the root word – cow – being a reference to a farm animal, whereas his "real" and inaccessible father had the military-sounding name Marshall. The two most famous homosexual killers, Gacy and Dahmer, may well have been taunted as youngsters with cries of "gay," "sissy," and "damn her," especially if, in the merciless world of children, they were at all effeminate in their manner or appearance.

First names also play a role, like any other voluntary act by the parents upon or after their children's birth. Once again, uncannily, ancient sagas and the monstrous transformations of modern-day antiheroes appear to coincide: reminiscent of Loki's evil father, who was named "Dangerous Striker," the fathers of Henry Lee Lucas and Ottis Toole beat and raped their children, as if to predestine them for a life of extreme violence. Comparing Ottis with Othon, "son of Odin," is, of course, far-fetched, but, if one adds the patronym Toole, the full name can be read as "instrument of Odin's son." Did these imaginary connections escape Toole's grandmother, a necrophagous witch who was well-versed in the ways of satanic cults? Whatever the case may be, she called Toole a "son of the devil," which reminds us that Odin's grandfather, who leaves a trail of suffering behind him wherever he goes, is named "Horn of misfortune" (*Bölthorn*).

Two cases suggest that vengeful behavior can be preordained by delusions that stem from a name: Wayne Williams (who murdered children and young adults in Atlanta, Georgia) and John Wayne Gacy, who is mentioned above, also a specialist in this type of crime.[1] John Wayne was Edmund Kemper's hero, and it delighted Kemper that they both had small feet and a tall build. Naturally, everyone admired the image of the cowboy hero from the West, but his role as an enforcer has been distorted by people in a state of complete disarray, who tend to interpret it literally. In the Gacy and Kemper cases, the criminals were on a solitary mission to purify and liberate. The name Wayne is close to "way," but it is also a homonym for "wane" (decline, diminish). One might also wonder about the "killer nurse" from Texas, named Genene, who killed twenty babies and was sentenced to life in prison in 1983.[2] "Genetic" transmission was clearly a problem for her.

George Franklin's acknowledged affiliation with the founding family of Franklin, Virginia, and thus his relationship to Benjamin Franklin probably added to the aura of scandal that surrounded his murder of one of his daughter's friends. At the moment she was giving birth, his daughter remembered how she had witnessed the act, twenty years after the fact. This double betrayal of loyalties – the murderer's betrayal, and that of his daughter, who had him prosecuted for the crime – seem to reflect an ill-fated family heritage.[3]

The theme of the family curse is universal, from the Atridae to the House of Usher. However, the scenario with which the United States is most obsessed is less the breakup of a family than the inability to found one, even in cases where descendants are given the same name followed by a number (as in Edmund Kemper III).

This is not an attempt to discover any real causality between names and actions, but rather to show that social commentary, beginning with the assassin's own observations about himself, seeks to explain fate and thereby has the effect of anticipatory or retrospective "creative predictions."

Louis Althusser's autobiographical memoir contains the same lesson, tracing back his slaying of his wife to the ill-fated implications of his name, which his mother gave him in memory of a lover who was killed during the war.[4]

Stories of Fate

Names are only an introduction to a more general question: why is it impossible to prevent the catastrophe of murder? Because, as certain murderers tell us, it has been foretold (something which name interpretation can only confirm). It has already happened and is therefore outside the realm of time. "What I am living makes me a stranger in the present," said Roberto Zucco, who at age nineteen killed his parents and five other persons before committing suicide at age 26 in the Vicenza penitentiary in Italy.

The criminal's often unconsciously fatalistic outlook is used by fiction writers, who give a voice to his silent beliefs. Stephen King cultivates such an aura of radical pessimism. As he writes in the introduction to a short-story collection:[5]

> I think that, as copulation tends toward self-preservation, all fear tends toward a comprehension of the final ending. [. . .] The horror writer always brings bad

news: you're going to die, he says; he's telling you to never mind Oral Roberts and his "something *good* is going to happen to you", because something *bad* is also going to happen to you, and it may be cancer, and it may be a stroke, and it may be a car accident, but it's going to happen.[6]

One may choose not to believe in this type of sign, or to try to refute it. But serial killers and their fictional doubles are there to tell us that the opposite is true: what is predicted today will truly happen; as a matter of fact, it has already started.

An excellent illustration of this pessimism principle is the extraordinary story *Thinner*. A friendly, stout American, who is the unfortunate victim of a witch's curse, begins to lose weight in tiny amounts of just a few ounces a day. But, as the chapters continue, whatever he does, he cannot stop slimming. The theme is amusing – even lighthearted – but King wipes the smile off of his readers' faces and leaves them trembling with icy terror as they await the daily verdict of the scales.

Unlike other authors, King does not try to surprise; instead, he exposes his subjects to a minutely detailed, inevitable destruction. He indicates the path to follow and the rules of the game, as if winding up a clockwork toy and then letting it find its own way to the edge of a table. This typically American author's international fame comes from the way he has transformed an oppressive systematization into a literary style.

Warning the People

The second factor in time suspension is the anticipation or foreshadowing of a catastrophe.

This procedure was in fact used by criminals long before its more polished literary interpretations appeared. For example, on 4 September 1913,[7] in the German village of Mülhausen, a masked man called Wagner fired shots in the street from two pistols. He killed eight adults and a young girl, and wounded twelve other people. The day before, he had calmly killed his wife and his four children; then, he had come by bicycle and train to the village to take his revenge on its inhabitants for "snubbing" him during a previous visit.

Ten years earlier, he had purchased the pistols, convinced that he would one day be pursued for having masturbated and engaged in sodomy (at age 27). He then made the decision to commit the murders and take his own life. In 1907, he began to lay a plan for killing his family. He waited to find an "altruistic" pretense for his murder, which was given to him by an earthquake in 1913. This "final" event, which in his mind was comparable to the burning of Rome and Nero's death, was his cue that it was time for the execution, which he described as taking place "like clockwork, totally mechanically."[8] Comparing himself to Shakespeare, Schiller, and Goethe, he said that enacting this drama left him feeling "both apathetic and excited."

He was institutionalized and became a model psychiatric patient before joining the Nazi party in 1929, where he supported measures of racial cleansing. Can one conclude from this that the Nazis secretly approved of the state of mind that is induced by such insanity, rather than seeing it as one of the forms of mental degeneration that eugenics was designed to eliminate? It would be hard to say. But one cannot resist drawing a parallel between the annunciatory technique which Wagner used ten years earlier to warn of his plans for murder, and the explicit warnings in Nazi propaganda about how "parasites" of the race should be dealt with. My point is that acts of pessimism and destruction which are programmed over a period of time and interpreted as the realization of a personal fate are among the various behavior patterns observed in individual cases of insanity and social and political psychopathy.

This early example gives us pause when we compare it with formal and rather foolishly "Cartesian" efforts of the American police, who make a fundamental distinction between mass murderers (unpredictable and defined by "bouts of insanity") and serial killers (premeditating, repeat offenders), "random" schizophrenic killers and "methodical" sadistic killers. For the Wagner case mixes together all of these categories. There is an element of sadism – whether conscious or unconscious – in sealing his loved ones' fate with a plan and then pulling the trigger at the preordained hour. Although Wagner committed the murders in only two or three days, two different, inexorable time periods are nested together: the very long period, which extends from the "impure act" and the supposition that others were aware of it to the days of the murders; and the period of the crisis, which is divided into three fast-moving moments, the "altruistic" murder of the family, a vengeful attempt on his brother, and the random killing of people in the village. In both time periods (similar to other murders, which we will discuss later), there is a progression from the private to the universal through a meticulous preparation of the sacrifice.

If we carefully observe multiple killings, committed either in public or in private (a common example being that of a person who kills his family and then, in some instances, takes his own life), it soon appears logical to search – in a number of serial crimes – for the long, inexorable period which precedes the crisis, often giving it a sense of pinnacle or climax.

The same organization of two nested time periods is found in the case of Charles Joseph Whitman. Whitman, a Texan with a long history of depression, had progressively stockpiled an impressive weapons collection. His first act was "private," as the victims were his mother and wife, but on 1 August 1966 he turned this "test run" into a public apocalypse, after climbing to the top of the University of Texas clock tower: from his perch, he shot down fifteen people and wounded thirty-one.

Anyone who likes slightly bizarre symbolism will notice that a university clock tower, a favorite place for mass murders in America, is highly symbolic, as it unites the inexorable march of time and an image of vast knowledge. This was not the first or the last time that a serial killer or multiple murderer would connect himself with an impossible mastery of knowledge and a desperate sense of the unrelenting movement of time.

This temporal dialectic of latency and sudden acceleration during the preordained crises is also found in the Chase case, which still remains exemplary in its atrocity.

The Sacramento Vampire

Most of Richard Trenton Chase's biographers agree that the young Californian, who was born in 1950 and committed suicide in prison in 1980, was not an attractive person: he was gaunt, his expression was dazed, he was dirty, and his clothes had holes. But this young junkie, with his stained T-shirts, would not allow his miserable surroundings to keep him down, and he emerged from them with acts of such horror that he acquired a public identity and a history. He helped to build this legend. He reflected for a long time on his destiny, which he conceived as a journey from one catastrophe to the next, each constituting an acceleration in tempo.[9]

Psychiatric experts have reconstituted his premonitory childhood as an assemblage of interpretations focused by the attitude of a "typically paranoid schizophrenic" mother, who destroyed her son's image of his father, whom she accused of cheating and of slowly poisoning her.

The psychiatrists construed this scene of looming disaster, but it was, in fact, Chase who first suggested it. If one reads the medical reports, one can anticipate the child's outcome, justifying his classification in the category of serial killers.

The message that various researchers, and Chase himself, trace back to his childhood was his parents' incomprehensible relationship and, consequently, the strangeness of his own existence. He did not understand how he could be the product of a father who betrayed and poisoned his mother.

His identity was carved out in this rift of knowledge, which incited him to crime, just as the ghost of Hamlet's father drove his son to madness, revenge, and suicide.

It becomes obvious that, because of his radical incomprehension of his own existence, he would experiment on these themes throughout his life. It was through his experiments to answer the looming question of his human origins that he transformed himself inexorably into an animal, a Jack the Ripper, a drinker of blood.

Casus perplexus

Observers apparently fail to see these acts as *in vivo* experiments, as if the inexorability of their violence must necessarily result from malicious intent and could not stem from a will for knowledge; as if it were wrong to consider a process of learning that is obstructed by a riddle as neutral; as if it were impossible to posit that a succession of inhuman acts could be prompted by a state of perplexity.

When Chase opened a baby's skull and ate the brain with a spoon, was his sense of curiosity any different from ours when we crack a nut and wonder what we will find inside? Probably not. The only problem is that, for him, a baby or any other human being, including himself, was nothing more than a receptacle full of poisoned organs. He explains this clearly when talking about his childhood: he saw himself as the product of a transmission of organic poisons. His naive question (whose dangerous effects one would rather avoid) was, if babies and pregnant women literally carry life within them, where are they hiding it? For, if it is not in the brain or the viscera, then humanity – his and ours – is nowhere.

This question influenced Chase from the beginning, but he did not look for the answer immediately. It was after he moved away from home that he began to sow his path with increasingly ominous signs. Like so many lost young people in California in 1976, he dabbled in hard drugs. But his eccentric behavior still seemed harmless: he believed that he was the reincarnation of one of the Jesse James gang, and placed oranges around his head before going to sleep so that the vitamin C would filter into his brain.

The evidence of his paranoid state of mind – i.e., aggressive behavior motivated against someone else – unfolded through a string of minor incidents. To foil the "plot" that had been set to destroy him, he shaved his head, in order to monitor changes in the shape of his skull and any bones that might begin to protrude through the skin. His internal organs were shifting places and his heart was shrinking. He checked in at a hospital, complaining that his pulmonary artery had been stolen and his blood circulation shut off. He was sent home. He began to kill rabbits, cats, and dogs, putting them in a blender and drinking the mixture to restore his blood supply. In May 1977, he killed a cat in front of his mother and covered his face with the blood. Another more disturbing form of provocation was his harassment, bordering on rape, of young girls. Complaints were filed with the police.

Yet it was not his nascent sexual aggressiveness that pushed Chase over the limit of socially recognized normal behavior: he began his career as a psychiatric case when he attempted to inject himself with rabbit blood. Rumor has it that the nurses in the institution where he was interned nicknamed him "Dracula,"[10] an uncanny foreshadowing of his future label, the "Sacramento vampire."

But, like others who have commented on him since, the nurses were wrong in their interpretation of the myth: vampires drink their victims' blood with gusto and gourmandise. Their eyes light up with desire in anticipation of these meals, and one can picture them with a trickle of drool running off their long fangs. Chase's case, by contrast, suggests no such craving. If he cooked organs or mixed blood in a blender, it was because he was attempting to figure something out. His murderous inclination came not from a sense of frustration, but from a lack of understanding of others.

Chase amassed a collection of revolvers and munitions. He had a consummate sense of timing, and spent long hours determining which route he would take and noting its main road signs and intersections. For researchers who know how the story ends, there is no doubt that he was preparing to become a "mad warrior."

But how can one explain the fact that nobody deduced the logical outcome of Chase's behavior at the time? It seems somehow inevitable that criminals are invisible before the disastrous facts. Everything takes place as though it were predetermined, with the witnesses' unconscious consent. Other persons' inability to "see what is in front of them" therefore appears to be part of the ritual preparation of the sacrifice, which seems almost to be desired.

Seen in their proper perspective, the eight killings were made in rapid succession (over a few days in December 1977 and January 1978). They also were organized like a progression of inexorable events, preceded by an announcement and preparations, and committed in increasingly horrifying ways. Unanimously considered to be a "random killer," Chase in fact committed linear acts, which took place in a restricted time–space structure. He noted the dates of these acts in a diary, purchased the appropriate weapons, and displayed a fascination for serial killings. He was very interested in articles on the Los Angeles stranglers, Kenneth Bianchi and Angelo Buono, who had perfected the technique of "carnapping."

He prepared by putting on a parka, which his father had given him. This one concession to a vague paternal symbol is another indicator of the material nature of sexuality in his confused perception: analogous to Kemper's father's bayonet, this object negates virility by turning it into a concrete sign.

Then, he set off on his hunt. Because his mother had refused to have him at her house for Christmas, he wandered around the surrounding streets and began to fire shots left and right at neighboring homes. He hit a woman, wounding her slightly, and aimed at a passing shadow, slaying a man. He then set fire to a barn and tried to break into a neighbor's house. He was not apprehended.

A few days later he achieved his crowning victory. He attacked a young neighbor who was three months pregnant as she was taking in her garbage cans, shot her at close range, raped and eviscerated the body, removed the organs, mixed them together, and drank the blood. On the same day, apparently unconcerned by his blood-encrusted clothes, he attacked a family, killing two men and a young woman, whom he then eviscerated. He brought their little boy, David, to his apartment and killed him in the bathtub. He cut up the body, mixed the organs with the blood and ate them, removed the child's brain and devoured it raw. His refrigerator was found to be full of human and animal organs.

A Pedagogical Killer

To anyone who is not too frozen with terror to see it, Chase showed that he did not kill for the simple pleasure of the hunt but that he was looking for something. What? We know the answer now, but he did not give his own detailed, maniacal explanation of the facts until he was incarcerated and put on death row at San Quentin, after which he committed suicide in Vacaville penitentiary, where he had been moved to protect him from the other prisoners.

Now that he was in the final lineup, awaiting execution, Chase revealed his secret, which researchers have interpreted as a Pythic message: he said he bore the star of David on his forehead (he was not Jewish, but David was the name of the child he had killed and with whom he identified) and was being threatened by extraterrestrials, who lighted the stars, which they came from by means of nuclear fusion.[11] The fusion – which was in fact his interpretation of his own conception – was poisoning him, because it was emitted from the soap scum that had collected in the bottom of a soap dish (representing his father's sperm). Because of the danger that his own blood might dehydrate, he had to drink other people's in order to maintain his circulation.

The circle leading back to his own childhood was thus complete. Chase could only understand the distance between his father and mother as something material (granted, he imagined it in terms of interstellar distances, but these are still physical), but at the same time he could not imagine his own birth as anything other than an encounter between two bodies which were already contaminated with poison and a damp rot. Had this encounter not occurred, he would not exist.

The progeny of this poisoned, natural copulation, he was not sure whether he was an extension of his mother or if he had inherited something from his father: sometimes he thought that the poison came from the mother, at other times from the father, and then he began to wonder whether it came from an intention, i.e., whether it was produced in the brain. In any case, his eroticization of the murders (the rape of his second victim) provided him the only form of certainty he possessed, that is, that the physical act had something to do with birth (he attacked pregnant women or women with small children). But, in all other areas, and especially in questions of manhood or maternity, the life cycle, and the reality of human existence, he was absolutely unable to believe any symbolic manifestation: he had to see for himself how the genital organs were formed, how they differed from the digestive system, and so on.

Unlike the myths that have been reported by Lévi-Strauss, in Chase's demented myth there is no distinction between the raw, the cooked, and the rotten; society and nature, or the nameless state that lies between the two. He was an incarnation of this middle state, and he turned himself into a system both of nature and of human life. In this sense, he provides an indication of the madness of any being, whether social or individual, that believes it is a system unto itself.

A Malevolent Rehumanization

Because of his revulsion for the paternal figure that produced him, Chase turned himself into a pure material element. His destiny, like that of a god, was frozen in stone. In his case, as in preceding cases, researchers and writers have been unable to come to grips with the self-destructive nature of a person who is unable or unwilling to symbolize an identity principle that joins together love and lawfulness. In order to provide a convincing rationale for aberrant behavior, writers tend to focus on perversion rather than madness, as madness is too inexplicable.

The result is a desperate attempt to stop. To escape the abomination of a purely "objectified" world, criminals and their observers try to convince themselves (and us) that there is a reason for these acts. Since the argument of sexual pleasure is not credible, the only solution is to invoke harmful intent.

To rehumanize a character like Chase, wallowing in a "state of nature," a commentator's only choice is to use a technique described in the preceding chapters: to lend him the same negative humanity that characterizes Satan. When he met Chase in prison, FBI officer Robert Ressler immediately made a connection between pure animal nature and the diabolical nature of his subject, saying that Chase's eyes reminded him of the shark in *Jaws*: two black marbles without a pupil, like the eyes of a demon.[12] This shift from bestiality (shark) to evilness (demon), described here as it occurs, clearly shows where the imaginary transition from werewolf to vampire, or from vampire to evil spirit, originates.

Freud makes the same argument in *Totem and Taboo*, his authoritative and yet highly criticized (except as a myth that concerned Freud personally) work, according to which the belief in demons is fostered by an animist renunciation of the all-powerfulness of ideas.[13] Have these demons also been the first to gain from a renunciation of the all-powerfulness of machines?

However, in the definition of a killer, the transposition of a real "animal nature" toward a spiritual "evil nature" makes it uncertain whether violence can be stopped. By transposing violence into the realm of superstitious rumors, one does not eliminate it, because it is projected onto another scene: that of contamination, which has both a "vampire-like" side and undertones of mass conversion. Authors of popular satanic novels have not failed to exploit these fantasies. This rift has also swallowed up an entire class of crime, associated with the horror of the afterlife and the spirit world, in which criminals' contribution to American cultural mythology is brashly apparent.

But Chase casts aside these romantic, superstitious constructions in one sweeping gesture: he brings us back down to earth, and even into the earth.

A Question of Existence

We should retain at least one key component of this pathetic character: in his example, the energy contained in extremely violent acts is not something organic, living or natural. It is entirely cultural, and is linked to an uncertainty about our existence as human beings. Richard Chase shows that the inexorable mechanism of a killer's fate can be driven by something very different from the romantic image of a hunter or a warrior – a lack of knowledge, a riddle about his origin – and that this can keep him going for several years. Basically, he asserts that life is merely a period of pure suffering, a type of limbo which precedes death, and this message seems to be repeated and refracted by many paranoid schizophrenic serial killers. When one comprehends the total horror that it implies, one understands why this message is not commonly recognized and even less frequently relayed by the media, which are much more likely to advance the well-established, narcissistic motives of rage, frustration, a will to possess, hatred, vengeance, or even an uncontrolled perversion, sadomasochistic practices, cannibalistic urges, etc.

Yet this raging question about human life which seems to motivate murderous insanity has a founding function. For, without these vagabond characters who are at once predestined and yet unpredictable in the nature of their attacks, one could not defend the idea that there is something within all individuals that transcends the socially accepted definitions of good and evil and the categories of socially controllable behavior. What is interesting about Chase in relation to Toole and Lucas is that he was not satisfied with merely drawing upon the energy of his dying victims, he gives us an interpretation of it: it is this search for the father that raises the dead and brings ghouls back to life. This quest animates beings who know neither what nor who makes them exist, and who have no knowledge of their own origins (as if such knowledge was possible, beyond the illusionary magic tricks that are played by any form of symbolism).

The thing which, since the dawn of time, has stirred ghosts, ghouls, revenants, and robots is that they do not know that they are dead. They are on a search. Like the knights of the Holy Grail, they have a quest.[14] The problem is that they do not search in symbols but in bodies. Their writing is set out in bodily fluids, other people's blood, the blood of animals, children, and especially women.

Psychosis as a Literary Process

Having observed the penchant of the criminally insane to warn others about the acts they plan to commit, Stephen King adopted this process as a literary genre, adding a sadomasochistic twist to it, perhaps in order to make its demented quality more easily digestible. He is certainly the first fiction writer to have systematized this foreshadowing technique to such an extent in the narrative process, both in his many short stories and in his longer novels. The only difference between the two is that, in the novels, the progression of days and hours which sets the scene is longer, which gives the reader a stronger sense of masochistic anticipation.

In *Roadwork*[15] (the story of a citizen's revenge on a construction team), the author uses his talent to its full effect to set the scene for the mad warrior's entrance. A gun-slinging Rambo in the making, his paranoid character matures slowly, sheltered behind a modest, sociable appearance that is belied only by minor but portentous incidents.

King's obsessive genius derives from the fact that he reveals the secret to the plot at the beginning of each of his books. By the tenth line of his short story "The Boogeyman,"[16] we know that the grieving father in the story blames himself for the death of his three children, who were frightened to death by a ghoul hiding in the closet. In "Shawshank," one of the short stories in the *Different Seasons*[17] collection, Andy Dufresne, a prisoner who was wrongly accused of his wife's murder, attempts to get himself released through a number of legal methods; but the narrator, a fellow detainee, soon makes it clear that in the end Dufresne escapes to a Mexican village with his money and his honor intact. It is precisely because we know the outcome in advance that our curiosity is raised: when will the "bad guys" in the prison stop inflicting sexual tortures on Dufresne, and when will he finally escape the rest of his troubles, which have condemned him to days, years, even decades of a living hell peopled by conmen and where the bathrooms are ruled by homosexual gangs? Readers also naturally wonder how he will manage to get out. But, even when the answer is finally revealed (he escapes through a sewage pipe full of excrement), we still want to know how long it will take him to crawl through the pestilential duct.

Similarly, in the first pages of *The Shining*,[18] we know that it was the isolated hotel in the snow-laden north that led to the former caretaker's breakdown and attack on his family, and we also know that the current candidate for the job, Jack Torrance – played in the film by an affable, albeit disconcerting Jack Nicholson – drinks too much, that he has a mean streak, and that he has taken his family with him. In fact, we already know that he is going to metamorphose into a wild animal, in exactly the same way as his predecessor. Because of this foreshadowing, which on the whole is not very credible, we want to find out whether the prophecy will fulfill itself, and we cannot tear ourselves away from the terrifying story until its long-awaited outcome has taken place.

This consonance between the killer and the writer therefore confirms the inexorability of the criminal destiny. Why? Because they both have an interest in underscoring the exceptional character of the criminal's violent nature, the killer as an argument in his own defense, and the writer because of his readership's strong inclination for sensationalism.

This in turn accentuates the mythological aura which surrounds this type of criminal in modern society and further reinforces the catastrophic tone of inevitability that associates society's tragic end with the excessive behavior of these antiheroes.

CHAPTER EIGHT

Twice Evil

I am Peter Stillman. That's not my real name. My real name is Peter Rabbit. In the winter, I am Mr White, in the summer I am Mr Green.

Paul Auster, *City of Glass, The New York Trilogy*

I Love You When You're Bad

The werewolf culture is America's signature culture. It is the collective expression of a people that lends no credence to the idea that its suppressed urges have been sublimated, perhaps because objects command a greater fascination in this society, which is still based on conquest, an enthusiastic use of physical force, competition, and takeovers. Things appear as if they were accessible treasures, glistening with beauty, like the goods which the shoppers in *Needful Things*, Stephen King's most powerful book, imagine they see in an evil storekeeper's window. On the other hand, Americans have not renounced their human nature, and so they may spend their lives wavering between two alternatives: the fetish and the need for love, the things that they can possess and consume and the never acknowledged things they are missing.

It was Freud who expressed this in the clearest terms: we are all a bunch of killers. Furthermore, in Anglo-American culture, before the kill we are rapists and sadists, and afterward we become cannibals. There is no way out. Paul Verhoeven, a rising star in American film noir, suggests the same idea through his well-intentioned detective character, played by Michael Douglas, who indulges in the worst imaginable horrors.[1]

However, there is a problem in the werewolf culture: it is incapable of acknowledging its urges. It feels obliged to label them as "bad." And, if it does not wish to give up these pleasures, it has to construct an elaborate defense system, an artful procedure by means of which it appears to be disgusted by the things it enjoys and to enjoy doing the things it hates. It is only normal that it should get somewhat lost in the confusion and have trouble recognizing its own offspring. Some, in their misguided good intentions, begin to worship repression, and sacrifice to it with acts that

119

resemble the very behavior they condemn; others indulge so excessively in forbidden pleasures that one has the impression they are trying to reach a sort of prescribed limit, which is highly reminiscent of the codes of conduct for assembly lines, offices, or the torture chambers described by the Marquis de Sade. As a psychiatrist friend of mine once pointed out to a murderer who told him that the devil had ordered him to commit a further thousand murders: "That devil is the worst boss I've ever heard of; he's got you working at a hellish pace" (indeed!). In short, the unlimited repetition of pleasure submits us to the most restrictive law of all. When savagery is given free reign, its self-constraint is more oppressive than that of any other liberty.

In general, however, the werewolf culture does not lead its followers to the borderline areas where they could reflect upon the philosophical effects of these paradoxes. This is precisely the werewolf's problem: he is impervious to the masterful theories of Blanchot, Barthes, or Bataille.[2] Instead, he lives in a state of pure contradiction between two urges: one for destruction, the other for order. The outcome is a form of delirium, which modern literature is loath to describe but which is overabundant in cheap novels and tabloid journals, and which is caused by a mental disassociation: since I can only exist by being evil, I have to cut myself into two "selves," a good one and an evil one. Naturally, I love my evil self and hate the good. So, if I try to destroy my good self and succeed, only my evil self will be left, the totally evil self that loves destruction and especially self-destruction. Mr. Hyde always gets Dr. Jekyll in the end!

This dilemma may be an old cliché, but it still lies at the crux of the werewolf's soul as he emerges, fully armed, in the ancient and modern Nordic cultures.

Who Possesses Me?

The theme of one part of the self exercising control over the other was treated by the ancient Germanic peoples. Human beings were possessed by a god whose name – Got or Wot – means possession or inspiration.

Modern Anglo-American literature uses and abuses the theme of possession by spirits, both under the "horror" label and in science fiction, which includes dozens of novels about extraterrestrials or computers that take over defenseless human minds. I have also noted that a number of multiple-offense criminals claim to be possessed by a dangerous personality that takes control of their good personality.

When this "good" conscience has not been erased, it pleads that it was forced to act on the orders of a dominant and, for the purposes of self-justification, demonized other being. The demon called Sam Carr dictated David Berkowitz's mission to him during his prowlings, on which he committed a string of arsons and murders in the suburbs of New York. The bizarre killer Samples was also inspired by a spirit, which "forced" him to slay and eviscerate women, both in Vietnam and in the United States.

Occasionally, this evil personality is not clearly defined. It is just a silent thing that lies in wait behind a killer's outwardly normal appearance. For example, during his trial, Ted Bundy was never able to present a focused image of the person that went out on the hunt to slay the dozens of hitchhiking girls he picked up. He consistently referred to this other personality in the third person and in the conditional tense. Bundy's commentators failed to see this as anything more than a form of denial: the day before his execution in the electric chair, with no hope of obtaining a pardon, a tearful Bundy was still unable to make his other self speak. At most, he described it as his "vampire" side, which was stronger than the affable, well-spoken young Republican yuppie he embodied during the day.

One can guess the function of this impenetrable separation: it prohibits access to the source of desire, since desires can only subsist and maintain their strength if they are forgotten and repressed.

The following account by another serial killer (a Russian) is enlightening:

> I cannot explain why I had the desire, but at the moment I killed her, I wanted to tear her apart. I cut open many of my victims and would take out their uterus and other sexual organs. On my way back, I used to throw their clothes and any other bloody things in a ditch or in the bushes. I was like a wild animal, and afterward, I didn't remember very clearly what I had done.[3]

Isn't what this real murderer fails to remember – the thing that makes him refer to his "animal" instincts – in fact the innocence of a "natural," primitive urge for fusional, aggressive, and nonverbal sensual experiences?

Twins

It is not inconceivable that a person could believe he had a conniving and totally "evil" self that took over his body while he slept and hid during the day behind his official identity. The Nordic sagas answered this question in a very poetic and guilt-free way: while the magician-warrior sleeps, falls into a catatonic state, or levitates, his internal being (or his *Hamr* in Old Nordic) escapes and goes about his business in the form of an eagle, a dog, a bear, a ram, or a bull. When he is in this state, the man is said to be *hammrammr*, or metamorphosed, transformed (from *heim*, the true self, and *hamr*, which means both clothing and soul).[4] The Viking Ulfr thus becomes Kveldufr, the Evening Wolf, and comes out to wander at night. Not surprisingly, Hrolfr Kraki (the King of the North), the offspring of a woman whose name means "she-bear" (Bera) and a male bear (Björn), metamorphoses into a giant bear.

A master of contemporary mythology, Stephen King answers the question "Where is your other self hiding?" in more pragmatic terms. The other self is simply there, in your gut, or on the surface of your brain.

> Thad Beaumont's brain was the color of a conch shell's outer edge – a medium gray with just the slightest tinge of rose. Protruding from the smooth surface of the dura was a single blind and malformed eye. The brain was pulsing slightly. The eye pulsed with it. It looked as if it were trying to wink at them. It was this – the look of the wink – which had driven the assisting nurse from the O.R.
>
> "Jesus God, what is it?" Albertson asked again.
>
> "It's nothing," Pritchard said. "Once it might have been part of a living, breathing human being. Now its nothing. Except trouble, that is. And this happens to be trouble we can handle."[5]

Of course, once the surgeon has discovered the eye and a few teeth and nails under his teenage patient's skull, the novel's entire purpose becomes to show the reader that there is no way to get rid of the presence of others in ourselves. Moreover, whether they are in the self or elsewhere, is it ever really easy to rid ourselves of others, of our fellow humans and the social community which is immediately formed when "other selves" begin to multiply?

The twin theme has been a classic in American film since Robert Aldrich's *What Ever Happened to Baby Jane?* (1962), in which twin sisters Jane and Blanche, each as evil and vicious as the other, vie to destroy one another behind a mask of innocence. In Frank Ozart and Jim Henson's artistic animation *The Dark Crystal* (1983), catastrophe occurs because the good side (which is benevolent but apathetic), which is made up of the wise men who founded the planet, becomes separated from the evil side, which is wicked but powerful. A mystical apotheosis is reached when the wise men are brought together inside a crystal, a common and ancient theme of fusion found in Druid mythology.

The principle of the mirror-image alter ego can be extended to include almost all of the superhero comics, including those that are farthest removed from Robert Louis Stevenson's "basic" Dr. Jekyll and Mr. Hyde model. In *Greystoke*,[6] the Tarzan character, a human animal (played by Swiss actor Christophe Lambert), is portrayed as a symmetrical counterpart to the English aristocrat. Is this a nod to the ancient legends of the noble hunter who comes face to face with his own beastly image in the animals he hunts? These stories, which are an integral part of the hunting ritual, sanctify the victim and justify a disgust for game meat, which allows the nobleman to distinguish himself from the lower classes by letting them eat the spoils of his hunt. But this phobic contrivance does not hide the fact that the hunter loves his victim because it is "like him," and because it is his double and reflects his own savage acts.[7]

One . . . or the Other?

We are therefore not alone in our own bodies. The experience of pregnancy, in which the body becomes home to another being, is not limited to women, at least not in the imagination. Children, both girls and boys, begin to wonder at an early age whether they took the place of another fetus that was either stillborn or eliminated voluntarily, for example because of a genetic defect. They may also fantasize that they smothered a twin sibling while in their mother's womb. This leads to the question: If I survived, does that mean that I am the evil twin? Or was the other twin the evil one? Stephen King puts this common fantasy into words:

> "This wasn't a cancer," Pritchard told him patiently. His hands went about their work as he talked. "In a great many deliveries where the mother gives birth to a single child, that child actually started existence as a twin, my friend. It may run as high as two in every ten. What happens to the other foetus? The stronger absorbs the weaker."
>
> "Absorbs it? Do you mean eats it?" Loring asked. He looked a little green. "Are you talking about *in utero* cannibalism there?"[8]

These doubts cannot be assuaged. Once one person exists, the search begins for the other, the lost soul sister. Once we can count to one, the narcissistic unit, our anxieties suggest that there might also be a two, or in any case a line separating two beings. One must have its two and, even if we can erase our mental image of this second half, it is always present in our minds as the missing part. Herein certainly lies the secret which connects counting sheep with insomnia: the same thing keeps coming back, time and time again. The function of reading mystery novels or horror stories to cure insomnia thus becomes clear: these sacrificial lambs that overflow from our inner duality must be slain somehow! This is why novels in which each chapter contains a killing, sequels in which each installment contains a murder, and biographies of serial killers are so effective: they attack the principle of repetition and thus the unbearable but inevitable return of the second self.

Aggressors do not attack strangers, but only those people who pose a fundamental threat to them: those who are like them or who reflect their self. By assaulting, killing, and attacking, they deny someone's existence, which is a way of acknowledging or at least encountering the other, even if it is to eliminate their intolerable, competitive presence, which reflects the awful truth about the self. The multiple aggression portrayed in American made-for-TV movies suggests this type of paradoxical desire: to acknowledge and eliminate, to recognize and deny, to welcome and destroy, to embrace and erase.

This strange, mechanical, inalterable dualism is refracted ad infinitum, primarily in the aggressor himself. He almost always divides himself into a likable public image and a dark side, a picture of perfect self-control and irresistible desires.

Moreover, this dualism works in both directions, suggesting that loving others immediately leads to death and, inversely, that an object of love must become a victim. Confusion arises between the meanings of love and hate, and also between who loves and who hates and who is guilty and who is innocent. In the story of Dr. Frankenstein, the creature Mary Shelley imagines (and which may have been inspired by Lord Ruthen, a vampire character created by Shelley's friend Byron) kills in a state of wild innocence, and it is its creator who bears the responsibility and remorse. Similarly, Dr. Jekyll is himself incapable of killing and yet he knowingly devises a formula that turns him into Mr. Hyde, a ruthless assassin who merely obeys urges that associate him with a class of demented subjects who are beyond the realm of the legal process. Tom Harris humorously chose Dolarhyde as his killer character's name, making money (dollar) the ruthless mirror image of the type of science symbolized by Dr. Jekyll (Hyde).

Mr. King and Dr. Bachman

Games with mirrors, cases of mistaken identity, false love interests that hide another forbidden attraction: Stephen King (again) is the past master of all of these devices, even in his description of himself as an author. In fact, the most urgent question he asks in his writing is, "Who is Stephen King?"

It is now known that, in the 1970s, King wrote a number of excellent, realistic, albeit dark and pessimistic novels under the name of R. Bachman. As he has since explained, this division into two authors (Bachman–King), which he abandoned in the 1980s, stemmed from a desire to write separate, realistic works, as well as fantastic fiction (dealing with the effects of supernatural forces). And, indeed, one can divide King's writing into novels in which the characters are taken over by a natural fate, and those in which the supernatural intervenes to make impossible, childlike desires come true. The author of the denunciation is therefore separate from the author of the confessed desire.

Almost all of the Bachman books belong to the first genre,[9] while those of his contemporary, King, belong to the second. Later, King's fame spilled over onto Bachman, and he began to write both genres under his own name,[10] using a more subtle, consonant style. As Clive Barker put it, King had now constructed a more elaborate reality that was more conducive to creating horror. Also, by arranging an encounter between repressed desire ("censorious realism") and confessed desire ("supernatural pleasure"), King makes people's refusal to admit their need for primitive violence appear even more perverse.

This is not all. A careful reading of *The Dark Half*[11] reveals that the hideous twinship between Thaddeus Beaumont (the good supernatural fiction writer) and George Stark (the evil detective novelist) is a reflection of the King/Bachman pair, as well as of myriad other author–character pairs that play a dangerous game with the limits between fiction and reality.[12] King writes in his afterword to the novel that Stark's creation, a merciless criminal named "Alexis Machine," is borrowed from a novel by Shane Stevens (*Dead City*), who was obsessed with the aberrations of the criminally insane mind. It remains to be proved that Stevens, if he really exists, is not in fact Stephen King!

King is not the only writer to have played on the idea of an unborn twin whose ghost takes its revenge years later, in a kind of back-and-forth relationship between dominator and dominated, like a contest pitting Cain against Abel and Abel against Cain. Evil twins are also portrayed in Frank Norris's *McTeague* and Dreiser's *Sister Carrie*.[13]

Unlike ancient sagas, *The Dark Half* has a happy ending because, as King explains, the good author, Thaddeus Beaumont (King), begins to understand that, in order to prevent a blood bath, he must solve the problem himself. He was the one who created Stark; it is up to him to finish him off.

This solution seems only partially reassuring to me, for, according to the werewolf myth, when the forces of good (no matter how intellectual) ferociously destroy the forces of evil, the victory may in fact be that of evil. If the forces of good are represented by the American-controlled UN democratic forces and the forces of evil by a second-rate eastern monarch who has annoyed the superpowers, it is hardly more reassuring. Have Hayek and Rawls's burial of Marx and Lenin truly set us free? Modern society has already begun to judge.

The Woman in the Man

As we saw earlier, in the section on vampires, doubles are also represented by the opposite sex as an image of the self observed from the outside. This may be a key to understanding the mysterious role of the Valkyries, who pick over and rouse the dead in the Nordic sagas. In many traditional societies, it was the women who both tested the survival instincts of their children and laid out the dead, although both functions have now been confided to the technical and medical professions. But the myth's logic goes deeper, for it examines what happens once these central characters of lore have decided which fallen warriors will be brought back to life after their heroic battle is over.

The riddle of the Valkyries is elucidated if one considers the logical problem they help to resolve: the dead hero does not know that he is dead. He therefore cannot remember his deeds. His glorious death cannot be evaluated objectively. Moreover, not all dead warriors have necessarily reached their ideal, since they may have been killed before they themselves were able to kill any enemy soldiers. They may have acted in cowardice and recoiled before their chance to attain glory, even if this was part of a strategy or a measure of prudence.

In other words, only the warrior can judge the value of his acts. But, because his career has ended in death, he is not there to make this judgment. Therefore, a female character must do so in his place, because she represents his double and his soul and does not take part in the combat (as a male double would). Like the tiny secret pouch represented by the womb, she collects the warrior's truth and nurses it back to a second life that is just as mortal as the first, for as a mirror image of virility this female figure is not a bringer of peace.

Duality and duplicity can nonetheless become intertwined, especially when there is a "deceitful woman" in the story. In *Alien III*, there is such a character, who is pregnant by a voracious extraterrestrial monster, and the film's director plays on the question – which is also foremost in the audience's mind – of her maternal instincts. Even though she is carrying a horrendous chimera, won't the human mother be tempted to spare its life or at least to prevent it from suffering? Can she truly feel hatred for her own flesh and blood?

Self-hatred and Hating One's Kind

Duplicity, whose seeds lie in duality, is not only something female; it is the accusation made against any self-image that suggests strangeness. In the first *Alien* movie, it is an astronaut (a "surrogate father") who unwittingly introduces the beast into the spaceship. His punishment is to have his stomach explode.[14] Suspicion becomes rampant and, although they are totally blameless for their contamination, the half-dead vampirized victims propagate their ailment with as much vigor as the demons that inseminated them.

The other dangerous self may be a repressed side that prompts people to indulge in "mixed marriages" and to cross forbidden borders. In *Apocalypse Now*, by Francis Ford Coppola (1979), the plot is only minimally concerned with the Vietnam War. As in Joseph Conrad's *The Heart of Darkness*, from which the film was derived, the real hero is a colonel in the secret service (played by Marlon Brando), who becomes the guru of a Vietnamese sect and is sacrificed in the end. The real enemy here can only be the self, especially when it opens up to other cultures.

This theme of ambiguity between the legitimate violence used against an enemy and acts of terror against the people one loves ultimately derives from the logic of the werewolf myth. Wes Craven explains this in a commentary on one of his films about the Americans people's "inner" violence:

> (Interviewer) – Let's talk about your latest film, which I happen to think is your best. *The People Under the Stairs* is based on a real event which was reported in the newspapers.
> (Craven) – Yes. I read it in one of the local Santa Monica papers. It is the story of a woman in a middle-class neighborhood who sees a group of blacks robbing the house next door in broad daylight. The people in the neighborhood were terrified by the idea that they might be robbed by thieves from the ghettos. The neighbors knew that the couple next door was at work, so they called the police, who found the door forced open but no trace of the robbers. They kept

ransacking the house until they heard a noise, and then they thought they should try to trap the robbers inside. They called for reinforcement officers and broke into part of the house that had been barricaded and where they expected to find the robbers, since the couple had no children. But instead they found three children, pale, mute and frightened like Truffaut's wild child, who had been held prisoner in the house since their birth and who no one ever suspected existed. What I find paradoxical is that these people, who were terrorized at the thought of being robbed, robbed their own children of their lives.[15]

The loving but paranoid father in *The Shining* is, from this point of view, frighteningly realistic. It is because this main character adores his son Danny that he resents him to the point of pursuing him relentlessly. It is precisely because of his failure to act naturally with the child that his destructive energies, aroused by the evil spirit that haunts the hotel, transform his paternal relationship into a monstrous power that is no longer recognizable as human. Before he turns his weapon on his son, he shows his fatherly face one last time:

> The face in front of him changed. It was hard to say how; there was no melting or merging of the features. The body trembled slightly, and then the bloody hands opened like broken claws. The mallet fell from them and thumped to the rug. That was all. But suddenly his daddy *was* there, looking at him in mortal agony, and a sorrow so great that Danny's heart flamed within his chest. The mouth drew down in a quivering bow.
> "Doc," Torrance said, "run away. Quick. And remember how much I love you."
> "No," Danny said. "Oh Danny, for God's sake." "No," Danny said. He took one of his father's bloody hands and kissed it. "It's almost over."[16]

In *Satyricon*, Petronius's character Niceros observes that, behind the wounded werewolf, there is a man in pain.

But, inexorably, the monster reemerges and tears away at his fatherly appearance, which is the final obstacle to his metamorphosis into a beast. The father's disguise of flesh and blood then becomes fully possessed by madness, and the murderous chase begins again.[17]

Was King aware that his image of a madman whose face and body are bathed in blood was reminiscent of a custom reported by Tacitus? Germanic warriors covered themselves with red paint to frighten their enemies. The "Harii" also used a *tincta corpora* when they waged violence of the same type, which the ancient Celt and Nordic cultures feared would be turned against their families, relatives, or fellow citizens.

A Balancing Act

Authors can counteract the presence of evil within the self rationally. For example, the two figures (good and evil) can be localized or made to alternate over time.

With King, duality appears in space, in the same way as ancient Nordic cosmogony separated Asgard, the city of heaven, from Urgard, the peripheral world of hell. In the postapocalyptic America portrayed in *The Stand*, the few survivors are grouped together by affinity, some in a good city run by a mystical nun (which was founded when the apocalyptic epidemic was released from a military experimentation laboratory), the others around a sort of satanic Mafioso, who makes his base in a ruined metropolis before launching his attack on the "good" characters. This is the same scenario as in the *Gotterdämmerung*, in which the good heroes assemble together before the final confrontation that leads them to their death.

In a more classic construction, the good vs. evil theme is set up vertically, between the surface (human) and the underworld (demonic). We should note that, oddly, creatures from outer space are occasionally associated with evil: in *It*, the monster that lives underground comes from a distant star, similar to the extraterrestrials whom the insane criminal Chase accused of transforming his internal organic composition. Do these examples hark back to the legends of Loki, who was the god of mischief, both in the heavens and below the earth, or to uranic myths, in which the gods in heaven form a blind, selfish power?

The underworld, whose tumultuous movements are so frightening to serial killers such as Wagner, Mullin, and Chase, is in literature a predominant symbol of evil. In "Graveyard Shift," as the workers who are cleaning out the basement of an abandoned factory descend deeper and deeper, the rats in the cellar become bigger and bigger. In a fair turn of events, it is the illiterate foreman who humiliates a college student working with the team who is the first to be eaten.

In most of King's dualistic novels, we never know whether the momentarily subdued evil forces will appear elsewhere. At the end of *The Dark Side*, the good writer's criminal double agrees to disappear. But he also disappears at the beginning of the story. Who is to say that he will not turn up again?

In *Needful Things*, the demonic shopkeeper is exposed and runs away, cackling to himself, on an airborne motorcycle. This leaves us with the certainty that he will continue to exploit the basest forms of human unkindness again in another place and time. *The Stand* ends with a stalemate between the forces of good and evil, in which one can easily detect the precariousness of the balance. This delicate equilibrium, which derives from the Zoroastrian and Indian traditions, is present in the Nordic culture but not in the model of Olympus, where Zeus (day) is the sovereign ruling over Hades (nonday, night). Like most contemporary writers of supernatural fiction, King is therefore closer to the Nordic mythology than to the Greek and Roman traditions. He does not believe in the possibility of a human order establishing lasting laws, but instead in a sort of infinite shifting from one order to another.

The Cult of Loki

The theme of ruse as a means of reconciling good and bad is hardly a modern one. One of its most fascinating prototypes is Loki, the most "mischievous" of the Viking gods. He represents a principle of evil reappearing within good. Initially unassuming, but increasingly insistent, he brings forth the savage life forms that will kill the gods in the final catastrophe. He is also a changeling and a master of disguise. He is the patron of obsessive psychotics, who try to hide their real nature and thus maintain the impression that they are good, although their irresistible, wild urges are apparent.

The son of a giant named "Dangerous Striker," who is a transparent symbol of primitive violence, Loki is introduced into the city of heaven and then adopted by the gods. Because he is small and deformed, his only way of escaping insignificance is to reveal his wicked side. In the same way as many killers in modern America are a reflection of their symptomatic childhood, he also gives clear warnings of the adult he is to become, although he does so in small ways, from behind a moving, mutating appearance (he is also called Loptr, meaning air) and changes of sex. A kleptomaniac before the term was coined, he steals small, magical objects that belong to the goddesses (youth-making apples from Ideunn, hair from Sif, a necklace from Freyja) or to the gods (iron gloves from Thor and a ring from Andvari). He drinks mead brewed from human blood with the gods, but his jealous and abusive nature leads him to instigate the murder of Baldr, the "wisest of men." With his magical powers, he fashions a terrible rod, which is capable of killing the bird named "Broad Vision." Because he is intelligent, he initially acts as Odin's helper, but he soon betrays his adoptive kin. He is a cheater and a player of dirty tricks.

When he is punished by being chained to a rock, he creates a "wicked wife" for himself, named Angrboda ("bringer of distress and trouble"), and sires three cosmic demons with her, whose alliance ultimately takes over the present world: Fenrisulfr, the wolf, Jörmundgand, the snake that surrounds the earth, and Hel, the goddess of death. Now one of Odin's sworn enemies, Loki joins the battle against the gods in the final test of powers and helps the troops of hell lead their assault on the city of the gods.

The differences with comparable Greek myths are obvious. While the justice of the gods of Olympus triumphs in the end by dint of ruse, in the tales of Loki a primordial brute force takes command by destroying the ephemeral order, with the help of the hero's ambivalent feelings. In the end, Odin's Loki-like characteristics are stronger than Loki's Odin-like characteristics.[18]

This is more or less the conclusion that the American masters of epic science fiction, Roger Zelazny and Thomas T. Thomas, reach in their book *The Mask of Loki*, in which Loki is made to triumph over Odin in a battle that lasts several thousand years. The two gods wage their fight disguised behind the outwardly human appearance of two human protagonists, who meet in different periods of history: during the Crusades, the French Revolution, and the Vietnam War, in the United States, and in a future war in Palestine. When he confronts Odin and his multiple human personalities, Loki disguises himself as different war heroes, in particular as the Knight Templar Thomas Amnet, and as a twenty-first-century American cyber-punk called Tom Gurden. After he has killed several times, Loki finally unmasks his identity during a state of trance, whereupon his medium, Tom Gurden, reveals that his "self-father" had many different names in different languages: Hazard, Pan, Puck, Old Nick, Quixote, Lucifer, Shaitan, Mo-Kuei, and Jack Frost. Now that he has finally succeeded in gathering all of the sacred weapons which together will break his old adversary Odin's spell, Loki exalts in having succeeded in this supreme deception, which raises him to the level of the highest gods and brings him universal triumph.[19]

This passion for retelling the Nordic sagas as a kaleidoscopic vision, in which heroes shed their masks one after the other and which ends in their cosmic deification, may seem to "Latin" readers (who have grown unaccustomed to epic tales of bold knights who dare to challenge entire civilizations[20]) to border on insanity. Even though these novels have come out in paperback translations, Latin cultures still find it difficult to identify with the passion for them that has taken over in America, and which began as an obsessive neurosis but may very well be turning into a psychosis. Indeed, what other word can describe the disappearance of the object of desire and its replacement with the sheer terror of a confrontation between a person's two selves? What is this fascination – which has only increased with young Americans' growing taste for heroic role-playing games (played with or without a computer and virtual-reality mask) – with multiple identity and its dangerous, inevitable outcome if not a psychotic tendency caused by a de-eroticized love of repeated symmetrical images?

CHAPTER NINE

The Beast Within

It Starts in the Head

This role-playing game that hides other identities "takes over the mind" in the same way as Kvasir (representing intoxication in the Viking culture) struck at the head before being struck down himself and broken open like a bottle of champagne, spouting forth a great geyser of fermented blood.

It is therefore no accident that Stephen King localizes writer Thad Beaumont's evil double in his head. By contrast with the rest of the world, of all the body's organs, Nordic Western tradition identifies most with the brain. It is by means of the intellect and knowledge that it has – like Odin, who was well versed in the use of all sorts of magical powers – established its hegemony and preserved the belief that it controls other peoples. Nor is it surprising that feelings of an evil presence are rooted in the brain. From Dr. Frankenstein, who mistakenly transplants the wrong brain in his creature, to Hannibal Lecter, Tom Harris's mad psychiatrist character who devours his victims while healing their minds, the process starts in the head, like the multiheaded missiles that our armies keep pointed at their adversaries in a peace-keeping salute.

This was the thinking of the paranoid schizophrenic Trenton Chase when he ate animal and human brains; of the patricidal Edmund Kemper when he kept the severed heads of female hitchhikers in the trunk of his car; and of the serial strangler Jeffrey Dahmer when he collected the painted skulls of his seventeen victims. Their possession of the head as the final outcome of an agonizing tête-à-tête with their own self-image was, therefore, quite literal.

In an early case from the 1930s, the Papin sisters put out the eyes of the authoritarian, up-tight woman for whom they kept house. A model of paranoid homicide, their case was analyzed by the surrealists and by Jacques Lacan, and later re-created by Jean Genet in *Les Bonnes*.

More recently, a Russian serial killer named Tchikatilo, who was arrested and sentenced in 1991, blindfolded his victims while they were alive and put out their eyes once he had killed them, because, "according to an old belief," the murderer's face could remain imprinted on the retina of the victim.

Clive Barker, the new master of English horror fiction (recognized as King's heir), was therefore not the first to imagine a character who, in his acquisition of all-powerful satanic powers, turns against his master, starting with the obliteration of his vision:

> "Don't," Kissoon began, but the knife dared to descend before he could forbid it, sliding into his wide open right eye. Kissoon didn't scream this time, but expelled his breath as a long moan. Jaffe pulled the knife out and stabbed again, the second stab as accurate as the first, puncturing the left eye. He drove the blade in to the hilt, and pulled it out. [. . .] With both his fists wrapped around the knife, Jaffe delivered a third blow to the top of the shaman's skull, then went on stabbing, the force of the blows opening wound after wound.[1]

What is the significance of this obsession for the head and eyes? It probably stems from the fact that the face creates an intolerable confrontation with another self, as if seen in a mirror.

Jacqueline Carroy[2] can be credited with having recognized the historical affinity between myths of a double personality and the "head" of nineteenth-century scholars, which was somewhat divided between science and the occult. She recalls that the Dr. Jekyll and Mr. Hyde parable was inspired in Victorian England by a number of reported cases of sleep-induced double personalities and of physicians who practiced magnetism, hypnosis, and hysteria.

She also points out that the pathological obsession with "doubles" was more prevalent among scholars than is commonly believed. It is widely unknown that Gabriel Tarde was not only a serious "sociologist of imitation" but also a judge, a psychologist (female hysteria being the model for his theory of imitation), a philosopher, a raconteur, and a cynical, and possibly slightly demented, futurologist. He believed that, following a "solar apoplexy," humanity would retreat underground to wait for a better world in a totally urbanized refuge.[3]

One can compare his worried observation of "reciprocal aping" among human groups with a parable used by Lacan, describing cybernetic machines that are programmed to imitate each other and which, through their mutual imitation, become stuck in ludicrous contortions. Imitating others does not create a community and, by spreading the belief that human society is based on "rational" affinities, liberal sociology actually undermines society's bearings and drives it and its scholars of sociology mad.

This is certainly the reason why mythical teachings have for thousands of years observed that the only way to stop this game of mirrors is to replace the face of the loved and hated alter ego with a figure that is farther removed and more symbolic.

One such figure, which has always been available, is that of an animal.

"Cousin *Bête*"

"Violence, hatred, and fear eat away at the thin veneer of humanity which dictates our behavior in times of peace, and lead to the appearance of an unsuspected animal nature. The war in Bosnia proves that this is not native to cultural environment or to a particular ethnic group."[4]

We attempt to prevent our "bad side" from becoming a real double or a twin, because, if it did, it could take over our identity. We do not, however, want to forsake the spontaneous impulses that make life interesting, even if they are cruel. Our animal nature therefore strikes an excellent compromise: we are descended from animals, but not directly related; they remind us of our place in nature without reducing us to a state of nature, since their hides and their forms have become too different from our own. We can love animals without (normally) becoming excessively attached to them, and we can hate them without (normally) feeling too guilty.[5] We share our shortcomings, our afflictions, and our diseases with them, as Laville de la Plaigne wrote: "Epilepsy, insanity, and rage are one and the same disease in man and in animals."[6]

Like Saint Hubert, who had a vision of a glorious cross rising up between the antlers of a white stag, we can play upon an identification with animals to justify a desire to kill and to sublimate the object of this desire. In such cases, the hunted, a free being who is identified with the hunter, becomes a taboo, because of the hunter's desire to destroy and devour this other self. By sanctifying the prey and refusing to consume its flesh, which is left for dogs and scavengers, the cannibal desire becomes transformed into a sentiment of noble purity. Renunciation of the animal totem hence contains a logic that justifies a disdainful, aristocratic attitude toward flesh-eating slaves but does not preclude fantasies of a wild hunt.[7]

Inversely, in human sacrifice, the mortal blows are aimed at the animal element. When Roberto Zucco spoke about the crime of killing his mother, he carefully dehumanized and animalized his victim, as if to rationalize committing such an act: "My mother looked like a dead rat when I hit her."[8]

If animalizing the victim excuses the act, the animal metaphor also allows violent criminals to attribute their destructive energy to the beast whose skin they are in or whose appearance they assume through a transformation of their own bodies. This is the first stage in werewolf metamorphosis, the partial loss of one's human nature and the adoption of an animal identity: "Transformation itself can be complete [. . .] or partial [. . .]: the eyes become closer together, deeper-set, the teeth develop in form, thickness, and sharpness, the nails become claws, hair becomes fur, physical strength is doubled, the desire for blood sweeps away all other urges and all cultural taboos."[9]

In the 1980s, hyperrealistic special-effects films began to indulge in savoring every single stage of this metamorphosis. John Landis's 1981 film *An American Werewolf in London* includes a long sequence showing the progressive bone distortion that takes place in the hands, the back, and the jaws of the unfortunate person undergoing transformation. It also shows, with humorous overstatement, the bloody shreds of audience members being spewed from the doors of a cinema (where the film-loving werewolf has managed to slip in), like an explosion of sticky steaks. Landis also made a film in 1992 in which French actress Anne Parillaud (the murderer in Luc Besson's *Nikita*) plays a feline vampire who bites deep into the necks of New York Mafiosi, which ultimately only envenoms their crusade against the FBI. In *The Company of Wolves*, human skin tears apart like a cocoon to release the hairy fetus of the wolfling.[10] Synthetic imaging will surely never surpass this film, which is a classic of the genre.

The animalization of human beings almost justifies the appearance of violence, but it can also introduce a new element of fear, especially when the two natures oscillate. In one of his most terrifying texts,[11] King uses the oscillation of contrasting images of pet and wild dog. The reader finds himself in the place of the victim, Jessie, who lies immobilized on a bed, and must try to distinguish in the expression of a stray dog, now gone wild with hunger, between the signs of a not completely forgotten tameness (from his days as a pet) and those of pure beastliness: the battle between human and animal nature can be read on the features of the face, but, to our horror, in this case the face is that of an animal. Once the dog has tasted the husband's body, which lies, after a fatal heart attack, at the foot of the bed where his wife Jessie has been bound and tied for a sadistic game, the question is when will the dog dare to attack the woman? When will what is left of the dog's "human side," which it acquired through a mixture of fear of and affection for its master (and, indeed, the dog obeys Jessie's weakening voice), be overcome by a more urgent need to plant its fangs into flesh, living flesh?

This question has been one of King's obsessions since he first posed it ten years earlier with Cujo, the beloved Saint Bernard and family friend, which has the misfortune of being stung by a diabolical insect.[12]

We should note the difference here with a "Latin" treatment of bad dogs, such as the horrible but hilarious Baxter, whose only thought is to kill its master's child, the object of its jealousy. Here, there is no shift between a (rather naive) human nature and animal nature (which is unambiguously and unhesitatingly portrayed as despicable). By way of contrast, Alain Jessua's *Les Chiens* is the story of a megalomaniac animal tamer, who turns out to be worse than his subjects, whose savagery he magnifies with the commands he gives them. But, whatever the approach, it is not fear that dominates in these examples but rather a sense of indignation in the face of inhuman behavior.

Definitive human transformation is portrayed admirably well as a marvelous and joyous event in Charles Perrault's fairy tale *Beauty and the Beast*, of which no film version can equal Jean Cocteau and Jean Marais's 1946 *La Belle et la bête*, the animated Disney version being no more than a mediocre remake. The moral of such tales is diametrically opposed to the werewolf story: who could ever imagine that the handsome prince would turn back into a monster once he wed the princess?

Therefore, it is not so much a complete and sudden metamorphosis that creates fear, but rather a hybrid association of two characters (such as the Minotaur, a man with the head of a bull) or, more terrifying still, a progressive, irreversible transformation, hesitation, and oscillation between them.

Half-human/half-animal characters are frightening. They border on another very ancient idea, that of mixing human and animal expressions and body parts into griffins and chimeras, which belong to both natures. Long before H.G. Wells described his character Dr. Moreau producing such crossbreeds in the secrecy of his private island, sagas told how the mother of the Nordic king amused herself by producing first a centaur, then a dog-footed creature, and, on the third day, a man. The many different versions of a cross between a man and a fly, whose monstrous fusion is caused by increasingly sophisticated technology, show that the "fear value" to be drawn from this vein is inexhaustible.[13]

In Tim Burton's *Batman II* (1992), the main characters are partially animalized in order to encounter Batman on his own semi-beast-like terrain. The heroine is a dead woman, who has been resuscitated by a pack of cats and invested with the soul and wardrobe of a feline. The "bad guy" is a penguin-man, deformed since birth; and even Batman owes his nocturnal (and animal) side to a childhood wound that has never healed. The icy penguin swallows raw fish, and the heroine, who is possessed by the ghost of a female cat, has both the penguin's taste for seafood and a liking for mice, perhaps even bats . . . This makes Batman insecure, and gives him doubts about the sense of his mission.

These different uses of the animal motif confirm that Anglo-American culture is preoccupied with the ambivalence and the continual, hesitant shifting between human and animal. Such shifts connect the attributes of both natures to the same essence, which is one of a universal savagery, in which all animal natures are equivalent. In the novel *Wolf*,[14] which is the story of a serial killer, the author tries to convince us that the assassin intentionally seeks out his beast-like nature by means of self-control, intelligence, and intuition (all of which are eminently human qualities), and thus obeys his hunter-killer impulses.

The devil himself indulges in fantasies of the human animal and becomes their servant. In Terrence Fisher's classic tale *The Curse of the Werewolf*,[15] a young Spanish peasant girl, who rebuffs the advances of an aristocrat, is raped by a wild man, who makes her pregnant. The demonic character who appears at the moment when the child is baptized (and who is probably just a shadow cast by a gargoyle) is enough to convey the story's meaning.

In the mythological world in which the werewolf appears and acts, everything tends to signify, imitate, and encourage the relationship between beast and human, which are considered to be equally hateful and greedy, heinous and destructive. This even extends to plants, such as wolfsbane, a strong poison, which grows faster on nights of the full moon and provokes the metamorphosis of any werewolf in its vicinity.

Metamorphosis

The myth of the werewolf tells us this: if you want to avoid destruction, do not waken the beast within, for, once he has started, the wolf will never stop. Once he has been unleashed, he will transform into a huge pair of jaws, swallowing up Odin and the entire universe.

Versions of the wolf that turns into a devouring machine include "The Mangler,"[16] a giant dry-cleaning machine, which, in Stephen King's story, swallows not only shirts but people, and manages to tear away from its hinges and go off on a bloodthirsty rampage throughout the town, where no one is able to stop it.

This is also the theme in Clint Eastwood's film *Unforgiven*, made in the style of a classic western. He plays the role of a poor American whose past as a gunslinger is revived when a group of prostitutes is harassed by cowboys.

With regret, like a former smoker who has a cigarette after years of absti-
nence, Eastwood's character rediscovers the pleasure of killing. Introduced
behind the mask of justice, his taste for murder gains strength and becomes
independent of him, although the man never consciously realizes this. On
the contrary, he experiences it more as an obligation to do his duty, while
for the other characters and the audience it is glaringly obvious that he
gets a thrill from the massacres he instigates.

If we go back further in time, to Great Britain, we can discover the other
half of the myth. Just as the vampire must never be allowed to cross the
threshold of a house, so the uncontrollable urge must not be aroused. It
must be fought and repressed and artistic interpretations of it censored,
just as Stanley Kubrick's 1972 film *A Clockwork Orange*, after the novel by
Anthony Burgess, was censored (and, as many people do not know,
continues to be censored) in London. Several years earlier, the British
censors had also banned Laslo Benedek's film *The Wild Ones*, which
recounts the antics of a motorcycle gang and was judged "likely to incite
young people to imitate the violent acts portrayed."

Contamination

While the story of gratuitous murder written by André Gide[17] has become
lost in oblivion, the savage frenzy of kidnappings, mutilation, and theft
perpetrated in *A Clockwork Orange* by three young English boys against a
background of electronic Beethoven is still just as powerful and chilling
today as it was twenty years ago. What is even more powerful in this film is
its portrayal of repression: judges sentence the "heroes" to antiviolent
behaviorist conditioning, which is in fact the most unbearably violent
component of the film. I suspect that the censors wished to repress this
aspect (which contains the essential meaning of Burgess's novel) more than
the scenes of exaction, for the pleasure in the judge's eyes as he tortures
the young delinquent is twice as apparent. Jumping ahead to 1992, in
California, it was said that it was also because of its portrayal of a law-
enforcement character who is contaminated by guilty, evil pleasures that
the film *Basic Instinct* was given an X rating. But isn't the same type of
contamination present in the American police force when an eminent
member of the FBI suggests that criminal instincts should be tested as
follows:

> You would need a system similar to the one psychiatrists use for criminals who
> rape and kill children: they attach electrodes to the criminal's penis and a machine

measures the flow of blood to the organ when the subject is shown pictures of nude adults and children. If he prefers the pictures of children, the fantasies are still there.[18]

He does not suggest that observers of this interesting device should also have their penises tested. Yet, if one assumes that this secret cruelty we possess is universal, all-invasive, and constantly contaminating everything that is good and civilized, police officers and psychiatrists should also be required to be tested for social aptitude. But who will test the testers and guarantee that they are humane? Who can guarantee that they will not succumb to the thrill of control?

In reality, the shifting between wolf and hunter, killer and avenger, and good and bad is a misleading simplification. An excellent example[19] is the way in which the media covered a recent event concerning the latest "mad warrior" in France:

> "He's a famous wolf hunter," school teacher Laurence Dreyfus is reported to have told the six children who were held hostage with her, trying to reassure them by inventing a game in which the hooded, armed intruder was a character out of a fairy tale or a fable. No one will ever know what the kidnapper thought of her courageous performance, especially when his meticulously planned, extraordinarily masterful, and mad scheme seemed to tell the opposite story: that he was the wolf; that he had decided to play this role because, in a crazy world, men and wolves run together.

Immediately afterward, in a totally thoughtless commentary on the event, the weekly periodical *Globe* ran an article entitled: "What makes people crazy?" One could send the proverbial ball back into the *Globe* editorial team's court and ask: how can society have become so crazy that it forces human beings to rot in a world of senseless existence, unemployment, war, and pollution?

Commensurate with the confrontation between the self and its double, the occurrence of conflicts and instability between the werewolf's human and animal faces increases. This is the principle of contamination: "A single bite, a tiny wound, a mere scratch and there is a new wolf in the pack," recalls Jacques Finné, a specialist in the abundant "werewolfesque" literature.[20] This provides an excellent pretext for revenge, which, appropriately, is also sought in series, as portrayed in a 1985 film in which an American hunter engages in the methodical extermination of an entire village of werewolves.[21]

Despite its obvious connection to the animal world, the werewolf has failed to counterbalance the desire to kill that overcomes the mad warrior, for whom it is only a metaphor. It has been no more successful in preventing this pessimistic mutation than the devil in the Christian tradition has in controlling the dark eschatology of Odinic mythology.

Of course, the wolf is one of the most traditional totemic animals, and its function is to focus violence upon a specific object, to act as a catalyst for the passions, and to free the human element, as distinct from nature. But, by creating an unpredictable, inexorable vacillation between man and animal, the werewolf suggests, on the contrary, that human desire will never be freed from its wild, untamable origins.

The Practical Use of Werewolves

The werewolf myth has therefore maintained throughout the ages that all human beings are of one nature: that of a savage, brutal, voracious, vicious being which needs only to rise to the surface, and which single-handedly holds the civilizing force of repression in check.

This conviction is hard to dispute, for two reasons:

1. It draws upon a fear that is easily awakened by the slightest frightening occurrence.
2. Even if one has doubts, one is forced – cynically – to admit that such beliefs have a practical side, because they justify maintenance of the forces of order and law enforcement.

Anyone who takes part in this dialectic – between the fear of real violence and the common sense that underpins fundamental myths – adheres to its logic in the end.

Initially, its effects seem beneficial: on the one hand, fear activates the collective interest and, on the other, myth is an outlet for a kind of imaginary deliverance, for, although myth is a way of suppressing violent urges, it does not deny their reality. At last, it becomes possible to talk about "real" hidden passions, and things that the moral code deems so horrible that it cannot deal with them are given back their status as desires and pleasures.

All of the energy that is deflected onto fiction is thereby neutralized, and hence satisfying the imagination becomes a way of preventing such thoughts from being put into action. This is in fact the explanation given on television. In an interview for French television, actor Christopher Lee justified his acting career, which contained a long string of bloodthirsty vampire roles, by stating that everything which is acted out in the mind will never be acted out in real life, and even that, if such films did not exist as a release for the imagination, the real world would be much more violent. This therefore demonstrates the "cathartic" function of horror shows.

However, one begins to realize that, once the myth of inborn violence has firmly taken hold in society, it is not totally without consequences. First, there is a tendency for it to stimulate constant anxiety. Anywhere, at any time, a creature displaying the instincts of a beast may suddenly appear. To make matters worse, innocent children will be lured to follow it, for the beast may take the form of their neighbor or a trusted friend. And if you suspect that your neighbor is a beast, then he must also suspect you. Any nosy neighbor spying from behind the curtains can spoil a person's reputation by insinuating that he has an odd appearance, has a strange way of dressing, or associates with strange people. If something happens in the neighborhood, the police will turn their defiant looks on this ideal suspect. Even if the offence is nothing more than a divorce, the defense lawyers will always find witnesses willing to testify to such a person's infidelities or tendency toward domestic violence.

So people act as if they were being observed, and at the same time they keep an eye on what is going on around them. Because of their mutual presumptions of guilt about each other, people create a sort of diffuse totalitarianism, mutual surveillance, and general state of anxiety. Signs posted on their front lawns warn potential burglars that "Citizens are watching you."

Now, we begin to see the other aspect of the problem, but it is rather late. The system works well, and therefore represents the general interest. Peddlers of real or fictional televised terror become rich and maintain the climate of insecurity, reaping maximum profit for all institutions that live off fear: the police, the justice system, industry, and the weapons and security trade.

Just when we want to backtrack and tone down the game comes the "clincher": we are really afraid. We really believe that we cannot let our children walk to the school bus alone. There are so many crazy people, drug addicts, and derelicts around. Even among fine, upstanding citizens, fear itself becomes an excuse for expressions of hatred and demands for revenge: an elderly person who kills a delivery boy who mistakenly rings at his door, because he thinks he is going to be attacked; a boy killed by attack dogs while on his paper route; any form of vigilantism.

We forget the causes of these chains of events. In fact, only one thing is present in our minds: that dark feelings of hatred have been awakened all around us. You feel the same hatred mounting within you. You may still be a liberal antiracist democrat, but now you keep a can of mace in your pocket and your father's army pistol in the glove compartment of your car.

If you really think about it, you are forced to admit that, behind your intentions of pure self-defense, you may be projecting anger on possible aggressors, or even entertaining an imagined pleasure at the thought of finally taking revenge on the gangsters who rule the rough neighborhoods in your city. Of course, you would never go beyond legitimate self-defense, but you know that behind your middle-class, responsible appearance as a family man or woman there is a werewolf in you, just waiting for the right time and place to get out and finally have some fun.

Can you therefore deny what you already know about your own true nature?

CHAPTER TEN

Beyond Hunger

Mad Warriors or the Living Dead?

Serial criminals apparently get carried away by urges, which are intensified by alcohol, drugs, or what they symbolize: inebriation from drinking blood. Their passion for murder seems to derive from a limitless need for stimulation, which subsists behind their phobia for flesh or sex.

But we have stumbled upon a difficulty: by satisfying his desires, the warrior loses his human qualities, becomes incapable of pursuing even a destructive plan, and may continue to degenerate even further. This begs the question, "What is the force that drives him?"

"Criminogenic" hostility comes from an inexhaustible greed, which is more a material urge than a biological need. What is this uncontrollable energy? If we could make a composite profile of these criminals, the result would not be an image of gluttons overfed on Coca-Cola and fast food, but rather a portrait of the living dead. The force that drives these monsters has an affinity with death itself. It sustains emotionally and psychologically dead criminals, such as Lucas and Toole, and pushes them along a bumpy road, where their ramblings are more reminiscent of a medieval *danse macabre* than the ballad of a lonesome cowboy.

In 1968, two years before Lucas began sowing his trail of murders across the United States, George A. Romero's *Night of the Living Dead* was released, a film which *cognoscenti* still consider as an unparalleled masterpiece.

Each of the "undead" in the film has the combined characteristics of an ogre and a serial killer of the same type as Lucas. They are brought back to life by a wrenching hunger for murder and flesh and become carried away in a voracious hunt, threatening all living things within their reach. People who have seen the film remember with (delicious?) horror the little undead girl who kills her mother with a trowel and goes off to eat her father's body in the basement of the house.

Dead heroes are traditional literary characters. Odin, unlike his son Baldr ("courage") and other symbols of life, is not resuscitated after the

Armageddon that ends this saga told by the Nordic oracle. Strangely, therefore, one of the principal Scandinavian gods is a dead god. Devoured by the cosmic wolf, he can never return, whereas his Hellenic alter ego Dionysos, who is murdered by Lycurgus ("he who acts like a wolf") is brought back to life by Demeter.

There is hence a negative side to these "hit-or-miss" warriors' wanderings: they become undead and unable to coordinate their movements, which are dictated by a spastic energy. Their hunger is senseless, since, like corpses, they are incapable of digesting what they swallow. Even in the most subtle film makers' movies, when the living dead ingest a meal, it immediately comes squirting back out of an enormous wound in their neck or stomach. The undead symbolize an energy that is expelled in death, only to return to its source: thus, the *Einhedjar* (or solitary warrior, a member of Odin's guard) is brought back to life by a Valkyrie, the robot repairwoman, only to die on the battlefield the next day. The meaning of the name Valdemar,[1] one of Edgar Allan Poe's characters in a grim short story about hypnosis,[2] recalls this force of death. It is as if the energy that causes corpses to decompose could, through the evil effects of magnetism, be reversed, thus suspending the natural process of death. Once released, death hastens to make up for lost time, leading to a horrifying scene in Poe – as well as a multitude of film interpretations – of the accelerated decomposition of a "living" cadaver.

This fascination with life's destructive energy is illustrated by the film *Braindead*.[3] Underneath its comic aspect, this is the most systematic of all the horror films in which the main activities are chopping and liquefying. Its farcical side does not hide the fact that two-thirds of the movie is devoted to the tearing apart of human bodies. Inspired by a Stephen King short story, in which the narrator is minced by a flesh-eating lawn mower, Jackson's vision of things is more all-encompassing: he puts all of the characters (the guests at a surprise party) literally though the blender. He has a good reason: as they dance and exchange "nibbles," the guests become undead. Their dismembered body parts continue to wreak havoc (including a digestive tube that leaps onto a loudspeaker like a rattlesnake), and so they must be totally ground up, taking care to avoid the bits that overflow from the blender and which can still attack! The autonomous nature of the body parts (heads that speak, severed hands brandishing swords, eyes that continue to see after they have been torn from their sockets, etc.) is a specialty of the most venerable mythologies.

In the end, all of the puréed flesh in *Braindead* looks the same, and it merges together to form a single, enormous monster in the shape of the hideously deformed body of the main character's mother. It takes no less than a bomb to make the thing implode and finally perish in a fire that consumes the ruined house. The moral of this story is: beware of your mother, especially if, like this mother, she has been bitten by an evil monkey.

Anthropologists, on the other hand, may interpret this as the age-old theme, in a logic of total destruction, of transformation through the four states of matter. The solid is attacked and reduced to a liquid, but it is fire that reduces things to the impalpable, nonexistent state of air. This is what Ottis Toole was insinuating when he said that he was never as sexually excited by intercourse and murder as by fire: "You know, I really love fire . . . it does something to me, like shooting up . . . makes me feel relaxed . . . I like the really high ones, with three-story flames."[4]

His masturbating before a burning flame (as if associating sexual pleasure with the friction of a magical lighter) is like a literal manifestation of his grandmother's belief that he was the son of Lucifer (the bringer of light or kindler of fires). Like multiple murderer David Berkowitz, who set hundreds of fires in New York in the 1970s, Toole and Lucas acted out a game from the Scandinavian sagas, which pitted Loki (also called Loptr, "Air") against Logi ("Fire"), in a contest to determine which of the two could devour a banquet of flesh the fastest. As a counterpoint, we could compare this with the Arabic proverb which teaches that the lion begets other lions, but that fire only begets ashes.

The Ancient Ceremonies of the Living Dead

From voracious gluttony, we have come to a rapid halt before the smoldering, icy figure of the living dead. Yet the living dead are not a recent invention. Although they are mainly associated with American horror films, they also constitute one of the most frequently recurrent themes in European tradition. The *Odinsjagt* (Odin's hunting party, mentioned by Orderic Vital in 1092) is a band of living-dead hunters, led by a giant one-eyed king, who steal from the living, take their food, kill them, or lure them to their death. The coincidental fact that Henry Lee Lucas was very tall, had one eye, and was described by Ottis as the leader of their murderous orgies is too provocative to resist.

The *Odinsjagt* is itself a German reconstruction of ancient variants from the Germanic tradition (the Familia Herlethingi, mentioned by Tacitus), the Celtic tradition (the hunt in which King Arthur assumes the role of Odin), and the French tradition, which includes *Mesnie Hellequin*, in which one finds the archaic name of King Herle (Harilo), yet another of Odin's nicknames, meaning tearer or harasser and which is softened, via the Italian *Arlecchino*, to become Harlequin, the clown with his garment of "many pieces."

Highly present in Christianity, the theme of the wild hunt (*Wuotesher*) was seized upon by the Church to arouse the fears of sinners. The members of the hunting group were said to be children who had died before being baptized and people who had committed suicide, died by murder, committed adultery, killed, disturbed a religious service, or broken their fast during Lent. In *Hymne des daimons*, Ronsard describes how he is frozen with fear at the idea of being carried off by the members of the wild hunt.

In modern American society, a combination of the Christian All Saints' Day and the Germanic/Celtic feast of the dead resulted in Halloween, whose etymology, according to the dictionary, is *(all)hallow(s) + e(v)en*, Allhallows Eve, the evening of the saints.

It should be recalled that, on Halloween, the dead are celebrated, mainly to prevent them from coming back to life. The handing out of candy to children who go trick-or-treating, dressed in more or less frightening costumes, is a metaphor for this. An even more obvious metaphor is found in the assaults that have been committed on these children: razor blades in pieces of fruit, poisoned candy, and so on. Thus the terrifying undead are attacked through their young impersonators.

The popularity of Halloween is due to a confluence of Nordic and Celtic traditions in the religious feasts of the winter months. The time of rebirth in spring was requested through sacrifices, in which the first victims were human. The Druid variant is said to have been the *Oidhche Shamhna*, the wake of Saman, the god of the dead. A hidden source of the Germanic version of Halloween might be the *Alfablot*, a bloody sacrifice to the elves, which was practiced in the ancient Germanic world. Repressed during the (late) conversion to Christianity, these practices led to fantasies of hungry revenge and, in their condensed form, they consolidated the terror (and fascination) of pagan rites, which are identified with Satanism.[5]

In a remarkable coincidence, the two serial killers Toole and Lucas – who clearly had a sense of showmanship – displayed an extensive knowledge of necrophilia and Satanism. Toole told anyone who would listen that his grandmother had taken him, from the age of five, to cemeteries around Florida to dig up bodies, which she then used in various necromantic rituals.[6] In Scandinavian mythology, Harthgrepa, the daughter of a giant, also woke the dead, so that they would read her fortune. When his mother died, Toole went to lie in the cemetery, believing that he heard her calling him to commit suicide in order to join her, which is reminiscent of the myth of Orpheus or, in the Nordic tradition, of the myth of Odin descending into hell in search of a necromancer (Odin is also called the "father of the slain").

In any case, Anglo-American superstitions and fiction consistently situate multiple heinous crimes around the Halloween season. A journalist who conducted an investigation into the murders by the criminal who struck in San Francisco under the pseudonym "the zodiac killer" has tried to show that the murderer concentrated his acts around the period of the solstices, and particularly around Halloween, and that his messages were full of mystical and satanic references.[7]

An American journal that deals with Satanism once observed that many "revenge crimes" take place on Halloween. For example, on Halloween of 1991 in Killeen, Texas, George Hennard drove his van through the window of the Luby diner, shot twenty-three customers dead, and then committed suicide.

Certain events are said to repeat themselves every year on Halloween. On Halloween day in 1986, a New Jersey postman killed fourteen persons. Five years later, in the same state, Joseph M. Harris, a postal worker who had lost his job, killed his former boss and his girlfriend during the Halloween weekend and threatened the gathering crowd with grenades and weapons. This is reminiscent of Clive Barker's novel, in which the main character is a postal worker who is planning to kill his supervisor and then becomes the hero of a dark, eternal Druid war taking place in the time–space continuum.[8]

After this first repression of demons on Halloween comes yuletide (from *Jul* or *Jol*), a Germanic celebration of rebirth at the new year, which was later more or less overshadowed by the celebration of the birth of Christ. The theme of sacrifices to Odin is not lost in the tradition of setting out food before the hearth or eating a Christmas goose. For the celebration of *Jol*, the peasant tradition was to slaughter a pig and perhaps, less than 2,000 years earlier, the occasional child.[9]

It was Odin who acted as *Jolnir*, the "Jol master" (a model for Father Christmas?), who led the hunting party, made up, as described earlier, of violent living-dead hunters, which have since been "softened" into reindeer pulling a sleigh driven by a kindly old man with a white beard. The only thing that remains of his monstrous nature is the blood-red color of his coat, the snowballs he has in the place of buttons, and the enduring legends about kidnappers who dress up as Santa Claus to steal little children.[10]

Odin's hunting party roams the earth for a cycle of twelve days and nights until New Year's Day, and during this period his dead slaves can also come back among the living.[11] Raising of the dead can be performed by burning incense before the oracular wishes for the New Year are made. Later, in the spring, comes Walpurgis Night. According to legend, on this night the witches come out and dance on the grave of Saint Walpurgis, whose name is said to be a Christianization of *Val-burg*, "the city of dead warriors."

All of this may leave readers with a strong sense of rationalism incredulous, but it is absolutely standard fare for young Anglo-Saxons, Scandinavians, Welsh, Germans, Estonians, Latvians, Lithuanians, or Finns, and can be found in all sorts of children's books, science-fiction novels or comics, and even in oral or culinary family traditions.

If the neo-Nazis and their "intellectual" supporters have espoused a "traditional" interpretation of these holidays, this should not hide the fact that this secret obsession with death has arisen – to the point of permeating international culture – from the Gothic British novel and later from American syncretism and its fictional film versions. It was not by "purist" Nordic-culture enthusiasts selling earthenware incense burners decorated with swastikas that this myth was introduced, but, more trivially, by the sale of Halloween gadgets and the international toy industry. Plastic pumpkins shaped like scooped-out heads are exported to the entire world from Taiwan. Their eternal symbolism of a ghost whose mind continues to illuminate an empty skull has become even more effective, since this universally recognized fairy-tale character cannot be traced back to its author.

Soldier or Lone Wolf?

Odin-like characters, who are at once living and dead (ogres, harlequins, or Santa Claus), never go alone but are accompanied by their people. The aspect of these living dead as a "number" or even a "collectivity" that has banded together, like an invading army, also constitutes an aspect of serial killers' self-mystifying behavior. In Toole's descriptions of satanic orgies, other members of Jacksonville society take part with him. There is a high altar on which the victim's throat is slit, after which the blood is drunk and, occasionally, the body cooked. Sometimes, new initiates slit the victim's throat and have intercourse with the dead body and then with animals, which they kill afterward. Then, there is a large celebration, during which a human victim and the animals are eaten.[12]

The serial murderer thus creates another serial setup, in which the members of a peculiar community must be repressed as a group. Serial killers relate strongly to this popular, punitive mythical judgment. In their dead state, they have formed a people from hell, a counter society that mirrors the society of "the good."

But this portrayal masks another aspect of the truth: the mad warrior is never really a member of any society, not even of a society of assassins. He is alone and wretched, consumed from the inside by his refusal to accept a common identity. He is, in fact, an exact personification of the original meaning of the word crime: something that has been sifted or filtered, as with a *criblum*.[13]

CHAPTER ELEVEN

A Malfunctioning Robot

Hobbes maintained that a human being's darker side could be controlled through social structures, but only at the risk of mechanization of the spirit. From Hobbes to Locke, from cyberneticians to the Chicago Boys, such plans have been predicted to triumph today in an "end of history" stabilized by the global market order, a sprawling untamed machine, which is at once a civilized form of violence and a shield against the violence of the wild.

Without judging the value of such predictions, we can examine how werewolves and especially the human animals for which serial killers take themselves respond to the theory of an automated society; i.e., how they react in concrete terms to the idea that society and natural energy have a mutual control over one another, through the transformation of human nature into a cybernetic machine.

It then becomes obvious that this strange hope for a society made more equitable by metamorphosing werewolves into cyborgs (half-human, half-machine) will be disappointed by the spectacle of serial killers, the real human machines.

The Automation of a Killer

What is gained by shifting from an animal state to a mechanized state? Regularity. What causes an assassin's inevitable degeneration into a hideous, indescribable thing is not so much his transformation into a beast but rather the predictable alternation of his human and animal phases. This alternation produces a mechanical rhythm that borders on biological death.

By becoming "mechanized," multiple criminals refuse to sustain their animal side and aim for inorganic existence. We should recall that, after a bout of possession ("going berserk"), Odinic warriors were hanged in a sacred ritual and attached to a rock, with restraints that grew tighter and tighter, reducing them to a catatonic state in which they lingered between life and death. Multiple killers are similar: something about them is reminiscent of a self-destructing machine. The increasingly rapid repetition of death acts recalls a robot that has gone out of control, causing its parts to convulse and ultimately fall apart.

The serial killer's fate can be illustrated by two sample groups, which I will refer to as "impotents" and "killing machines." In the first group, the affliction of sexual impotence makes repeated acts the criminal's last shred of human dignity. In the second, even this pretense disappears, and the now totally robotized criminal can lead a "normal" life.

Among sexually impotent criminals, pain still manages to register, whereas for a pure killing machine there is only a functional split between types of acts which are equivalent to eating or sleeping as far as their perpetrator is concerned. Everything, including violence, takes its place in the order of a perfect system of consumption (which is hence radically different from anything human).

Impotence in Relation to the Other

Certain murderers' "impotence" should not be understood as a feeling of helplessness with regard to women or life, but rather as the image of a robot slipping and falling on a carpet or a remote-controlled car grinding its wheels in a sand trap. The more its action proves ineffectual, the more the machine repeats its attempts, until it finally wears down, succumbs to shock, or runs out of energy.

In some murders that have been provoked by a woman laughing at a man's impotence, one might believe that the motive is vengeance. But when Richard Lawrence Marquette murdered three women in succession, each time apparently because of their amusement at his expense, and then cut them up into small pieces, his motive was different. When, between 1980 and 1983, John Joseph Joubert, a young, innocent-looking Air Force soldier, stabbed three adolescent boys in the back, whose bodies were later found naked in the woods, it seemed that this was the beginning of a repeated series not of failed but of impossible acts. He was acting out of a parody of homosexual relations, which he was apparently incapable of engaging in. The Joubert case can therefore be summed up as the impossibility of producing a penal orgasm from a knife.

In cases in which such series of acts run their course without being stopped by the police, a more distinct pattern emerges. For instance, in the category of "impotent automatons," the example of the Russian murderer Tchikatilo[1] helps to elucidate certain American cases. Tchikatilo taught in a technical training school, was married with one child, and killed fifty-three teenage boys and girls between 1983 and 1990. Knives and cries of pain and fear were the conditions for his sexual performance. Unable to penetrate his victims, he ejaculated while pummeling them with his fists. During his trial in 1992, Tchikatilo revealed the extent of his psychosis by stating that he had become a woman and that "it was time for him to give birth." Had he finally found a solution to his impotence?

Albert DeSalvo, "the Boston Strangler", who struck in the early 1960s,[2] was in his forties and had been neglected as a child. He married a German woman, whom he met during the occupation in Europe, and had a daughter with her, who was born with a permanent birth defect. He associated this "failure" with the painful experience of his sexual problems: an "abnormal" need and premature ejaculation. His urge to commit hundreds of rapes and then to murder thirteen women within a matter of months, before finally seeking psychiatric help, therefore arose from the stigma of impotence (or, rather, of a "maladjusted" sexuality, in terms both of desire and of results).

DeSalvo's first objective was to find a way to enter these women's homes. In this at least, he was successful, since he had a masterful technique for setting traps, for which he used various disguises (repairman, plumber – his father's profession, etc.). His method was almost always the same: he went in, waited for the victim to turn her back, delivered a blow to her neck (he was very strong), pushed her onto a bed, and strangled her (he especially liked to use the victim's stockings). Then, he raped, sodomized, and contorted the body in obscene or degrading positions (placing objects in the vagina, etc.), before ransacking the apartment inch by inch.

As with Tchikatilo, one notices a sort of progression in the horror of his acts. DeSalvo's first six victims were aged between fifty and sixty. Then, he attacked young women, nurses, factory workers, and students. The series came to a strange end. DeSalvo later claimed that, all of a sudden, he had been horrified by what appears to be merely a macabre detail in relation to the rest of the atrocities he committed: after forcing a broomstick into the vagina of his last victim, age nineteen, he left a New Year's greeting card at the foot of the body.

This strategy of closing in on the victim recalls somewhat the Kemper case, with the series of concentric circles leading to his mother, and his abrupt halt, like a deprogrammed machine, once he had cut her throat. But, with DeSalvo, the pattern is reversed. He went from older women to young girls, and finally to the suggestion of birth with the New Year. DeSalvo seems to have used his murders to regress to an *in utero* state, to return to a sort of nonexistence, in which he could define himself as a stillborn child. One might wonder whether what he was looking for, when he searched his victims' apartments, was (in Freudian terms) a missing baby, or one that was impossible to conceive.

Criminal Output

If the impotence of their faulty machinery is stressful for some serial killers, it is not for the second group, who will be the protagonists in this final scene of serial killings. The total divergence between their human masks and the automated atrocities these criminals commit is considered – both by them and by some of the people who have studied them – to be the result of a positive quality: a talent for disguise and methodicalness.

An example of how cold calculation is sometimes equated with professionalism and skill is illustrated by Ressler's tendency to link criminal typology with levels of intelligence and education: "'Disorganized offenders' (supposed to be more insane) have a low IQ; the 'organized' ones (presumed to be more perverted) are smart, cultivated and show social skills which make them able to seduce their victims."[3]

If self-control is connected with well-mannered, socially acceptable behavior, Ressler does not speculate on whether in these criminals intelligence (Kemper had an IQ of 135, higher than the others') or self-control might instead be manifestations of insanity. In other words, it may not be because they are intelligent that they are better able to commit a series of murders without being caught, but, on the contrary, because they are "killing machines" that they develop what is termed intelligence in the vocabulary of standardized testing. Their calculating coldbloodedness is only a functional component of their pathology. One clue that points to this is contained in a letter written to the *San Francisco Chronicle* by the man who "so cleverly" hid behind the zodiac killer alias.[4] He states that he does not fit in the least the descriptions that have been published of him, and that he is in fact quite an ordinary man, except during critical moments.

Is he boasting about his ability to fool people? His tone does not suggest this. I think that he is simply making an observation: that his personality is truly split up into separate boxes.

A Link in an Ecosystem

Ted Bundy, a preppy student who murdered several dozen young women (possibly more than a hundred) between 1971 and 1978, was arrested in 1975, when there was still no direct evidence against him (although a certain

"Ted," who fitted his description, was being sought for the kidnapping of a number of young women). He was implicated by a number of circumstances, including the discovery of bones buried in different public parks, but fiercely denied any involvement.

Before his trial, he escaped from prison, thinking that he could begin a new life on the other side of the United States. But, just after settling down on a university campus in Tallahassee, Florida, he broke into the Chi Omega sorority house armed with a log and, going from room to room without being detected, bludgeoned three women to death in their sleep and wounded two others. On his way home, he attacked, wounded, and raped yet another woman. This uncontrolled orgiastic bout was like a way of making up for the lost time he had spent in prison. One has the impression that he was eliminating a "surplus" of intolerable female figures.[5] His last victim, a twelve-year-old girl, was killed shortly before he was taken in, exhausted and filthy, by the local police. The machine's amazing efficiency had been worn out and the functional split did not work as well as before. Bundy was executed in Florida in 1989.

What is striking in the Bundy case is the contrast between the make-believe aspect, cultivated both by the criminal himself and by various institutions (the justice system and the media), and the meaningless repetition of the killings, which were reduced to a mere blow to the head.

Because these snapshot-like acts are not photogenic, made-for-television versions of the Ted Bundy story have cultivated a contrast between an absorbing intrigue built around an appearance of innocence and a virtual absence of images surrounding the murders. There is no equivalent for Bundy in the history of film making: killing machines like the anthropoid robot in *Terminator*, in which Arnold Schwarzenegger provides the flesh-and-bones wrapping,[6] are too romantic. They kill with jerking movements, roll in the dirt and inflict wounds on each other that are so enormous you can see through them, tear off each others' arms and legs, crush each others' skulls, etc.

Bundy, on the other hand, offers a true lesson in sobriety. He would find some pretext to lure a young girl into his beat-up Volkswagen (too many books to carry, a fake cast and a pair of crutches, etc.), or else would wait in a parking lot wearing a stocking with eye holes over his head. Once his victim was within reach (or seated in the car), Bundy would hit her on the temple with a chisel or a wrench. She would lose consciousness and fall backward onto the reclined passenger seat.

"He"[7] strangled the victim with his hands and a piece of rope, and then got on with the "chore" of getting rid of the body. Sometimes, "he" allowed himself a few sexual indulgences, but, on the whole, these were not frequent.

Bundy explained that he did not take pleasure or draw any kind of gratification from wounding or frightening the people he attacked. He did not try to torture them, since fantasizing about the crime was always more exciting than committing it. The sociologist Elliott Leyton observes that Bundy enjoyed possessing his victims in the same way as others enjoy rewarding themselves with an expensive gift, like buying a Porsche. But the primary characteristics of Bundy's style were speed and stealth. His killings were not acts of possession, but summary executions. The fact is, "he" was pressed for time, he had to resurface in his social circle, or go into town for dinner with his friends. Not that "he" needed an alibi, but seeing "his" friends was as important as killing.

Psychiatrists have in fact found Bundy to be totally normal and to have a strong sense of reality, emotional stability, sensitivity, etc. As he has said himself, "After conducting numerous tests and extensive examinations, (they) have found me normal, and are deeply perplexed (. . .) No seizure, no psychosis, no dissociative reactions, but in no way crazy. The working theory is that I have completely forgotten everything."[8] This is the kind of explanatory pseudo-concept which is found in Ann Rule's biography of Bundy:

> The Ted Bundy the World was allowed to see was handsome, his body honed and cultivated meticulously, a barrier of strength against eyes that might catch a glimpse of the terror inside. He was brilliant, a student of distinction, witty, glib, and persuasive. He loved to ski, sail and hike. He favored French cuisine, good white wine, and gourmet cooking. He loved Mozart and obscure foreign films. He knew exactly when to send flowers and sentimental cards. His poems of love were tender and romantic. And yet, in reality, Ted loved things more than he loved people. He could find life in an abandoned bicycle or an old car, and feel a kind of compassion for these inanimate objects – more compassion than he could ever feel for another human being. [. . .] On the surface, Ted Bundy was the very epitome of a successful man. Inside it was all ashes. For Ted has gone through life terribly crippled, like a man who is deaf, blind or paralyzed. Ted has no conscience.[9]

This somewhat simplistic Jekyll-and-Hyde-type interpretation (which Bundy always refuted) fails to take full account of one thing: Bundy was perfectly at ease in society. He once described himself as being totally integrated into the university "ecosystem."[10] The choice of words is interesting, for he refers to the social world as if it was purely natural and as if the natural world of social activity enveloped that of his crimes. When asked whether he remembered the effect that some of his crimes had on him, he answered by asking whether, when someone eats bouillabaisse, he remembers the difference in taste between a clam and a mussel. The impulse to kill seemed in his case to be like a need to let out a yawn, with no greater significance than eating an apple or smoking a cigarette.

But, if everything was so natural, why was there such a carefully defined line between Bundy's two lives? He tries to convince us that this was the best way not to get caught and to continue enjoying the other aspects of his life. This splitting of his personalities was a way to control the "entity" within him, to keep it out of sight and remain in mainstream society.

Bundy's demonstrated inability to talk about his crimes should therefore not be chalked up to his "technical" double life. On the contrary, it should be seen as the subject's inability to detach himself from the magma of the circumstances. It was not due to a sense of horror for his acts, but, from his point of view, to their meaninglessness, in the same way that we do not think of sleeping, urinating, or eating as subjects of conversation. For this man, who was at ease with himself and his ecosystem, and who had visions of sorority houses like maternal wombs, the act was indistinguishable from the being. His "asocial" acts were followed by socially meaningful acts, which were just as strong a statement about his circumstances as were the murders. Therefore, there is no point in seeking a symbolic sense of frustration. Bundy's message is all too obvious: he saw life laid out before him in its entirety. It was an endless thread of successive acts, in which the forms of murder and language were alternated. In short, it was completely natural.

In reality, things were not so simple. For Bundy, the natural state could not be taken for granted. Happiness could potentially come to an end and he could be banished from the ecosystem, a world which he associated with his doting mother, who had always been there to help him "prepare for his exams." To remain in this undivided universe, he had to eliminate any shortfalls or excesses. A daily dose of murder was prescribed to stamp out the superfluous faces of "other women," who, with their long hair parted down the middle, suggested the intrusion of a nonexistent symbolic kinship in his fishbowl-like existence.[11]

Somewhat like Kemper, who saw a girl's face staring back at him every time he looked in the mirror, for Bundy, the world was an all-encompassing female domain, in which sisters, mothers, girls, and women combined in a sort of murky incest, which was constantly straining toward an unbearable separation. It was this threat of loss, and this sort of female father figure, that had to be annihilated as regularly as possible to avoid psychical death. The result was Bundy's total incapacity to grasp the reality of his acts, which stunned the legion of police officers and experts who tried in vain, almost until the day of his electrocution, to extract an explanation from him.

The Story of a Killing Machine

What, one wonders, could possibly have produced such a machine, whose "nature" was to assassinate women? Let us consider the commonly assembled biographical elements, with (as in any form of mythology) both their suggested and their hidden relevance.

Theodore Robert Bundy spent his childhood years with his mother's family in a puritan Philadelphia home, which was characterized by the figure of his grandfather, a well-known painter, whose reputation included rumors of a bad temper, sectarian religious beliefs, and a secret fascination for erotic illustrations. This "chief of the horde" (whose wife was under treatment for depression) is said to have committed incest with his daughter, making Bundy both his mother's son and her brother.

Nothing is certain, but Bundy's grandparents at one point "adopted" him, keeping their daughter's pregnancy under wraps at a clinic for unwed mothers. Given his adoption by his grandfather and his illegitimate birth, Bundy had three explanations to choose from: he could be the son of an unknown father (possibly a sailor or a traveling salesman); he could be his mother's adopted "brother" of unknown parentage; or he could be both his mother's "real" brother and also her son, since his grandfather was also his father. Even in the event that the incestuous act was not con-summated, the fact that his mother allowed her son to be "adopted" by her own father rather than choosing another solution suggests that she was satisfying an unconscious desire for an incestuous relationship by "giving back" the child to her own father, something that occasionally occurs in real adoptions.

This uncertainty about the father is therefore combined with uncertainty about the mother as well. It begins at birth, since Bundy's mother con-sidered giving up the child anonymously and leaving him in the care of the clinic. It continued until Bundy was almost an adult, for it was only until after his mother/sister had left her parents' home, moved to another state on the West Coast, and married that she told him he was indeed her son and that she had hardly known his father. The revelation of his illegitimate birth may not have shocked Bundy as much as some believe. It was not the discovery that he was his mother's real son that surprised him (moreover, he must have known that he was her son, simply by virtue of her constant care and attention), but rather her admission that a lie might be separating him from his "real father," who as far as he was concerned was his grandfather, whom he admired and in many ways identified with.

Thus, Bundy's entire childhood was placed under the cloud of his elusive origins, his stolen parentage, and the fear that his mother would abandon him or even disappear by transforming into a sister, etc. This may have contributed to his absolute love–hate relationship with females, whom he saw as "parent snatchers" – his mother's invisible alter ego. It may also explain why he placed a circle of knives around his mother's sister, Julia, while she slept one night (see p. 175), and could account for the disappearance of Ann Burr, a girl who lived next door to him, while he was still in his teens.

The guiding principle appears to be that, in order to survive and to negotiate the passage between sexual pleasure and symbolism, which all people must come to terms with, Bundy had to eliminate the women who separated him from his mother and yet who were one of the conditions for reaching her. The problem in his case was not that he had to emulate a bogus father figure (as in the Kemper or Manson cases), but that he had constantly to regenerate the flow of vital energies that nurtured his identity by annihilating women, who, like the nurse who almost carried him off for good when his mother was considering giving him up for adoption, stopped the flow.

Bundy was therefore a murder "automatist," but more for his own well-being than for a fascination with productivity or numbers.

The Clockwork Clown

Among murderers who sought "high yield" and maximum efficiency, John Wayne Gacy was, by contrast with Bundy, quite a remarkable case. A paunchy thirty-year-old, Gacy in just a few years strangled and killed thirty-three young men in his home in the Chicago suburbs. He ran an interior-decoration business and was a model citizen, congenial and well liked. He had an active social life and dressed up in a clown suit to entertain the children, whenever there was a block party in his neighborhood.

The idea of a murderer in a clown suite has been used often in fiction. Ted Sullivan and Peter Maiken produced their film *Killer Clown* in 1983,[12] and Stephen King describes how the monster in *It* takes the form of a clown to lure children away to a circus, where they are devoured. There is also the character of the Joker, the snickering nemesis of the brooding but righteous Batman, or the character of Malcolm in the Kyrandia legend, a popular video game.[13]

In the evening, Gacy changed roles. He went to gay bars to pick up young boys and bring them home. If he managed to convince them to let him tie them up for sadomasochistic game playing, their fate was sealed. Gacy would slip a bar through a chain around the victims' necks and strangle them. Again, preliminary playacting or superficial torture were less important than the death act, which was relatively quick. Afterward, Gacy's careful cutting up and storing of the bodies in his basement were reminiscent of a collection of hunting trophies, or, as he wrote in a message to Ressler, a "harvest."

Gacy's feeble attempt to interpret his repeated urges as a form of pleasure, or even as a form of hatred for "pathetic queers" and his own "bad homo side," was not very effective. He had nothing in common with "real" sadists like Fish, Heidnik, or Schaefer. He belongs among the prodigiously efficient "industrial-style" murderers, who appear to derive from repetition something "beyond orgasm," which has more to do with the combined number of their acts than the satisfaction of a passing desire.

The Dissolving Machine

Let us take one last step to complete this blood-drenched circle with a discussion of a contemporary murderer: Jeffrey Dahmer,[14] who killed seventeen young men between 1978 and 1991, many of them black homosexuals.

Dahmer's case very closely resembles the old myth of the "dismemberer." But, unlike the bloodthirsty, cannibalistic vagrants Lucas and Toole, or other murderers who cut up their victims, he was not a polymorphous deviant. He never tortured; he killed quickly and painlessly (by dissolving a sleeping pill in the victim's beer), and limited his sexual practices with the bodies.

He was, however, a specialist in dismemberment, liquefaction, cutting, preserving, and remolding: in short, he was something between a chemist and an artist. But he worked with increasing speed, from one murder in 1978 to eight in a single year in 1991. He was caught because he could no longer sustain the pace.

Dahmer is also remembered in connection with a police scandal. A young Laotian man whom he had drugged managed to escape into the street, naked, his hands cuffed, and to call for help. The Milwaukee police called Dahmer in for questioning, but with stupefying sang-froid he explained that they had been having a homosexual argument and that the young man should return home with him. The police brought the man back, paying no attention to the putrid smell or other clues indicating violent behavior. A few minutes after they left, Dahmer strangled him and cut him to pieces.

Like Bundy's, Dahmer's coldbloodedness amazes people, probably because they do not understand the seriousness with which, in his insanity, he approached his "work."

Dahmer began to kill in 1978, in the small town of Bath, Ohio. He was eighteen years old and had been abandoned several months earlier by his parents, who had just gone through a very bitter divorce. He brought a young man home with him after a party, but, when he wanted to leave, Dahmer, terrified of being left alone again, struck him with a dumbbell and strangled him. A curious ceremony followed: he cut the flesh and bones into myriad minuscule pieces and scattered them in the woods behind the house. Since there was "nothing to indicate that a crime had been committed," he felt no sense of worry. He then went to Milwaukee, where he had been born, and moved into one of the highly segregated city's mixed neighborhoods. For almost ten years, he went through a quiet string of menial jobs, sexual encounters bordering on illegality (he served a short prison sentence for pedophilia), drink, and drugs. But Dahmer had plans. According to Don Davis,[15] he told one of his cell mates that he hated blacks and the he would like to kill a thousand of them. At the time, he had a job working the night shift in a chocolate factory. His cell mate laughed at the thought that a man like Dahmer would want to kill people.

In 1988 he began to use his "dissolving machine." He went to saunas or nightclubs to pick up young, homosexual immigrants, who were eager to integrate into society, and brought them back to his studio to show them photographs or discuss the possibilities of a job. He would serve the victim a (drugged) drink and then strangle him with a strap or a rope. Afterward, he began a careful dismemberment of the body, of which he photographed each stage in minute detail. To remove the flesh, he placed it in a large vat of acid (there is probably some relation to the fact that his father's field was analytical chemistry), kept the heart and certain other organs in the refrigerator, bleached the bones and skull and painted them gray, like the fake plaster skulls that are popular sale items in heavy-metal shops.

It is conceivable that extreme solitude during puberty could drive a child to drink or become violent, but it is not easy to comprehend the meaning of the dismemberment and systematic destruction of the bodies of Dahmer's growing number of victims.

Again, fiction, and in particular horror novels, can help us to understand. The following passage describes the fantasies of a first-time murderer after he has done away with his bothersome victim:

> It was only when he was clearing out his room of any sign of himself – eradicating every trace of Randolf Ernest Jaffe – that he regretted doing what he'd done.

Not the burning – that had been altogether wise – but leaving Homer's body in the room to be consumed with the dead letters. He should have taken a more elaborate revenge, he realized. He should have hacked the body into pieces, packaged it up, tongue, eyes, testicles, guts, skin, skull, divided piece from piece, and sent the pieces out into the system with scrawled addresses that made no real sense, so that chance (or synchronicity) was allowed to elect the doorstep on which Homer's flesh would land. The mailman mailed. He promised himself not to miss such ironic possibilities in future.[16]

Dahmer never posted bits of his victims' bodies, but the novelist's outrageous idea points us in the right direction: the act of dismembering a body is "sent out" as a message about the insignificance of numbers for a totally solitary person, whose own existence hangs on a miracle. Traumatized by his parents' divorce, Dahmer made it clear that, for him (as for many psychopaths), people only existed as names in a register of births, deaths, or marriages. Being the son of a chemist and an artist was, for someone who never believed that words and things could be independent of each other, purely a combination of information. As soon as this set of codes fell apart, every molecule of the people he had feelings for had to be totally disintegrated.

This type of insanity has cultural counterparts, especially with the belief in which the warrior's actions become indistinguishable from the law. This culture, with its Anglo-Saxon origins, has strongly influenced computer games, in which players must confront the following dilemma: either they fail to discover the secret code and will therefore never gain access to the dazzling virtual "nature" that the program has locked within its womb; or they succeed and thereby accept the notion that life is just a series of codes.

For Dahmer (and for a number of criminal computer wizards, including Crutchly and Kraft), the choice is clear: alone facing the machinery of a job market that is reduced to social codes, the only way to carry on living is to digitalize the bodies of loved ones by reducing them to an infinite number of information bytes dissolved in a cosmic soup.

Murderers Searching for Life

Dahmer, Bundy, and many other "mass-production" killers talk about an orderly, repetitive multitude of identical acts. They tell us that, unlike the mass-produced "dream" gadgets sold in urban shopping centers, these acts must be taken seriously, for they are not "virtual" but absolutely real. They can even be called absolute or successful acts: acts, because they change the body (both the body of the actor and that of the victim); and successful because they are irreversible (causing death or mutilation, etc.).

Leaving a trail of murders in one's wake, manufacturing victims (like mass-produced consumer goods), and dismembering their bodies after terrifying and torturing them seem, in their very madness, to be attempts to go beyond solitary existence or limitless repetition. They are pathological efforts to act in the outside world and on others, one at a time. They are figures of plurality, distinction, and the group, but they make a real effort to connect with others.

Such acts make up for the lack of social identity that removes the subject from the material and industrial flow of things and of postmodern society's quasi-objects and quasi-subjects. If a killer kills, it is not because he "has no conscience" but because, in his horrendous existence, things are all the same, so that by destroying some of these replicas one has the momentary illusion of making space in the world, space to breathe and to re-create differences.

But, since each murder of one's fellow is bound to create inconsistencies, it is always necessary to start over. To sustain consistency, the subject is driven to make new attempts and ultimately to engage in repetition. The death act is a search for life outside the machine . . . by killing in an increasingly mechanical way.

Like Frankenstein's monster, whose attempt to communicate with a little girl he sees tossing flowers into the water consists in tossing her into the water, hardened criminals do not distinguish between beings and things. The monster acts on the metonymy that little girl = flower and fails in his attempt to communicate, although the realization of what he has done causes him to panic.

Such efforts are tragic, for in the succession of death acts the murderer discovers no other, whether in the person of the victim or in the deepest recesses of the victim's body. These attempts to create a community in a social desert all end in failure. Like the vampire who does not see his own reflection in the glass, the "heroic" existence of a serial killer, a mythical monster or a character in a horror movie, is necessarily surrounded with "omnipresent" things and "departed" persons. Since he cannot temper his fixation for "finishing" others (in the literal and figurative senses of the term), a mad warrior is only conscious of his fellow man when he breaks him, like a mirror that is hiding something else. Even Henry Lucas's closest friends had to end up cut into pieces and stuffed in a suitcase, "do-it-yourself"-style.

Through these repeated crimes, the mad-warrior culture exhibits a real cognitive deficiency. The increased number of acts of violence and the series of combats and victims are symptomatic of despair: a despair of ever finding the key to the passage between numbers and subjectivity.

Multiple personalities, mechanized killers, and dismembered cadavers strewn along the highways (and raised from the dead in popular fiction) expose, through the voices of horrified social commentators, something that David Riesman prophesied forty years ago: we Americans, the avant-garde of free society, are a lonely crowd.[17]

By showing that a world filled with a multitude of manufactured objects is necessarily a solitary world, serial killers affirm that postmodern society has been the death of meaning. They do not express this in lyrical philosophical terms, like Baudrillard; more prosaically, they commit acts in which the "word" truly becomes the "deed."

Anglo-Saxon philosophy has been pondering for over a century where the symbols that humans use have their roots in reality. It should turn its attention to serial killers. For they have found the answer in the form of a spiritual or moral impulse that ultimately leads to the creation of inert matter.

PART FOUR

The Criminal, Witness to Culture

Truth, Repression, Pleasure

Up to this point, we have simultaneously explored three types of discourse on abnormal (i.e., heinous or criminal) acts:

1. Commentary on multiple killers in North America.
2. Horror fiction and film, produced principally for, with, or by Hollywood.
3. The "fantastic" mythical sources of European Nordic cultures, particularly those that revolve around the theme of the mad warrior (from werewolves to vampires).

In the course of this exploration, it has become apparent that each of the three areas of study was echoed in the other two, constituting a field of crime-related symbolism.

With respect to their predominant styles, each area of study places greater emphasis on a certain aspect. By examining the recurrent aspects among types of murderers, which are reflected in the repeated murders themselves, biographies of serial killers posit that the most horrible acts are not acts of desire, pleasure, or rage, but rather desperate attempts to find an opening in cases where the absence of the father has locked the killer up in a closed world of twinned images and insoluble conflicts between pure forms of the self.

Unwilling to deal with this reality, fiction and film attempt, on the contrary, to relate automated killing to a kind of sexual release, an indulgence, or a sadomasochistic perversion. In its reconstruction of criminals as polymorphous perverts, the art of horror, especially in America, tries to ignore the coldest, most poignant reality of murders: that they are performed as acts of mental survival by annihilating the obsessive image of an identical "other." By demonizing murderers, artists and police investigators help to spare their culture from this most radical form of atrocity but at the same time close their ears to the criminals' message of absolute pessimism.

When Stephen King laments the consequences in a person's life of having an all-powerful sadistic mother, the main effect is to make us forget that the worst form of violence is not domination but an inability to differentiate.

Another neurotic, as opposed to perverse, way of rejecting the messages of psychotic killers is to interpret their "animalistic" violence as the negative swing of a pendulum in a binary system, whose positive component is the law and society itself: this is what I have referred to as the "werewolf complex," the principal reference here being myth.

I have pointed out that the myth of Odin, which is the paradigm for all binary legends, contains predictions of catastrophe of the type that we are constantly led to expect from hardened criminals. For there is more to the myth than the symmetrical forms of conflict versus civilization: it also anticipates (and secretly desires) a final breakdown of the mechanics of physical violence.

American culture has, as a society, fed the debate among these three principal forms of discourse: the impossible truth of a robotized murderer, the horror of an unacceptable and perverse pleasure, and the ancestral myth of a balance between good and evil. The pattern that emerges is in fact quite simple: American society (and the culture that imitates it in the rest of the world) has chosen not to go beyond the neurotic model of constant vacillation and cyclical irresolution between savage aggression and lawful repression, for this has allowed it to enjoy the indirect benefits of the spectacle of crime, while continuing to deny crime's deepest message.

It therefore draws upon the two other forms of discourse (the "cold" discourse of the criminal and the "hot" discourse of the artist) in the following way:

1. The criminal's perversion as interpreted by the artist allows one to infer that he has an excessive libidinal energy. The existence of this desire makes it possible in turn to deploy an equally powerful phobic repression and to present the justice system as an innocent counterforce or, rather, a counterforce that is unaware of its own strength.
2. The automated coldness of the act is not attributed to the human being, but to a natural, physical, and social reality. It is therefore necessary to control reality's tendency to create formal structures by giving it a fresh dose of "free agency."

If, as we shall see, attempts to reconcile these opposing factors and at the same time play upon the themes of cold versus hot, or of violence versus the law, are raised to an art form in Anglo-American culture and resolutely upheld as a universal political ideal, they are also at loggerheads with two forms of "degeneration" that are very difficult to control:

1. On the one hand, the perverse temptation to fantasize about the supposed pleasure of extreme violence can be unpredictably and uncontrollably transformed into ultrapuritanical forms of phobia and hysteria. American politics, which has been pervaded by religious fervor, is at constant risk of a sudden resurgence of this "witch-hunt" phenomenon, reminiscent of Arthur Miller's *Crucible*.

2. On the other hand, the machinery designed to regulate and repress can turn into the very thing it is supposed to prevent: pure, natural violence. This means that not only psychotic individuals but in fact the entire society could become trapped in a mechanism with no subject, an obsessive game of symmetry.

CHAPTER TWELVE

Good

The Serialization of Killers

Serial killers, like all real or potential assassins, or any normal person for that matter, are unique, inimitable, "unserializable." All people possess, at the very least, one characteristic that is truly individual. But branching off from this unique core there is a collective commentary – a societal saga that is propagated both by the murderer and by the dozens of people who interpret his actions. It is here that the categories of half-man/half-beast, or monster, are created, and these are solidly opposed to the categories and sequential chains that exist in normality. It is also here that, promoted by the criminal himself, the negative ideal of a "bad nature" is honed and can be used as an argument in favor of efficient, well-directed attempts at elimination. The Eric Schmitt hostage-taking case in the Parisian neighborhood of Neuilly was an example in which psychologists assisting the police investigation spread the idea in the press that certain methods were capable of "targeting" deviant psychological profiles in order to "control" and indeed to prevent or predict their actions.

This love of order and hatred of people who are "unfit" for life in society is not total nonsense, since it indicates a certain comprehension of the supposed adversary. But one must be aware of its limits and potential abuses.

For years, VICAP in the United States, with the assistance of the FBI crime analysis bureau, has been working on the definition of the serial killer. A special group called the Behavioral Science Unit (BSU), composed of twelve special agents, nicknamed the Dirty Dozen (directed by a character named Jack Crawford in Tom Harris's novels), observes crime at long distance with the aid of videotape and photographs, and then links cases via its database with crimes that bear similarities, even if they are inconsistent. Thus, VICAP has gradually constructed a sort of statistical portrait. Most serial killers are white, young, heterosexual, eldest sons who were raised in the 1940s and 1950s; 51 percent have a high or superior IQ;

80 percent are middle- or upper-middle-class and had fathers who held a steady job. On the other hand, in 47 percent of these cases, the killer's father was absent or left the home before the child was twelve, and in 66 percent of the cases one observes a dominant mother. The majority of this type of killer exhibits sexual problems or alcoholism.[1]

The VICAP specialists have more precisely classified killers according to whether they are "organized" or "random" criminals. The first type generally were brought up in financially stable conditions but lacked discipline, whereas the opposite is true for random killers. Organized criminals live with a partner, own a vehicle and travel frequently, plan their crimes, personalize their victims, and demonize them. They leave few clues at the scene of the crime, try to avoid the police, and only rarely resort to suicide.

Random killers are completely opposite. They tend to have pathological mothers and often have a past history of psychiatric disorders, they live alone or with their parents, travel little, behave violently, kill in a nonsadistic way without taking precautions, and are more prone to suicide.

The BSU has also discovered some obvious, and less obvious, correlations: if a victim's face is disfigured or crushed, it is generally the case that the assassin knew him; murderers who clean a bloodied bathtub, for example, are likely to have been institutionalized in a psychiatric hospital less than six months before the crime, etc.[2]

Abuses

This type of police procedure is not new. In the 1950s, when an organized manhunt was arranged to track down a bomber, the police were already using psychiatric statistics. Professor Ernst Kreshner studied 10,000 patients while compiling his portrait of the bomber, whom he suspected was a paranoiac. He concluded that 85 percent of paranoiacs had an athletic build and a symmetrical physique, that their handwriting was well formed, that they tended to dress fashionably, etc., and these hypotheses were borne out when the bomber was finally apprehended.[3]

The problems begin when numbers and clues must be given a value, and especially when one attempts to interpret them. In general, the number of cases on which the police can base these portraits is small – a few dozen at most – but this does not prevent some people from presenting them as a realistic and generally reliable model. Thus, Ressler develops his theory of "normal" and "abnormal" fantasies, which is reminiscent of overzealous attempts in postpenal psychiatry to perform the behavioral adjustment, à la *Clockwork Orange*, of "deviants" (so called because they are criminals):

"Whereas the normal person fantasizes in terms of sexual adventures, the deviant links sexual and destructive acts. Normal fantasies of interpersonal adventure are fused with abnormal attempts to degrade, humiliate, and dominate others. Most normal fantasies have at their center the idea that the partner will have as much fun as the dreamer."[4] With this idealization of "normal" fantasy, the master sleuth has clearly strayed into a domain where his authority fails him. The antiseptic nature of his mechanical, adaptive conception of desire, and its total disregard for the advances of Freudian psychology on the underlying violence present in all fantasy, could conceivably be used to cast guilt on any form of hatred, whether repressed or not, because it is "abnormal."

Despite the risks of abuse, ideologues, the police, psychiatrists, commentators, and even murderers seem to be in agreement that one should abandon inductive reasoning in favor of pure and simple deduction, and support the principle of criminal predestination. For example, Ressler uses this quotation from Monte Rissell, a youth who killed women: "They should have noticed it at school. So excessive was my day-dreaming that it was always in my report cards. I was dreaming about wiping out the whole school."[5] Did Ressler also dream about wiping out criminals at this age? No one has questioned him on this point.

By employing this type of naive comment, the experts' ideological writings transform individuals into sociopaths. Their normative tendency virtually stigmatizes as future criminals all young persons who present the same early signs as those that are detected in real criminals:

> Adolescence in these troubled youngsters was dominated by increasing isolation and "acting out" behavior, with lots of day-dreaming, compulsive masturbation, lying, bed-wetting, and nightmares as concomitants of the isolation. [. . .] Cruelty to animals and to other children, running away, truancy, assaults on teachers, setting fires, destroying the property of others and their own property – these acts begin with adolescence.[6]

This might seem convincing at first. Readers will recall that Kemper's childhood was characterized by feelings of hatred within his family. When he was still a child, DeSalvo, the Boston strangler, was sold as a slave by his father. Abandoned in the Boston Navy Yard, DeSalvo lived with a group of wild children, who killed stray cats and tramps with the same indifference. From the age of three, Ted Bundy showed strange signs of aggression toward his young Aunt Julia and one night placed a circle of kitchen knives around her as she slept. At age six, Joubert fantasized about strangling his baby sitter and devouring her until there was nothing left.

One is therefore not surprised when an isolated event occurs, irrevocably setting the criminal on his path: "People whose childhoods have been deeply impaired do not go on to live wholly normal lives; they become the alcoholic mothers or the abusive fathers who create home environments that perpetuate the cycle of abuse and make it highly likely that their children will become offenders."[7] But, if we are willing intellectually to accept this theory of inevitable predestination, we may find we are on a very slippery slope ourselves.

From Profiling to Suspicion

Although in certain types of crime criminals have stated that they were intimately aware of their own destiny, we must not forget that the idea that a coherent profile exists is supported by manipulations of social phenomena; inevitably, this profile is corroborated by numerous indicators, whose purpose is automatically to trigger our mistrust as soon as we recognize certain signals. Here, we enter a world of surveillance, where everything can be used as a "clue" for police officers on the trail of deviant behavior.

Once the police have adopted this logic, the process of investigating an entire population with a fine-toothed comb based on criteria of deviance appears to be no more irregular than the arbitrary aspect of the criteria themselves. The fact that there are a multitude of individuals who will never become murderers and yet who match the characteristics that describe the serial killer does not cool the investigators' enthusiasm.

Classifying "risk groups" is no less dangerous than defining the criminal by his chromosomes. In a society that indulges in mutual mistrust and keeps a close watch on strangers (when it is not spontaneously reporting them to the police), these ideas can aggravate reciprocal feelings of suspicion, especially when they are corroborated by the authority of the FBI.

The serialization of killers and the categorization of the serial killer have not, however, discontinued the serial killer's potential for yielding trendy byproducts.[8] For, in order to create a scapegoat, one must first relate an individual's behavior to an identifiable form, and this process of classification is facilitated by the fact that the police are hardly the only social agents with an interest in grouping people into tidy categories.

For example, anyone who sells goods that are linked to a certain lifestyle has an interest in serializing modes of consumption in order to create an effect of emulation that will encourage people to make the same purchases as their friends, classmates, or colleagues. Peddlers in the sex trade find it effective to serialize perversions in order to define markets for mass-produced goods, even if they never correspond exactly to the personal characteristics of an individual's sexuality. Government authorities also have an interest in defining various behaviors as "factors" in order to use them as evidence of the effectiveness of their policies: a 5 percent drop in the number of smokers, a 2 percent reduction in automobile accidents, etc.

So, beyond the police, all professions that have some relation to repression, justice, or administration need categories to facilitate their management, labeling, analysis, branding, control, etc. In short, series make it possible to use other people as instruments, and a society that is governed by the alliance between officers of repression and merchants is willing to accept a general serialization of what conforms and what does not.

Serial killers, however, cannot be serialized, except as examples of a diffuse cultural disorder. Those who try (consciously or unconsciously) to act as examples do so by introducing themselves into the social and political debate as emblematic, sphinx-like figures, but rarely as "types." However, a society that will not even question its own motivations is loath to acknowledge the enigmatic oracular side of criminals, and so, when compared with the emblem, the "type" has the advantage of facilitating normative and repressive reactions.

CHAPTER THIRTEEN

Evil

Destined for Evil

The imagery of monstrous crime feeds our desire for police-like control. But at the opposite end of the spectrum – i.e., the desire for deviance – it also indulges our love of catastrophe.

A fascination with the apocalypse is shared by the public and by criminals like Manson, Berkowitz, and others. It is also a craving for disaster, an imaginary collective release, and it is extrapolated as the outcome of the holy terror of criminal destinies. This ill-fated course toward catastrophe is accepted as a general model by believers in the "mad warrior." It reveals a secret desire that exists in the self but which virtuous behavior and social repression attempt to smother for as long as possible: the desire for the end of society.

This is because, in Nordic mythology, political order is not a condition for welfare or even a compromise between powers, but rather a tragic attempt to contain and channel each party's destructive energy (which, of course, none wishes to surrender) for the longest possible time. The apocalyptic belief that underlies Viking myths[1] applies both to individuals and to society. The element of truth in the discourse on serial killers is that there is a natural tendency toward an inexorable outcome, which may be followed by redemption. By repeating their crimes and dismembering their victims, negative heroes exhibit a temporality that is drawn toward disaster and repetition. This is also true of criminals who, within a matter of hours, commit massacres that are the outcome of long periods of paranoid or mystical maturation.

The same message is conveyed in films that center on increasingly destructive and intoxicating violence, from one generation of film noir to the next: from Stanley Kubrick to Abel Ferrara, and from Terence Fisher to Clive Barker or Quentin Tarentino. These directors always carry the hard edge (the same hardheartedness that Nordic warriors had to possess and which was echoed in the names of the most noble among them: Gerard,

Richard, Harry, etc.) of their movies one degree further, building up toward
a sacrificial slaughter and a rebirth of the kind that is promised by the
suicidal or homicidal sects that flourish in the United States.

Works of fiction are organized by rules similar to those that, according
to commentators, govern the urges of real killers. Consciously or unconsciously, their authors draw an outline of the werewolf culture, which
follows the irreversible march of a lone wolf, mortal encounter after mortal
encounter, toward a blood bath, a dismembering and liquefaction of bodies,
and finally a defilement of the entire planet, which is both the sacrificial
culmination of the story and the condition for repeating the experience
with an even harder edge.[2] Alejandro Jodorowsky's film *Santa Sangre*, with
its imagined swimming pool filled with blood, makes a first step toward
this type of implicit "hope." It alludes to the holocausts under the old
Mexican regime, but also recalls the ancient Norwegian saga, in which the
gods used a vast cave to store the blood of Kvasir, their equivalent of
Dionysos, before drinking it.[3]

It is true that North American productions contain a thousand different
messages. The world of fantastic fiction alone has branched out into an
incredible variety of Hollywood genres. Specialists will tell you that the
vampire is not a werewolf, a golem, or a Frankenstein's monster; that the
Tommyknockers, the Blob, and the Alien have no more in common than
Gremlins, psychokillers, Satan, witches, and the living dead; that a chase to
the death and the story in *Jaws* do not derive from the same myth and that
they are not even related to the tales of Count Zaroff. They will tell you
that discriminating American audiences never watch Z-series or Freddy
Kruger[4] films, which are dumped on the foreign market or movie theaters
in the American slums. They explain that good cartoons and Walt Disney's
childlike animals (including the big bad wolf) have nothing to do with the
bloodthirsty monsters in splatter films, that Stephen Spielberg is not
Stephen King, and that Freddy does not belong to the Adams Family.

Granted. But, regardless of what critics who do not bother to delve
beyond clichéd analyses may say, this bustling universe follows an order in
which the plot line is always the same: good (the socialized world) is
threatened by a rise of evil surging up from its own insides, rushing to the
surface, and spreading across the universe. Occasionally, an individualized
point of resistance crystallizes a reversal of the situation and good is
reinstated *in extremis*.

The writings of Stephen King or the mystical murderer Charles Manson
can shed some light on this subject. For both of them, evil rises from the
bowels of the earth, from far below its crust, and tries to lure away the
inhabitants of its cities so that it can devour them one by one. In the

tradition of Lovecraft, King denounces this in horror, while Manson desires it and refers to it interchangeably as God or the devil; but their fascination with it is the same. The lid that has been placed over a stale democracy and a boring white middle-class life style is thus lifted, releasing a torrent of irresistible passions until the next cycle begins.

Naturally, fiction writers and crime researchers object to the idea that there is a criminal destiny. But, at the same time, they confirm it, and their belief in catastrophe-bound, solitary wanderers has left its mark on two centuries of Anglo-Saxon fiction. Starting in the 1970s, this was driven home with frightening monotony, while, in counterpoint to the "white riots" ordained by the punk-rock movement, films from all over the world portrayed heroes who wandered alone in a landscape of deserted skyscrapers and who were capable of feeding the women of their dreams to a dog.[5]

America's Obsession with Nazism

The fragile nature of Nordic myths and the fact that they do not inspire a deep sense of civility probably derive from a single characteristic: they conjure up fantasies of their monstrous mirror image, and it takes only a single wrinkle in the pattern of history – a short circuit in the meditations of a civilization – for these fantasies to become reality.

This is what happened in Germany when the Nordic myth encountered the myth of the state. Adopting Napoleonic centralized power in a culture comprised of different communities was tantamount to setting a cultural time bomb, since decentralized mutual control had been designed to counter the evil model of a central sovereign. To deal with the incoherence of their state-divided ethnicity, the Germans fabricated a delusion that naturalized the Leviathan of the Prussian state.

This delusion consisted, on a pretense of racial purity, in reconciling a warrior's nature (savage, valiant, spontaneous, etc.) with a state culture (orderly, repressive, rational, etc.). I will not discuss the contradictions between the trivial bourgeois brutality of Nazi sympathizers and the romantic facets of the Nordic myth they cherished. But I should recall that Hitler is said to have addressed the SS "Werewulf" division, which specialized in terrorism and execution, with a speech that extolled the independence and ruthlessness of beasts of prey.[6] With these words, the Führer epitomized the perfect contradiction in his regime between a violence that was disciplined by the logic of the state and the purely "natural" individuality which he tried to promote as his official ideology.

Twenty years earlier, in *Mein Kampf*, it was the Jews that Hitler had compared to individualistic wolves: "The same pack of wolves which has just fallen on its prey together disintegrates when hunger abates into its individual beasts."[7] In its ambivalence, the wolf metaphor totally escapes ideological coherency but lends itself to any sentiment that focuses on pure hatred and a fight to the death between the self and its double.

Now that this psychotic quest has been ended, there is hope that, rather than create a war between human animals and Jews, or between Jews portrayed as animals and an ethnic state, the contradiction between brute force and civilization has hopefully been overcome by Germany's introspection into its own culture.

Disneyland and the Apocalypse

I would not say that the same is true of the other major branch of Nordic culture, the Anglo-American one, which today is approaching global proportions. The ingredients for metaphysical pessimism are just as present here, although they follow the flow of artistic trends and do not pose a threat to the official neo-Kantian discourse of the rule of law.

People may laugh or weep at the fact that unified international culture resembles a huge county fair, where the human race is enticed to visit twopenny attractions where nightmares and dreams are peddled. But this is the way it is: the poor majority has been torn away from its ancestral bearings, like the errant groups of American settlers as they made their way West, and it needs uniform symbols to guide it. As long as there are carbonated sodas, hamburgers, and penny arcades pointing the way to heaven or hell, people feel at home in any part of the world – who cares about the local Amerindian, Greek, or French culture!

The pioneering spirit has spread across the globe, and the advancing masses distinguish themselves from those whose sedentary life style has left them to stew in their own quirks, using the traveling bazaar that caters to them (and which is made up of multinational giants today) as the emblem of their freedom. There is nothing scandalous per se in the fact that American manufacturers have taken the lead in this dream crusade, or even that they make billions of dollars from selling tiny bubbles in sugary water, film footage, the numbered pixels that make up virtual images, or management consulting services. Small or large, they are all part of the fair, masters of illusion, whose trade is, after all, perfectly respectable.

Yet a problem remains: these snake-oil sellers are so completely fused with their errant crowd of customers that they are incapable of preparing for the next phase, in which people will begin to rebuild societal values, this time on a universal scale. Not only are these mega-wheeler-dealers unable to contribute to producing new values, they snarl at their very existence. Once again, violence raises its sharp-toothed snout.

The masters of "global democracy" have become so comfortable in their temporary role as the pathfinders for uprooted migrants who have regressed into adult children that they no longer want to grant them their emancipation. And the "big babies" (a cliché which will never run out of willing analysts) refuse to grow up. Since their nerves are saturated with pleasant sensations, they can only imagine the adult age as a source of frustration. The idea of being expelled from the consumer ecosystem gives them an intolerable sense of injustice. After Günter Grass, the author of *Drum* and *Dog Days*, prominent American science-fiction novelist Thomas Disch has described in no uncertain terms[8] what happens to a character who refuses to grow up, cannot put up with the slightest annoyance, and is eager to wield the almighty powers he has inherited with the gift of an evil caduceus given by the god Hermes (alternatively, Mercury, Odin, or Saman): in the end, he creates a super-AIDS virus in his laboratory and sets it loose on the entire world.

Truth is not far from fiction. If someone wants to live in a world of make-believe, someone else will inevitably replace his joystick with a real trigger, shooting real missiles, aimed at Baghdad or Somalia. People who were raised with the idea that all needs are satisfied by the same cosmic force, and who become enraged at the slightest frustration, find it normal to shift imperceptibly between game and reality, fiction and atrocity, laughter and tears, or competition and tantrum.

Knowing that these risks exist, is it right to take the sellers of macabre tales and their sales pitch with a grain of salt? Can we laugh at them in the same way we laugh at harmless Disney characters? Laughter is certainly one strategy. We can join our favorite cartoon characters and make marvelous fun of their adversaries. It is very relaxing. But beware the day when Mickey Mouse is painted on the sides of bomber planes flying over Dresden, Hiroshima, Hanoi, Mogadishu, or Sarajevo, and when Billy the Kid's colt turns into a blast explosive or a bacteriological weapon. For, that day, the words "no future" will begin to realize their full potential.

Stop Laughing

The great film director Costa-Gavras, who has so accurately captured the features of the cultures in which he has lived (France, Israel, the United

States), perceived under an appearance of impeccable moral legitimacy the erratic alternations described above, and used them as the basis for his superb yet disturbing film *The Music Box*. In the story, a young and brilliant American lawyer takes her own father's defense when he is accused of having acted as a torturer for the fascists in Europe, and in the end she discovers "the truth." Although the evidence is slim and might be the result of a manipulation, she not only denounces her father to the court, but reveals his crime to her son "for his own good," something that would seem inconceivable to Latin European audiences, and thereby forever destroys the image of the child's grandfather, who is his only male hero.

What Costa-Gavras is saying is very clear: belonging to a democratic America requires that one sacrifice one's origins and family loyalties.[9] The denunciation is presented as a civic duty. To enforce this, modern America is capable of making an educated woman do of her own free will what Nazi Germany had to force its youth to do after anesthetizing them with a program of military training: denounce their parents and sacrifice their descendants for a public ideal.

By portraying what America is capable of pushing people to do under cover of a perfectly democratic ethic, Costa-Gavras only grazed the surface, so as to avoid shocking American public opinion, which is loath to accept even the slightest criticism.

Because of their prickly reactions, it is possible that no one has ever really pressured the Americans to debate this monstrous aspect of their conception of civic duty, which reduces blood ties to a function of universal social control. Despite what one reads in the newspapers about the effects of frayed family bonds, this society continues to produce individuals who throw themselves into legal disputes against their own relatives. The extreme cases include that of a man who sued his mother for having caused his birth defect (by neglecting her doctor's advice during pregnancy), an insurance company that publicly rewarded a man for reporting his pyro-maniac son, and a woman who sold the story of her son's death to a television company for a handsome sum of money.

It is only right that telephone hot lines should be available to provide police protection for battered children: it is an acknowledgment of the tragic deaths caused by child abuse. But a collective Big Brother is watching all normal parents as well and reducing parental responsibility. This "Swedish" side to the United States, where the white majority is largely made up of Nordic and Germanic strains, should not be forgotten when speaking about the chaotic liberalism that seems to prevail there. The tendency cannot be dismissed as puritanical hysteria, for it draws on a deeply internalized ancestral belief in the need to control all forms of deviance in order to strengthen the force of social order. This cultural model binds deviance and repression together in an endless cycle: the cycle of the werewolf myth.

Adopting a more tolerant picture, which is closer to "mythical maturity," is not impossible, but it cannot be done without risk, since the psycho-sociological structure organized by the myth considered here only allows for openings as inlets through which it can suck in a catastrophe. Separation can be painful, and even lead to insanity; for, as serial killers remind us when their borrowed identities begin to crumble, there is a void, and with it violence and despair, gaping behind the beauty of symmetry.

One senses this tendency in the very fabric of America society, in all of the minority groups that have been hardened by vindictive or puritanical sectarianism. Pure violence is there, sure of itself, waiting for a war in Somalia or a riot in Los Angeles or elsewhere so that it can emerge with a clear conscience. And, if Cornwell (alias John Le Carré) has summoned the "last superpower left" to finally show its authority without measure, let us hope that this will not give rise to a general metamorphosis into a society of "mad warriors," or spread the fundamental pessimism of this metaphor, which is reminiscent of the frustration some adolescents experience when they fail to come to grips with adulthood and, ultimately, reject it.

The Young Criminal Mind

It amuses the ennobled spokespersons of the global county fair to give lessons in financial management. But, as they prepare for the end of the world, they forget that if they lock their flock of suckers into a system of mindless consumption they may become truly hostile.

Very few stories tell what becomes of the keepers of this "house of horrors." When the visitors have grown tired of plastic skeletons and wax figures, tomato-juice blood spurting from throat wounds, and ghosts made of sheets, what do they do? They attack and devour the owner, his assistants, the popcorn vendors, the guards, their dogs and grand-mothers. Once someone has seen the charred carcasses on display at Coney Island (which was the first attempt to create a sedentary amusement park), they understand why there are so many security guards at Disneyland. Those who play on people's basic instincts will eventually reap what they sow. Hasn't it been said that moviegoers really long to satisfy their secret desires and that fiction writers project their own fantasies onto their characters?

We have already seen how the collective fantasy is structured. Serial killers make it obvious enough: through an alternating cycle of satisfaction and frustration, it is a progressive descent into distress, drifting, and despair, a march toward everlasting solitude.

Nordic sagas, which are a condensed version of the fantasy, also echo it in their many adaptations. When communication among people becomes trapped in a machine, the force of desire inevitably is transformed into a longing for death. Some have tried to control this force and use it to make money, but, as with Disch's caduceus, negative energy grows commensurate with any attempt to make it follow a rational course and to segment it into smaller "consumer units." As it accumulates in increasingly large quantities at various points in the system (in the form of money, or in the physical form of human beings), this energy will use any means to release itself, including the very market forces by which it is driven, the power by which it is channeled, or the network through which it is disseminated.

The Nordic culture of pessimism has always maintained that, ultimately, restraining natural violence is a waste of time, because the principle of life demands retribution and a violence equal to the violence with which it is repressed. One can therefore only resign oneself to deferring the inevitable final explosion. At best, fighters will be compensated for their disinterested heroism when the Valkyries[10] select them as the most deserving among the dead on the battlefield, a triage that destines the chosen few for celestial clashes even more bloodthirsty than those on earth.

The desire for catastrophe, which is the real basis of the pessimism in Nordic culture, often remains hidden, repressed or denied behind fashionable postmodernism, triumphant liberalism, and the current mania for political correctness. If it raises its ugly head too often within the skinhead or hard-rock movements, it is merely denounced as a local resurgence of Nazism. But one of the merits of the debate on mass crime is that it recalls the common reality of this deep pessimism, and that to do so it literally subjugates hundreds of millions of spectators of their acts.

The imagery of the great Odinic warriors' grim violence is just as much a threat to democratic England and America today as it was to Germany, even when it is firmly gagged and bound, forcefully exorcised, or dismissed as simple fantasy.[11] It could even be argued that the memory of Hitler haunts these countries, because they have portrayed him as a devil (unlike other cultures, where he is seen "merely" as a barbaric madman). In numerous cases for the prosecution, one of the criteria (used by the media and sometimes by the lawyers themselves) for establishing that the accused is guilty of inhumane behavior is to ask him his opinion of Hitler. If a defendant can be found to have made favorable remarks about Hitler, the members of the jury are certain to be aghast and to "understand" why he may have been led to commit the horrible act in question.

This test also appears in fiction. In his novel *The Dead Zone*, Stephen King shows how the hero, a man with extrasensory powers, is able to foresee that an extremely popular presidential candidate is in fact a villain and future dictator. An inner voice constantly asks him: "Suppose . . . just suppose you could hop into a time machine and go back to the year 1932. In Germany. And suppose you came across Hitler. Would you kill him or let him live?"[12] King once again gives in to the mandatory ritual in the Anglo-American world of disavowing Nazism in a somewhat childish, hysterical tone. The hero's answer is that he would drive a knife as deep as he could into the assassin's black heart and twist it in the wound, but, first, he would coat the blade with rat poison.[13]

We go from childishness to dementia with James Herbert, who in his book *The Spear* identifies Hitler with Longinus, the soldier who stabbed Christ in the heart and then became one of the original characters in the occult quest for the Holy Grail. With quotations from *Mein Kampf* as chapter headings, this mysticofantastic epic adventure throughout the ages, in which knights of old are reincarnated into Nazis, ends in a victory of good over evil, when an incorruptible American detective finally recovers the relic, after a string of misadventures in the time–space continuum, and plunges the spear into the rotting body of Heinrich Himmler. But the ambivalence of his disgust, which hides his pleasure, is revealed in the same scene, when the hero suddenly becomes aware of the eternal nature of the struggle between light and dark.[14]

What the author is interested in is not the victory of good, but rather indecision, repeated images of battle, and a constant and fascinated fixation with the ambivalent and changing relationship between the devil and Christ, Christ and the devil.[15]

Nazism is also portrayed as a form of Satanism in the film adaptation of King's *Needful Things*. Once he has been unmasked by a good cop, the demonic storekeeper in the book manages to escape on his motorcycle from the small American town where he lives, whereas in the film he flees in a 1940s Mercedes. In the book, America's fascination with consumer goods is criticized through the character of the smooth-talking salesman. In the film, which is much more politically correct, since it was made for a young audience that does not read books but instead watches videos, a cultured and hence suspicious European (played by Max von Sydow, who mysteriously allowed himself to be roped into this nonsense) is portrayed as the criminal through a plethora of redundant signs: World War II model airplanes, bits of dialogue in German, newspapers from the Nazi period in his basement, etc.

Everything seems to indicate that, by developing a phobic fixation on

Nazi demons (which has nothing to do with the moral and political implications of the totalitarian, racist Nazi regime), a stratum of Anglo-American culture is expressing a fear of desires that it continues to harbor under a thick shell of liberal democratic principles. Of course, such death wishes are not the sole prerogative of this group, but it entertains them as if it recognized something kindred in them, although this it fiercely denies.

It would be wrong to believe that this type of novel, film, and now computer game, which brings together geopolitics, history of war, space opera, fantasy, and horror, is an isolated phenomenon. Such works are legion on the shelves of bookstores in English-speaking countries and, despite Europeans' (especially in the Latin cultures) lack of tolerance for stories of depressing and endless epic battles, many are available in translation. On every page, they confirm that the inspiration for the images that now define North American culture derives from real-life models of "changeling warriors," the world's great political or civilian criminals.

As a last example, there is British writer Robert Harris's novel *Fatherland*,[16] in which (like Philip K. Dick before him) the author imagines a victorious German Reich. A police officer rediscovers the Shoah, the evidence of which has been almost totally buried in the victors' congested archives. The book has some instructive historical interest (as it recalls the real documents used to design the peace), but at the same time it discredits itself by the jabs it makes at the plan for a united Europe, which it considers merely as a smoke screen for German hegemony.

But, most of all, by portraying the hero as a young SS officer who "discovers" the awful truth while wandering through Berlin, wearing his stylish uniform (like the many clean-cut American actors who have worn the Nazi commander's outfit so well in films), Harris endorses the idea of committing harmful acts without feeling remorse. The novel offers a good example of the pleasures that are authorized by phobic genres, which, as we saw with the film *Falling Down*, are an important resource for a violent culture that is superficially restrained by political correctness.

CHAPTER FOURTEEN

The Delights of Hesitation

Nature should thus be thanked for fostering social incompatibility, enviously competitive vanity, and insatiable desires for possession or even power. Without these desires, all man's excellent natural capacities would never be roused to develop.

Immanuel Kant, *Philosophical Writings*

The werewolf culture is fascinated with the hesitation between nature and culture and between barbarianism and civilization. But what does "hesitating" mean for a society or a social group?

To take one example, it means fantasizing about returning to a non-existent mythical past. Hence, the large "Africanist" movement among American middle-class blacks preaches a fantasized return to the continent of their ancestors, using a literal and politically correct interpretation of the term "African-American."

This is probably a radical black version of the public's general engrossment with the distant past, which, among middle-class American whites, has been given the misleading label "New Age." For the descendants of the country's Anglo-Saxon Protestant founders, this distant past is found in their Nordic origins. In *Backlash*,[1] which is feminist Susan Faludi's indictment of the return of male chauvinism in America, the author writes a revealing chapter on the poet Robert Bly. Bly was known as a pacifist and conscientious objector before he became Shepherd Bliss, the leader of a men's movement that sought to discover the true male nature through the ancient Viking myths. In this New Age environment, he took his followers on weekend retreats in the woods, where the participants, wearing tribal masks, disguised as animals, and beating on drums, were able to rediscover "the beast within."

Faludi observes that this was Bly's way of "climbing back onto the media throne," and that between 1985 and 1990 hundreds of men (lawyers, judges, CPAs, businessmen – in total, more than 50,000 adults who "had a life") enrolled in his workshops, paying $55 to attend lectures and $300 for weekend retreats. Bly is editor of the journal *The New Warrior's Gazette*, and he has written books on the sacred image of the phallus, in which he exhorts men to break away from their mothers and the women who "have transformed American males into yogurt-eating little boys." He tells them to "look deep within themselves" and "accept their dark side," by meditating on Grimm's fairy tales, the *Iliad,* and the *Odyssey.* Faludi ridicules Bly, without stopping to consider that, as she expatiates about the desexual-ization of society, her own puritanical vehemence makes her a perfect sparring partner for this mad warrior. This duel between a rusticated macho and a feminist crusader sums up what I mean by the hesitation in American culture between two neurotic phenomena.

Ethnologists must be careful neither to scoff at this antagonism nor to lend it too much credence. It should instead be seen as another example of the constant shifting in Anglo-Saxon imagery between irrepressible violence and violent repression. It reflects a desire to refrain from spon-taneous violence but at the same time a reluctance to cut oneself off from the "dark side," without which the social cannot be established.

On my left (the hand of desire) is the "macho" thesis, consisting of a fascination with spontaneity and frenzied violence. When these are part of a narrative that filters the horror and softens the sharp edges, they become almost likable, in spite of the dangers they pose. They are what gives the devil his charm, as portrayed by John Updike in the iconoclastic, seductive, and hairy-chested character Daryll Van Horne. Like the primitive leaders of the legendary horde, Van Horne impregnates women, this time in the quiet village of Eastwick, where he brings out the witch in all of them.[2]

On my right (the oath-taking hand) is the thesis that brutal instincts must be repressed, since the majority of serial killers are males who rape and kill women.

In the middle, we have the intellectual – a figure that has always been ambivalent in America – or his rascally reincarnation, the horror-fiction writer.[3] Mild hysterics, intellectuals try to act as mediators. Their powerful brains weave complex solutions that are both logical and attractive.

The "Hobbesian solution," for example, which reconciles animal energy and human nature through the intercession of the Leviathan, is not just a cold conceptualization but a delightful, admirable, and thought-provoking ideal. It is a "marriage of heaven and hell,"[4] as the poet and painter William Blake imagined it in the eighteenth century. Blake depicted good as the equivalent of repressive rationality, and considered evil to be the natural expression of a basic psychic energy. In the "Proverbs of Hell," he extols heroic energy. In *Visions of the Daughters of Albion,* a forerunner of Wilhelm

Reich's work, his heroine Oothon (another name with an Odinic root) attains new-found pureness through the pleasures of the flesh. For Blake, the symbol of innocence is the lamb, which has been domesticated by the tyrannical god of "repression," while the symbol of experience is the tiger, which embodies energy and the forces of love and cruelty, as in his famous verse:

> Tyger! Tyger! burning bright
> In the forests of the night
> What immortal hand or eye
> Could frame thy fearful symmetry?

The "tragic dilemma of humanity" between these two principles is captured toward the end of the poem: "Did He who made the lamb make Thee?"

It appears that Blake conceived one of the first prototypes for the fascinating symmetry between an energy that is free but cruel and the citizen who has been tamed by a repressive legal system. Of course, the "fearful symmetry" that Blake wrote about, and for which the Scandinavian werewolf was an even earlier model, is also found in a long tradition of Anglo-Saxon tales of obsession: Jekyll and Hyde, Dorian Gray and his portrait, Van Helsing and Dracula, Batman and the Joker, the evil slime and the Ghost Busters, *Alien* versus *E.T.*, Graham versus Hannibal Lecter, and so on. Some authors of horror tales acknowledge their affinities with the English pre-Romantic writers. For example, Tom Harris's dark hero was given the name Red Dragon as a reference to Blake's painting of a red dragon and a woman basking in the sunlight.

Rather than merge together the white knight and the black knight, good and evil, or light and darkness in a single character who can courageously confront the reality of his own desires, this culture is infatuated with the continuous vacillation between twinned beings. It wants constantly to watch man's transformation into a wolf and then back into a man again.[5]

An example of American culture's rapt attraction to the symmetry between good and evil is Barry Sonnenfeld's excellent film *Addams Family Values*.[6] The author shows that the most terrible monsters (the Addams family contains elements of everything America hates or fears most, from Latin machismo to outrageous romanticism, from outdated aristocratic snobbery to wildly nonconformist individualism) are not what we think, but rather the designated victims of a virtuous, upstanding America full of boy scouts, Walt Disney clichés, outings in the woods, corrupt policemen, and widows dripping with diamonds – an America that is highly representative of the lack of symbolic castration. Like many American women, of whom (as Sonnenfeld suggests) she is only a slightly exaggerated caricature, the widow in question, an attractive platinum blonde, who introduces herself into the outlandish Adams family as the agent of a demented normality, is characterized by her incredible greed. She wants everything, right away, and is willing to marry a monster with a skin disease in order to steal his money. In comparison, the Adams family children, who play poker with cards that are illustrated with famous American serial killers, attempt to execute their little brother with a guillotine (with the "Marseillaise" playing in the background), and roast the camp counselors who force them to watch Mickey Mouse cartoons instead of the Thanksgiving turkey, seem infinitely more likable. In the end, it is the children who discover true love, the love between rebels, like Romeo and Juliet. In short, the bad guys here are the good guys, and vice versa, and the eternal ambivalence of the symmetry between good and evil appears once again, with an uncontrollable energy circulating between the two poles.

A Confirmation of Values

Let there be no mistake: Anglo-American culture's attachment to this symmetrical relationship is not a minor issue that only concerns imaginative detective novelists and literary critics. It is a belief that is anchored in the social and political identity, a habitus[7] that creates the coherence between attitudes in many aspects of life. This is why, when North American society and the English-speaking peoples in general translate multiple crime into fiction, they do it with vital urgency, for in so doing they show that crime contains the principle of evil, which is the sine qua non for the appearance of good in response.

This urgency must be comprehended if one is to understand the indignant reactions that are raised by any criticism of "banalized" American culture. The critics, believing that they are only delving skin-deep, scratching the surface or challenging a vile, consumerized indulgence of people's desires, are in fact attacking the core of this particular world view. The balance between good and evil, which is repeated in all forms of fiction and commentary on crime, is not just a hackneyed, simplistic, or childish idea, but in fact the very foundation of Anglo-American values, which attempt to lock freedom and order, and energy and social control, in battle for as long as they possibly can.

In contemporary Nordic and North American culture, the criminal's metamorphosis into a werewolf, an asocial human animal of ancient legend, fills a logical function: it is the negative condition for a human order; at once the precious treasure and the secret aim of that order but also the thing that it must keep underground (or under the table, like the left hand, which many Americans prudishly keep on their laps during a meal).

Kant in fact makes the same point when he describes the necessity for man's negative, rebellious, or wild side in the process of civilization: "All the culture and art which adorns mankind and the finest social order man creates are fruits of his unsociability. For it is compelled by its own nature to discipline itself, and thus, by enforced art, to develop completely the germs which nature implanted."[8]

It is not my position that Americans are any more morbid than other people or that they have any particular enjoyment in hearing about human sacrifice and dismembered bodies or murdering frenzies in which an instinct for mass killing is released. On the other hand, I do maintain that, in this culture, people have, in perfect confluence with the Kantian theory, a stronger belief than elsewhere that violent but supposedly life-giving energy is impossible to eliminate and that institutional control is needed simply to regulate the general state of combat.

At best, the ideal solution would be to alternate collective repression and the emergence of individual energy, at the calculated risk of the roles becoming reversed. People believe that, all things considered, it is better to support a neo-Zoroastrian alternation between the principles of good and evil than to allow evil to run free behind an appearance of good – i.e., of government authority and autocratic legitimacy. A psychiatrist interviewed by one of Jeffrey Dahmer's biographers, speculating on why America produces more serial killers than the rest of the world, has offered this explanation: it is because this country, the standard-bearer of a New World Order, is a cultural melting pot. Clashes are inevitable, and susceptible individuals absorb and reproduce situations of violence.[9]

Of course, choosing liberty over dictatorship opens a realm of possibilities so vast that anyone would risk getting lost in them; but this heroic solitude (reminiscent of the Protestant work ethic) seems to be the price of freedom.

The ill effects of freedom are just as clearly recognized. Police psychologist Roger Depue analyzes the unfortunate consequences of mobility in these terms:

> Over the years, the American family has lost its moorings and its traditional bearings. In the past, members of the same family used to live in close proximity to each other. Neighbors often had known each other for several generations. But good-neighborliness has disappeared and been replaced by a society of strangers. We have become a nomad society. Every year, almost 36 million

Americans move, which corresponds to slightly more than 10% of the population. On average, a family will move twelve times before their children turn eighteen.[10]

But this development is seen as the result of the people's choice to live in a state of general mobility and competition, in other words, to have a free society in which all opportunities can, and must, be taken on the run. The observation is therefore less a criticism than the observation of an ideal: that of the original state of a nomad people on a perpetual quest for new frontiers.[11]

The Pleasures of Phobia

Americans' adoption of a culture based on hesitation and the equilibrium between principles of violence and the law does not derive simply from their ideal of society. And the logical interdependence between freedom and savagery does not suffice to explain their intense support of this ideal. A double form of eroticizing is involved, contrasting the "dark side," our hidden store of wild urges, with Victorian prudishness and its intangible order, which lends value to the forbidden forces it represses. Without the civil, high-minded, clean, and innocent side, the murderous, wild, merciless core would not be able to sustain itself; but, inversely, without the dark energy of this core, the belief seems to be that civilization would have no reason to exist as a rampart against barbarianism. The two worlds of life and law are therefore dependent on one another and, as in phobic obsession, the object of desire is at once rejected with disgust and yet ever present, so that not one drop of its unknown pleasures will be lost.

This dual, cyclical culture is therefore not laxist. On the contrary, it is heroic and repressive, because there is a major subsidiary incentive: the pleasure of continuing to engage in violence, whether it is legitimate or not.

Communing in a State of Pessimism

It is through virtuous combat that the American urge for violence is expressed. Beyond the interests of classification (by the police, the courts, the market, the government, and indeed criminals as their collaborators), repression is an essential temptation, because it promises pleasures that are equivalent to the supposed pleasures of crime. Freud recalls this when he explains that the reason why crime is repressed is because the same desire is bound to be kindled in all the other members of the community [. . .]. [T]he punishment will not infrequently give those who carry it out an opportunity of committing the same outrage under color of an act of expiation. This is indeed one of the foundations of the human penal system and it is based, no doubt correctly, on the assumption that the prohibited impulses are present alike in the criminal and in the avenging community.[12]

This question is a matter of concern for writers and for the police. In Robert Ressler's interesting book *Whoever Fights Monsters*, there is a quotation from Nietzsche which is frequently used by Stephen King and other authors: "Whoever fights monsters must take care not to become a monster himself. For, as you stand looking deep into the abyss, the abyss is looking deep into you."[13]

Such ethical overinvestment is likely to worsen rather than resolve the problem of Anglo-American culture, which tends to provoke and preserve images of monstrosity at the same time as it fights and represses them. In fact, the Anglo-American world does not stop at punishing individuals: first, it turns them into mad warriors, of the sort which are a menace to society. The police have helped to build a hall of fame of superheroes who are hellbent on destroying the heavenly existence offered by the "best system in the world." Hence, another phenomenon can be added to complete the one that Freud describes: by construing criminals as a menace to society, America takes a secret pleasure in imagining society's destruction.

A Functional Duality

There is another reason for this culture's evident need to maintain the symmetrical relationship between social violence and social control as an intangible truth. It is because the relationship's ideology has been very helpful in justifying the dual division of the same society into a world of "the damned" and a world of "the chosen."

Phobic about the world of evil with which it is in constant combat, the market-based democracy also has a vital need for an imagery of horror. As I have observed in another work:

There is no "liberal" society without its own Stephen King to describe the terror of getting lost in the woods, falling into the hands of demons, madmen or gypsies, witches or extraterrestrials, which all belong more or less to the same horde. A society formed around the pair *werewolf/social control* must also have its "people of the damned" as evidence of its own existence. Hence, through the manifestations of their poverty, lack of control, riots, and delinquency, the masses of

poor blacks and Hispanics who are excluded from the market *serve a purpose* in
the ideology of a symmetrically opposite world of pastel colors and up-scale
neighborhoods and which represents the "real" society of reciprocal solvency.
In the eyes of its white Protestant inhabitants, a country like the United States
thereby becomes a sort of complete cosmos where the damned and the chosen
live face to face, mutually proving each other's existence, and this goes far beyond
the inevitability of social stratification.[14]

Reminders of the existence of this "dark side," therefore, not only
correspond to the perverse pleasure of "slumming"; they are also part of a
strategy of self-preservation. The social authenticity of violent film
occasionally appeals to certain European critics, although they do not
understand its inner meaning:

> We may learn more about contemporary America from these crude, violent films,
> whose mixture of pain and anxiety is supposed to teach us how to look at the
> world. It is to their credit that they do not convey fear through theories or symbols.
> Thus, the audience can capture, if only for an instant, the savagery and violence
> of which man is capable.[15]

This is true. But by internalizing the theory of a violent human nature in
this way one runs the risk of succumbing to the perverse aesthetic of
poverty, which American mythology feeds on, in contrast with the American
dream: the mournful, otherworldly beauty of the ghettos and slums, which
recalls that of cities destroyed by war.[16]

The transition from the ambivalence of the metamorphous warrior to
the rich/poor division has the value of stabilizing both sides of this
symmetrical relationship. The American middle class's almost maniacal
fixation on conspicuous consumption (regardless of risks of debt and
impoverishment), its grim resistance to any form of state-run social
security (which is seen as a siphoning off of sacrificial poverty-fighting
energy) cannot be explained by the American dream alone. These are
also due to the ancestral mythical fear of becoming submerged in
poverty, which is considered to be the punishment for a life of savagery
and violence.

A Victorious Religion

As an imaginary configuration with quasi-religious proportions, the werewolf myth can only survive if it is able to expand and convert and conquer
others.

For partisans of the theory of innate violence, it is time to go on an ethical crusade. The horrifying possibility that a nonviolent nature, or even a nature that is not exclusively violent, exists must be denied *urbi et orbi*. For, if such an idea were to prevail, the mechanism of mobilization and control (whose only justification is that it prevents the monster within us from emerging) would eventually collapse. How else can one explain the attempts to discredit anthropologists (such as Margaret Mead) who dared to imagine the possibility that there were civilizations structured by a different imagery, societies that were non- or postviolent, without werewolves or mad warriors?[17] Maintaining the myth of the mad warrior appears, by contrast, to be the duty not only of entertainers (the leaders of a cultural industry that wants unlimited, worldwide exposure) but also of many mainstream intellectuals.

In addition, the myth is projected as a factor of cohesion, a way of conquering and proselytizing other cultures. It seeks to gain ground in these other cultures and bend them, one by one, to its sacrosanct dualist principle. For example, Robert De Niro made his Hollywood debut in *Taxi Driver*,[18] in which he played a young champion of the Italian community in 1968 who quickly buys into the werewolf ideology. His solitary existence gradually transforms him into a dangerous weapons maniac, and in the end, for "a good cause," he kills three small-time pimps and is applauded as a hero. Scorsese's film, of course, conveys a rather negative judgment of the idea of all adhering to this culture: indeed, America will tolerate no more than a tiny dose of this kind of "European" snobbery when the general trend is clearly to join the ranks.

Occasionally, scenes of extreme violence are considered to be the cultural monopoly of Anglo-Saxon film directors, as reflected in certain remakes. For example, *The Phantom of the Opera* by Dwight Little in 1990 transposed Gaston Leroux's famous Parisian novel to London. Was it more credible to situate a close-up image of a woman having her throat slit and then being decapitated in the country of Jack the Ripper rather than in France, the country of serial killer Landru? The film's producers offer an interesting reason: "We did not want to give the characters a heavy French accent."[19] Does this mean that the natural language of extreme violence has become the universal English language?

It would be an overstatement to speak of America as having a culture that sticks fiercely to its values when in many ways it seems to have shed the ethical, authoritarian ideals that continue to plague the Old World. If "visible" minorities and individualistic, cultural, or linguistic pride are accepted as components of the melting pot, they are not tolerated unless they concede to the "best system," embodied by the market, the

Constitution, and American lawmakers, which regulate circulation between natural energy and social order.

Of course this world view, which has triumphed today, strikes a contrast with the most ancient forms of community solidarity, based on the exclusion of strangers. But a culture in which humans must be conceived of as uncivilized beings, in order to counterbalance this with a single model of the system of civilization, tends to reject those who do not conform to the general norm. It does not "officially" exclude African-Americans, Hispanics, different language groups or myths, traditional modes of consumption or production; but it can eliminate anything that oversteps the boundaries or becomes autonomous, and can stir hatred against anyone who is unwilling to conform.[20]

To the extent that this cultural system has become international and continues to spread to other countries through the sale of television programs and the mass distribution of films and books (such as those of American authors Stephen King, Peter Straub, Tom Harris, or English writer Clive Barker), my interest is to understand its implications and limits. The werewolf complex, reflected in the different representations of the ambiguous struggle between madmen and avengers, seems to depend on the three main motifs of fascination, impotence, and, finally, radical pessimism:

1. A fascination with the other self reflected in the mirror of the crime.
2. An impotence to comprehend the multitude of human beings as a community that begins with the individual and with a moderating "condensation" of others.
3. A pessimistic belief in an eternal conflict, which is occasionally suspended by a succession of foretold apocalypses.

We should note that these tendencies echo trends in another society whose warring past still maintains a strong presence: that of Japan. It happens that the mythology of an everlasting battle also corresponds to a certain Japanese military culture. One may consider comic books to be harmless, but the "Akira" series by Katsuhiro Otomo recounts the birth of an all-powerful child on the site of an atomic disaster and his propulsion into an apocalyptic future. The series, which is very popular among adolescents all over the world, because of its flattering portrayal of rebellious youngsters on motorcycles, takes place against a backdrop of asphalt and merciless warfare.

Is it "reasonable" (to use the favorite word of John Rawls, the cantor of Western democracy) for artists in two of the world's leading cultures to join their efforts to promote this imagery of a world bent on death and unbridled power among young people?

It is difficult to believe that such images will never have effects beyond the world of paper and film, not because of the mechanical influence of the media, but because they are a breeding ground for broadly shared secret convictions.

CHAPTER FIFTEEN

Lessons in Inhumanity

I would rather be a cyborg than a goddess.

Donna Haraway, *Simians, Cyborgs and Women*

All societies wonder whether unbridled individuality and social order can be compatible. Some have devised theories that allow for both an irreducible conflict and an association between the two. Others, including the computerized postmodern society, have returned to the venerable dualistic myth, which brings private and public, necessity and freedom, and society and the individual into perfect symmetry.

To illustrate the exchanges between them, this myth imagines a pendulum-like movement, a shifting back and forth between madness and reason. This is the classic form of the werewolf myth and its obsessive neurosis, of which I have mentioned several manifestations. But its current form, which is especially developed in the United States, aims to go beyond. It posits that the entire cycle of culture and nature can be mechanized and thus made natural. It is a thesis of painless emotional pacification, which is found in the ideal of human automation that originated with the golem myth and recurs in the cyborg myth, as well as in theories of a self-regulating market. This proposition, which is supported by a belief in the pure naturalness (predetermination) of human life, nevertheless signals a possibility that social neurosis may degenerate into collective madness.

It is at this point that the serial killer's message becomes truly interesting, which is probably the reason why it has continued to fascinate Americans, like an unsolvable riddle. If in the United States there is a seemingly endless supply of commentary on heinous crime, this stems from the fact that "killing machines" are both the ultimate "proof" of man's animal nature and witnesses who constantly cry out the underlying truth about automation and repetition, which Anglo-American culture sees as an ideal and would like to substitute for society.[1]

The ideal of self-regulation was introduced three centuries ago by Hobbes, as his panic-stricken reaction to the "werewolves" that were turning

the politics of his era into a tragic killing field.[2] It was indeed to eradicate
the disorder in the human world that he sought to draw upon the hope of
a nascent science which – from Galileo to Descartes, who were his contemporaries – presented a new cosmology, according to which order no longer
flowed from a fixed center but from the reciprocal control of forces in
movement. Far from being a terrifying revelation, this discovery of reality's
energetic nature produced, on the contrary, an extraordinary opportunity
to restore order.

Hobbes's work is an attempt to imagine how the laws of man's animal
nature ("*homo homini lupus*") could be used toward a productive end by
channeling their energy into a conventional institution (the Leviathan). As
a sublimated animal force, the conventional will thus becomes the instrument for making man artificial and for rebuilding him as peaceful. In
construing his theory of a government machine that is powered by the
human animal's natural energy, Hobbes loyally places himself in the Nordic
tradition of a confrontation between crime and the law, foreshadowing
the encounter between Frankenstein and the werewolf, a classic theme from
nineteenth-century Gothic romanticism to mid-twentieth-century British
horror fiction.[3]

Of course, several contributions from culture's "rational" fields were
required before the project could become realistic: among others, these
were Newton's appropriation of systems of measurement, Locke's appli-
cation of an effective regulatory device to market forces, and Darwin's
determination of the long-term effects of the survival of the fittest. Two
centuries would pass before, with the emergence of computer technology
– the brainchild of cybernetics and classified information technologies –
the dream could start to become a reality and the wolf (individual violence)
could be bound together with the system in a single self-regulating machine.
More than 1,000 years have passed since the earliest rendering of this ideal
in the Nordic myth of Fenrir, the primordial wolf that is tethered to a rock
by Tyr, the god who embodies the social system, and which unleashes its
voracious hatred against him in a sort of mutual act of castration.

For Norbert Weiner, one of its founding theorists, cybernetics is,
explicitly, the creation of a new human world, a "golem" founded on
communication between beings that are adjusted by technology. This idea
reappears in "technologist" feminist Donna Haraway's outlandish (but
significant) work ordaining a replacement of sexual urges with the
controllable, more democratic, and supposedly less male-chauvinist flow
of a mechanized body. The great universal machine made possible by an
autonomous interlinking of smaller machines, which are in turn grafted

from humans, could therefore bring about peace, mutual understanding, fairness, and happiness.

Yet the irrational side of these recurring ideals is exposed openly by the most archetypal murderers, those who have carried out the experiment successfully by mechanizing their acts, as opposed to mere "number crunchers," like Crutchley and Kraft, technical-school instructors, like Tchikatilo, or speed demons, like Wilder. Of course, we can always refuse to listen to them, on the grounds that their acts disqualify them from commenting on society. But their words are not just commentaries or mere opinions. What these criminals are telling us is much more frightening: their acts are reality tests, tests in which humans seek to confront (or even to merge with) the nature of things through technology and technological "series."

Is total communication between all beings and all things human and democratic? Ted Bundy shows that the opposite is true: in his "ecosystem," he says, a woman is equivalent to a good bouillabaisse, a classical music recording is comparable to a murder, and an evening out with a friend can extend naturally and without interruption into a night of dismemberment.

Richard Chase goes further. In practice, communication (between his parents, for example) totally eliminates the possibility of human identity, because nothing else exists but things and relations ("matter and information," as thermodynamic scholars would say). Similarly, Dahmer shows us that, far from being a factor of unity, the universal interconnection of solitary units is what makes him wonder where living beings hide their existence, thus fueling his urge to cut bodies into ever smaller pieces and to dissolve and pulverize them before symbolically "sending" them back to the world. Mechanization as a factor for increasing human strength is categorically refuted by the cases of Joubert, DeSalvo, and many others. In these instances, repetition and serial acts reveal nothing more than the powerlessness of a defective machine that constantly repeats the same function, until it breaks down.

Is automation an enrichment, a source of plenty and of multiple goods, a cultural enlightenment? Bundy and Gacy do not believe this for a second. Their harrowing "work" is utterly desolate and empty. The practiced, almost perfect death blows they deliver are an age-old reflex inherited from their prehistoric ancestors.

Moreover, as Bundy suggests through his very inability to express himself, communication simply does not exist. In a world reduced to equivalence, likeness, mass duplication, and a succession of purely sensory experiences, there is nothing left to say.

Monsters: Gatekeepers of the City?

It is possible to listen further. Serial killers do not just tell us that a communications-based society does not work. They also provide two other lessons:

1. They show us the weak points in the theory and the areas in which it is lacking.
2. They indicate a way to avoid the collective psychosis implicit in the generalized belief that government-run society can be replaced with a "natural" automation.

On the first point, the following observations have been made by all sources that discuss recurrent crime in the United States:

1. A multitude of encounters (Lucas, Toole) provides an escape from solitude, but, when these encounters are real and not symbolic, they result in a multitude . . . of dismembered body parts (Lucas, Dahmer).
2. Encounters should be disinterested and constitute a form of communication, but too often they are predatory (for blood, as in the case of Crutchley, for organs as in the case of Chase, or for individuals, as with Hansen), or entail domination, infliction and sustaining of injury, or an uncontrollable hatred of others, women or homosexual partners (Gacy, etc.).
3. Life in its concrete form is so fragile that it seems unable to endure pleasure, and yet pleasure is what makes life worthwhile. Moreover, at the first sign of aggression (cutting, striking, devouring, restraining, etc.), life becomes the object of an impossible act of consumption (Berdella); but, worst of all, it is impossible to preserve life in its ephemeral transition to death (Schaefer).
4. As the act is repeated in the quest to reach a receding horizon of happiness (DeSalvo, Joubert, Marquette), it reveals the absurdity of the will to control (Kemper), for, in effect, it constitutes an accelerating race toward doom (Bundy, Chase, Dahmer, and most other serial killers), even in cases where it corresponds to an ascent up the social ladder (Starkweather).
5. There must be subjects for these acts, but it is not known where they hide (Mullin, Chase, Bundy); they are elusive.

Using these fragments of logic, for lack of anything better, serial killers underscore the fact that their acts differ from the insignificant activity of everyday postmodern existence, which they nevertheless designate as their reverse side. The criminally insane and their commentators – who create their *mise-en-scène* – try to explain that the violence which guides (or fascinates) them cannot be reduced to a pure repetition of the same thing. It is reflective, not of a series, but of an attempt to place oneself in a family relationship, as one who holds a recognized symbolic position, something which in postmodern society has become increasingly difficult.

This unspoken desire may therefore suggest a less pessimistic outcome to the mad-warrior epic: that the inexorable progression from the human to the inhuman (which the mad warrior illustrates in the same way as horror fiction) could be interpreted in the opposite direction, from the inhuman toward the human.

Thus reclassified and reversed, our collection of mad warriors could indeed adopt a progression leading back from the wilderness toward civilization, somewhat like that of the ancient warrior Ulysses, when, still daubed with blood from the massacres in the *Iliad*, he makes his return, in stages, one island after another, toward the world of civic peace. Can the deep meaning of the *Odyssey*, which Vidal-Naquet explores in *Chasseur noir*[4] (but which seems to have escaped Robert Bly, the high priest of American New Age "masculinism," despite his numerous ventures into mythology), be anything other than the revelation through myth and poetry of a much more ancient purification ritual, which is part of the warrior's return to civilization?

In societies that still have a close relationship with the hunt, there is a countless number of lengthy rituals to purify hunter-fighters while they are still blood-spattered and inebriated by the kill, before they can even set foot in their own – human – world. The *Odyssey* spreads out and glorifies each step in this repatriation, steps that are acts of cleansing and gradual release from destructive fantasy.

Ulysses, who is still a terrifying warrior at the beginning of his journey, leaves behind a world of drugs (the land of the lotus-eaters), a world of cannibals, a world where magic tricks are used to capture and kill (by Circe), a world where the dead are made to rise by spilling blood (the land of eternal darkness), and even a world of simple political idealism (Phaeacia) before coming back to the real city of "bread-eaters," where order is maintained in his absence by the wise and faithful Penelope.

If we group heinous criminals together by "type," we find an arrangement that resembles the succession of islands, with their more or less inhuman inhabitants, in the *Odyssey*. With Toole and Lucas, we have an example of drug-taking killers, who are like two demonic lotus-eaters. With Chase and other dismemberers, we visit an island where people eat living flesh. The sirens, who automatically kill those who are seduced by their singing, resemble "killing machines," while killers who lure victims into their lair are highly reminiscent of Scylla. The Cyclops, who imprisons Ulysses's unfortunate comrades and then devours them, is comparable to the sadistic killers who lock up and prepare their prey for death. The last port that separates Ulysses from reality is the ambiguous land of the Phaeacians, which is too idealistic to be true and yet too human to be completely monstrous. It reminds us of the political debate surrounding the criminal himself, who lacks the tiny measure of courage he needs to shed his self-definition as a "great warrior" and acknowledge that he should be punished.

In other words, the Nordic myth of the mad warrior, which, as we have discussed, contributed to a large extent to forming the base of crime culture in America, is never very far removed from similar myths in the classical culture. Only a tiny detail makes it different: the absence of a reflex reaction that could reverse the path toward disaster and lead back toward humanity.

But why should the bloodthirsty adult children who are the dark face of the wholesome American dream have to live the myth backwards when they could go on their own odyssey through an imagined series of islands, where they would leave behind the shreds of their "inhumanity"? On the time–space island, they would shed their compulsion for mechanical repetition. On the nightmare island, they would learn to distinguish reality from fantasy (like Kemper, when he was in prison, who bitterly remarked that "reality is never as perfect as dreams"). On the island of witches and demons, they would remember how to relate the most atrocious acts to a bad intention or an act of personal will. On the island of temptation and phobia, they would tear themselves away from their fascination with excessive urges and hubris. Once this last bubble of mystical illusion was dissolved, they could return to the world of the "bread-eaters," of people who respect nature and live as united citizens.

Of course, society as a whole would have to agree to define its monsters not merely as the symptoms of something else, and it would also have to develop a mythological tradition in which a reversal of the hoped-for catastrophe and an acceptance of the shortcomings of civilization were possible.

We have seen that, in postmodern society, these conditions are far from being fulfilled. The reflex has not yet set in.

Conclusion

Why Compare Serial Killers, TV-Movie Heroes, and Odinic Warriors?

Have I sufficiently justified an apparently incongruous comparison of the Nordic past with the American present with regard to their treatment of violence?

I have argued that, in its quest for an automatically functioning civilization, American postmodern society has revived an ancient myth that was already almost completely structured as such in the "free" Nordic European societies, which resisted the Roman Empire and the state-controlled societies that came after them.

Fifteen centuries since the Vikings reached the height of their power, in the Nordic world (in the broad sense) the celebration of Halloween continues to preserve an imagery of irreducible social deviance. The offerings distributed to the ghouls embodied by trick-or-treating children symbolize civilizing energy, transformed by virtue of the law into a gesture of salvation toward the untamed forces of the wilderness. This syncretic rite, which is not common in the Latin countries, despite the cultural influences that have been carried over with the expansion of American trade, combines ancient Druid and Odinic themes from the entire northern European region. It is in fact the most highly concentrated example of what the rest of the world currently refers to as "American culture," since most of the cultural industry related to it is devoted very precisely to reproducing through the media and literature the symmetrical relationship between society and its monsters.

In exposing this homology between ancient myth and modern society, I of course do not wish to deny the evolution of history, but rather to contribute to refining our conception of it. Although I absolutely do not believe in symbolic archetypes, I do think that the solidity of certain myths, conceived in very different circumstances, can be almost blindly affirmed, in other places and periods, provided that certain resources are available for them to be reused or even elaborated on.

And, indeed, at least three similarities have been mentioned thus far between the "cultural ecology" of the medieval Nordic world and that of North America, which is still being conquered:

1. The competition between a centralized government order (Rome for the Germanic peoples, Europe for the Americans) and more autonomous, combative, and nomadic forms, which are nevertheless able to surmount the disorder of personal vendettas and corporative struggles with the type of highly legalized system characteristic both of early democratic confederations and forms of postmodern individualism.
2. The sparseness, relatively "natural" environment, and vastness characteristic of areas of human habitation: from the fifth to the fourteenth century, the demographic differential between "Latinized" Europe and the Nordic regions was maintained, as the Nordic regions were utter human deserts, hardly different from what one observes outside the large metropolitan zones in the United States and Canada today.
3. Finally, and most importantly, the existence in North America of a confluence of Nordic populations (Anglo-Saxons, Germans, Irish, Scandinavians), which are united by the strong kinship between their cultural traditions, the similarity of themes they share from "late Christianity" or the close relationship between Catholicism and the Protestant denominations, etc.

The Reasons for Cross-cultural Comparison

What interest, other than aesthetic, can be derived from observing the homology between such diverse historical periods?

The answer is that history is not merely a succession of entirely unpredictable stages and breaks. For one thing, what is referred to as our sense of history is in fact our ability to discover anthropological structures that require a large amount of time and a great variety of geographic locations to emerge in an unadulterated form. Lévi-Strauss describes such structures as becoming visible on a plane parallel to the great diversity of myths in various "primitive" societies. I believe that they display a similar pattern over time.

In other words, medieval Nordic society's culture–nature myth, which is characterized by an oscillation between discipline and energy, mechanical flow and savagery, "put itself on hold," storing up its potential over time until it could release it into the more receptive environment of American culture. The science and technology of automation have provided the "werewolf myth" with the conditions for fulfillment on a global scale. They have lent reality to the Hobbesian imagery of the Leviathan and of artificial, automated life forms, whose symmetrical counterpart consists of everything that is left untamed and uncaptured by the political machine: the savage, the human animal, the monstrous criminal. In this sense, Hobbes helped to contemporize the ancestral Nordic myth, for, in the time of Galileo and Descartes, he recognized his mechanizing metaphor's potential for modernizing the old Anglo-Saxon legend of civilization as a self-regulating form of barbarianism.

The lesson I have drawn from the extraordinary evolution of the ancient mad-warrior myth in postmodern society is not that history repeats itself but rather that it accumulates and anticipates the times and places that are conducive to realizing its raw potential.

Why? How? Perhaps the myth of Odin was an early portent rejecting the idea that all peoples will evolve to Greco-Roman-type civilizations. For it remained stubbornly fixed in a stage which the distinguished Hellenist Pierre Vidal-Naquet has termed the "black-knight" theme in Mediterranean mythology (an eternally adolescent warrior, who never reaches adulthood or the rank of soldier, hoplite, or *populus*). Hence, the argument used by "beserkers" to justify their freedom to remain barbarians, in a state of eternal youth, is an idea that becomes reinforced when attached to modern sovereign power, which the fathers of rational thought multiplied tenfold.

But, not least paradoxically, what flows from this ancient myth when it attains nationwide proportions in the United States is not only the kind of solution it offers to the nature/culture or barbarian/civilization relationship, but also the type of failure and despair that are inherent to it.

This extreme individualism has quickly moved into the political realm, where it has been able to spread with no fear of creating a civil war. Adorned with the virtues of a "freedom fighter," mad warriors can lay their plans. They hide their insanity behind socially acceptable neuroses, using religion and moral values as a cover-up.

Through the combination of his various militant beliefs, the angry white man is constituted piece by piece, and all his components fall into place: he is against the government, against taxes, against affirmative action, against immigrants, pro-NRA, pro-life and he belongs to a fundamentalist Protestant church or a sect. The creation in 1989 of the Christian Coalition, on the initiative of the famous televangelist Pat Robertson – and which now boasts a membership of more than one and a half million – is an indicator of the tendency to gather previously diverse themes under one banner of fundamentalist wrath, which then becomes drawn to join the general struggle in the name of good.

During his questioning following the Oklahoma City attack, with which former members of the militia movement in Michigan have been charged, Norman Olson, a gun salesman and Baptist preacher, who leads the Northern Michigan Regional Militia, stated that "warfare and armed rebellion" were inevitable "unless the spirit of the country [changed]."[1] Although it is fiercely denied, the relationship between the rise of mass criminal activity and the trend toward a second American Revolution is present in the psychological profiles of the real perpetrators of recent attacks. When Timothy McVeigh, who has been convicted of the Oklahoma City bombing, wrote in 1992, "Do we have to shed blood to reform the current system? [. . .] I hope it doesn't come to that, but it might,"[2] he foretold the inevitable catastrophe with typical paranoid certitude. But he also fits the description of the collective search to bring about a "final" confrontation through a major event, which characterizes the increasingly aggressive culture of these militias, thereby heightening their resemblance to eschatological sects as they prepare for a doomsday and occasionally even create one by setting off an incident the effects of which they hope will be devastating.

Mass murderers who later become political terrorists seem to long for such a fatal series of events to occur: they believe they can provoke certain reactions in society and thus send it into a frenzy of repressive action. And, indeed, society's reactions often fulfill their desire: witness the immediate commitment of thousands of police, investigators, judges, and legal experts to the fight against terrorism after the Oklahoma City bombing, and the lifting, requested by the federal government, of rules prohibiting electronic surveillance or preventive arrests. This appears to be a dangerous spiral, especially when one considers the growing number of death sentences, the "three-strikes" program, and other disturbing facts (such as the removal of 1,000 convicts from the Phoenix penitentiary, who were sent to live in a penal colony in the desert).

Perhaps we have entered a period in which individual violence and its collective counterpart are in open confrontation.

Today, the myth's central contradiction is being spread through global communications. By maintaining the wild-man image as a necessary motivation for self-repression, not only are we buying into the cult of an obsessive oscillation between two principles, but we are encouraging mutual destruction between gods and demons. The fundamental pessimism in the *ragnarök* theme (*The Twilight of the Gods* in the Germanic version, the "clash of powers" in the Icelandic version) is spreading throughout the world at the same pace as legends of the precarious balance between the warrior and the law or the werewolf and the village.

We must be especially careful not to make the error of thinking that only the German variant, derived from Gothic romanticism and distorted by the Nazi movement, contains the suggestion of an apocalyptic extinction of society, which the Germanic tradition in the broad sense regards as the "energetic process run amok." There is also a vast profusion of horror culture, which children today absorb under the indulgent gaze of even the most intellectual parents. As we have seen, this culture, like its spiritual leader Stephen King, sends out a constant message that some things are "destined for evil."

The fascination with the catastrophic saga of serial killers revolves around the same model. From the country that gave the world production-line automobiles, nuclear warheads, and multinational business, as well as more recent contributions, such as the multiple personality and the cloning of human embryos, this devotion to the underlying structure of a myth that produces symmetry, doubles, multiples, oscillations, and finally an irremediable conflict between different versions of the self, should give us pause.

If civilized behavior consists in suppressing an excessive belief in any form of mythology (which is supposed to be the job of clerics and intellectuals), we should first recognize that the conquering theme in the "berserker" myth has already materialized in history. Moreover, we have good reason to suspect that, in a postmodern development of this theme, its intrinsic pessimism would be inescapable, because it organizes the collective unconscious in such a way that desires are formed around the ideal of a conflict between symmetrical principles.

When we describe Disneyland cartoons as harmless fluff, we should not forget Hobbes's model of an automated commonwealth. For, of course, close behind them lurks their exact antagonist: the shadow of the big bad wolf, the real, totally wild one, in the form of a feral criminal on the loose, like *Fenrir* ("roamer of the plains") of the Icelandic saga, who swallowed the city of the gods and Odin with it. Roughly translated in modern terms, this could be taken to mean: the private sector will eventually destroy the public sector and private interests will demolish all forms of solidarity before finally destroying each other.

On the other hand, if we ourselves are attracted by this pessimism, then the young generation, which is so quick to translate our unconscious desires and act on them in extreme ways, has no reason not to follow our example.

In any case, let us not pretend that this "cultural invasion" has been propelled solely by the mechanical stuff of play or dreams, or by the fast-food restaurants and video stores that are so popular with teenagers. The only way these things were able to sprout up in the first place was because, in a democracy, the basic message of the culture that created them tended to attract adults and privileged groups first. Let's face it: we, too, have been taken in by the mirage of the nature–culture symmetry. We, too, have savored the ancient myths of barbarian heroism, recycled in the Darwinian struggle for survival in the market. We believed that they could revive the energy that has been trapped inside us in an "iron cage" of instrumental rationality. If we ourselves had not been captivated by this ideal, we would never have allowed our children to develop such a fascination for Stephen King, role-playing games, and murder stories, nor would we have pretended that we hadn't noticed it, or refused to admit it when we did.

What to Say to a Werewolf during Metamorphosis

If the hypothesis is correct that Anglo-American culture is polarized by the myth of the Odinic warrior, it would be ridiculous to try to prevent the media and other cultural agents from drawing on the oracular prophesies of American serial criminals. On the contrary, we must maintain a dialogue with any agent that sends out a repeated message of hope for a natural end, and hence of metamorphosis from human to animal, from animal to killing machine, and from massacre to end of the world.

This opens a debate that no one can refuse to join. I have tried here to decipher a barely hidden message, whose purpose is to make us react. For, indeed, we must react to the poignant juxtaposition of a Disney park beside the gates of historic Paris and at the feet of the venerable Sorbonne; not to laugh, criticize, or judge (even though few tears will be shed if the park is shut down), but simply to take part in a global intellectual dialogue.

In fact, reacting is the least courtesy one should pay to a cultural under-taking of this magnitude. Reacting to the development of internationalized Anglo-American culture (as opposed to simply stuffing oneself with it, defying it, or ridiculing it) can also help those who are partial to the culture to release their feelings of ambivalence (and often of fascination) and consider the possible consequences of an unconditional adoption of this type of ideal.

But how should one react? and on what grounds? What nation, state, culture, or continent can claim to be the sole embodiment of the ancient process of civilization that resisted barbaric heroics and their robotic double? Moreover, it is clear that the perversions or terrors in the werewolf culture do not justify the illusions, injustices, and inadequacies of the paternalistic state. As liberal Nordic culture correctly reminds us, through its myths and popular liberal philosophy, sovereign transcendence to power is never anything more than the long-term investiture of a warrior who has eliminated his opponents. The criminals of yesterday become the leaders of today and the potentates of tomorrow. Sovereign leaders may, over the generations, be increasingly restrained by the political machine from exercising real power, but power is not bound as a result to lose its violent, aggressive, and coercive nature. Rambo's repulsion for government regimes is not totally foolish. Assertions that the mad warrior (or black knight) will necessarily evolve into a citizen should therefore not be inter-preted as the formula for a clear conscience in a Franco-Greco-Roman model (of the type propounded by Charles Maurras[3]), which has never existed outside the realm of ideals and utopias, and which, moreover, is highly developed in North America, whose bureaucracy rivals that in Europe. Where should we seek the answer to this inexorable myth, for which serial killers are the emblem? In concluding, I will mention two possible paths, which relate on the one hand to the contents of the societal myth and on the other to behavior and styles of civilization.

Can the Werewolf Escape Damnation?

First, let us consider the contents of the myth: how is dialogue possible with a culture that believes only in the pleasures and frustrations of the criminal hero, who is perceived as a god, a demon, or a killer robot, rather than as a person who has "chosen" crime? Perhaps we should adopt a philosophy of "freedom in nature" to counter the ideological Darwinian dogma that evolution is purely determinational and hence that history is driven forward by the strongest individual and collective impulses. A number of conclusions may be drawn from science's recent observations on incalculability, nondetermination, and the multiplicity of possible out-comes. When applied to humans, these observations indicate that freedom is not only the mandatory choice between two imperatives or two natures (individual and social) but, indeed, a multiplicity of possible destinies, which totally resist the serialization of market forces or the political machine.

With regard to the theory of social control, which underlies all the trends in naturalist sociology that have been inspired by the werewolf myth, it can therefore be posited that, if a personality is both nondomesticated and fully civilized, it is no longer certain that this subject has an absolute predestination (whether biological or other). A philosophy (as yet little developed) of nondetermination as a source of freedom may help us to overcome the dilemma that confounded Cartesian or Hobbesian theory, i.e., how is it possible for man to be a political animal and an autonomous subject at the same time?

Acknowledging freedom not as the power to act on one's impulses but as a means of preserving multiple possibilities is tantamount to accepting plurality in a nonstandardized world (which is the only viable world order). We are not satisfied with the pairing of a political constitution and a self-regulating economy as the sole alternative to the ordeal of unsettled segregated ethnic groups; for there is a great risk that the diabolical couple formed by the system and its marginal groups, which is already wreaking havoc in urban areas, will reach global proportions.

One may not have to look far to find a key that can open Anglo-American culture to other myths that are not doomed to an obsessive oscillation between uncontrolled savagery and political correctness, compulsive aggressiveness and hysterical expostulating, private life and the public forum, personal freedom and "economic" needs. Like all evolving cultures, this one has within it the potential to move beyond fossilized clichés. Whether or not it uses these resources to strike a civilizing compromise, whereby nature and culture are reconciled, is another matter.

Both the culture of fantastic literature and the commentary on murder suggest ways of healing the werewolf. Thus, the world of violence occasionally allows for interpretations that portray it not as a strictly defined class of dangerous persons, but as a succession of mirage-like images of power, which, when they are abandoned, lead back in reverse succession to the human element. Like Ulysses on his return from the atrocities of war, we too can find the road home by leaving these islands of magic and death behind us, one after the other.

Another Kind of Tale

To break the circle of relentless heroic destinies, return to a life of kinship, tradition, and acceptance, and revive poetry and nondetermination, we must learn from the ancient European and Asian societies, which took the time to master the relationship between violence and the collective by means of narrative talent, humor, and lightheartedness.

We should remember how the sultan in *The Arabian Nights* was distracted from continuing the series of executions he was exacting on his wives, like a serial killer. It was not so much the ruse of interlocking tales that quelled his thirst for murder but the living presence of another subject (Scheherazade), whose storytelling kept him awake with its awesome ability constantly to produce the unexpected.

For us, the choice should not be between cynically ignoring the images that our children ingurgitate – the automated violence of cybernetic games and illusions created on videotape – and pretending suddenly to discover, amid distressed cries for censorship, how they have been entertaining themselves. Instead, we should simply compensate this serial effect with the effect of a constant physical presence, by patiently weaving a new narrative world for them.

What stories should we tell?

It may be best not to decide in advance, but rather to give freedom a chance to find its own way in this maze of inexorability.

Notes

Introduction

1. In recent years, namely since the collapse of an alternative ideal to postmodern liberalism (1989), crime rates have exploded in Western Europe: crime has doubled in Germany (5.2 per 100,000 in 1993), and it has risen even further in the Netherlands. It has also increased in France (2 points more than in 1990) and the United Kingdom (4.2). The lowest level is to be found in Ireland: 0.66 in 1993.
2. This information is according to the Uniform Crime Reporting Program (UCRP) established among large American institutions to synthesize available data.
3. The second amendment of the United States Constitution provides that: "A well regulated Militia, being necessary to the security of a free State, the right of the people to keep and bear Arms, shall not be infringed." The sale of combat weapons is therefore not contradictory to the Constitution, if the purpose is to train soldiers. There seems to have been no forethought of the fact that they could become insane. Let us wish President Clinton, who seems determined to take on the NRA and control the purchase of arms (reflected in his support of the Brady Bill, which requires a five-day waiting period prior to the sale of firearms to private individuals), good luck.
4. The Violent Crime Apprehension Program (VICAP) was set up by the FBI to track felons and apprehend criminals who commit multiple crimes.
5. Elliott Leyton, *Hunting Humans. The Rise of the Modern Multiple Murderer*, Penguin Books, New York, 1986, p. 12.
6. Reported by historian Pierre Darmon in "Le criminel-né existe-t-il?," *L'Histoire*, 168, July 1993, and "L'abominable chromosome Y," *L'Histoire*, 115, 1988, p. 50.
7. Robert K. Ressler, a famous member of the FBI's crime investigation bureau and creator of VICAP; author (with Tom Schachtman) of *Whoever Fights Monsters*, Pocket Books, 1992.
8. Ibid., p. 64.
9. Jonathan Demme, *The Silence of the Lambs*, 1990, based on the novel by Tom Harris (Yazoo, New York, 1988), sequel to *Red Dragon* (see n.10).

10. Tom Harris, *Red Dragon*, Dell Books (a division of Bantam Doubleday Dell Publishing Group, Inc.), New York, 1990, p. 92.

11. Ariane Chemin, "L'âge des fictions réelles," an article on the latest incarnation of "live television," *Le Monde de la radio et de la télévision*, 20–24 May 1993, pp. 16–17.

12. The battle raging in the United States against violence on TV and movie screens shows that this type of "phobic" shift is beginning to occur. But, if the restriction of smoking in public places coincided with a massive explosion of drug use, just as the prohibition period was conducive to the emergence of the American Mafia, can we really expect the elimination of bloodshed from made-for-TV movies to lower mail-order sales of P.38s? I am not so sure.

13. *Falling Down*, a Joel Schumacher film, 1993.

14. Stephen King, writing as Richard Bachman, *Roadwork*, New American Library, New York, 1981.

15. Stephen King, *Insomnia*, Viking-Penguin, New York, 1994.

16. This also holds true for Latin America, where, as in North America, the New World is characterized by overt social unrest, reflected in the existence of gangs and paramilitary groups, armed militias, etc. The theory of homeostatic equilibrium between violence and social control appears, however, to be specific to the northern culture.

17. There is something comical, or perhaps depressing, in the contest that is being waged in the horror-film industry between synthetic-monster manufacturers and mechanical special-effects operators as they try to outdo each other. But the fact that Anglo-American cinema has become a supermarket for horror gimmicks should not hide its chilling sources of inspiration: these are not the products of sophisticated special effects obtained through state-of-the-art image-synthesis technology (*Jurassic Park, Terminator 2*, etc.), robotics, or tomato juice (gore is on the decline), but, rather, dark and terrifying films such as *Clockwork Orange, Henry: Portrait of a Serial Killer*, and others that are not well known to the general public but which have been the basis for entire traditions.

18. J.R.R. Tolkien, *The Lord of the Rings*, vols. 1–3 Pocket, New York, 1991.

19. Paul Verhoeven, *Basic Instinct*, starring Michael Douglas and Sharon Stone, 1991.

20. Among comic books alone, a culture that is too often overlooked by researchers who study horror culture, there are several dozen titles that center on were-wolves, such as the *Wolverine* series (72 issues) or *Warwolf*, published by Marvel Comics. Encounters between other superheroes and werewolf characters are countless.

21. Songs by the Swedish group Ultima Thule contain exhortations to waken one's "Viking blood," with explicit references to Odinic themes as a justification for xenophobic rage. Such conspicuous displays should not hide the multitude of

"soft" or underhand forms of idealized violence that have invaded Western culture, in Europe as in the United States.

22. Roger Caillois conceived a system in which the genre of fantastic literature is organized according to varying levels of anthropomorphism (*Anthologie du fantastique*, vol. 1, *Angleterre, Irlande, Amérique du Nord, Allemagne, Flandres*, Gallimard, Paris, 1966).

23. Ibid.

24. Daniel Pennac, author of *La Fée Carabine* (Gallimard, Paris, 1992) and *La Petite Marchande de prose* (Gallimard, Paris, 1992), enjoys tremendous popularity in France.

25. *Fiorile* (*Floréal*, the eighth month of the French Republican calendar (April–May)), a Franco-Italian film by Paolo and Vittorio Taviani, 1993.

26. And where "warrior women" would truly castrate male warriors, who are described as rapists, as in contemporary news-making stories like the Lorena Bobbitt trial.

Part I

1. I should point out that this idea was applied to the subject of fiction writing in 1990 by French authors J. Baudou and S.S. Chéret in *Meurtres en série: les séries policières de la Télévision française* (Editions 8e Art, Paris, 1990).

Chapter 1

1. The strong relationship between the ultraviolent writing that goes unchallenged in works of horror fiction and a form of romanticism that displays neofascist tendencies can be seen indirectly. For example, *Ciné Fantastique-Mad Movies* magazine, one of the few such publications in France that is attuned to the popular trends among its young readership, published an exclusive interview with Jean-Marie Le Pen, the leading extreme right-wing politician in France (vol. 64, 1990). Le Pen is careful not to make any positive statements about horror film, and in fact declared after the interview that he would not buy the magazine.

2. According to Régis Boyer, Odin embodies "the state of trance and quasi-demented fury that takes hold of magicians, lovers, warriors and poets in certain circumstances and doubles or further multiplies their potential, making them capable of performing feats that are beyond the reach of common mortals in popular imagery. They become 'howlers' (*Hroptayr*) whose magical power, with its strong ecstatic, shaman-like undertones [. . .], forces things to stray from

their natural course" (*Les Vikings*, Plon, Paris, 1992, p. 347). We should also note the proximity between the roots vad- and vid- (to see), which create a kinship among the words "clairvoyance", "voyage", etc.

3. According to Claude Lecouteux, "The genealogies of the royal families of Anglia, Kent and the western Saxons refer to him as the founding father of their lineage" (entry for "Woden," *Petit dictionnaire de mythologie allemande*, Editions Entente, Paris, 1991). For Jean Markale, Odin is comparable to Myrddin (Merlin) of Celtic legend, who shares many of Merlin's characteristics (madness, magical powers, living as a hermit in the forest, clairvoyance, etc.) but is less human. The root *myrd* could refer to the sea (*myrddin*: merman) or to death (*mord*). In any case, like Odin, Merlin acts as a shaman, seeking initiatic bliss through the transports of ecstasy (Jean Markale, *Merlin L'Enchanteur*, Retz, Paris, 1981).

4. Especially during the Viking age and in Denmark.

5. The notion of the "twice-born" is an ancient Indo-European idea. The Brahman tradition, for example, separates castes that have been ritually cleansed (and thus twice born; the Ksatryas, the Brahmans, and the Vaysias) from those that are born only once and are the prisoners of their own nature: the Sudras and the Dasyus (casteless servants). This theme has been taken up again in modern symbolist anthropology, by Moscovici, who speaks of "the two births of man," in reference to the transition from predatory behavior to hunting and then from hunting to the adoption of predomesticated animals (S. Moscovici, *La Société contre nature*, UGE, 10/18, Paris, 1972, chapter 4).

6. Leyton, *Hunting Humans*.

7. Stéphane Bourgoin, *Serial Killers*, Grasset, Paris, 1993, p. 235.

8. Of course, a "series" of blood drinkers does exist, and it includes John George Haigh (in the late 1950s) and Crutchley (discussed later).

9. Lucas was sentenced to twelve consecutive life sentences for known murders in three states in the US, but his execution in Texas put an end to this multitude of lives, which mirrored those he had taken.

10. To take a contrasting example, in France, a killer named Plancke, who shot a girl in her car, was found in a matter of weeks. He did not have the option (although he may have had the need) of vanishing somewhere in a sprawling continent. In the new Europe without borders, however, this may be possible.

11. In whom we find the prototype for the Joseph Ruben film *The Good Son* (1994), with the young Macaulay Culkin in the role of the "bad boy."

12. Pierre Legendre, *Le Crime du caporal Lortie, Traité sur le Père. Leçons VIII*, Fayard, Paris, 1989. On Lépine, see the study by Hélène Meynaud, "Polytechnique gelée, 1989," *Sociétés et Représentations*, 1998, 1.

13. Leyton, *Hunting Humans*.

14. Bertrand Hell, *Faits et dits de chasse dans la France de l'Est*, MSH, "Ethnologie de la France" collection, Paris, 1985, pp. 61–125.
15. Whence the expression "to run amok."

Chapter 2

1. *Les Chasses du comte Zaroff*: this story by Richard Connell ("the most dangerous game", 1930) was made famous in a film by E.B. Schoedsack and I. Pichel released in 1932.
2. Robert Graysmith, *Les Crimes du zodiaque*, j'ai lu, Paris, 1990 (*The Crimes of the Zodiac, The Case of the San Francisco Killer*, 1976).
3. Pierre Vidal-Naquet, *Le Chasseur noir. Formes de pensée et formes de société dans le monde grec*, La Découverte, "Textes à l'appui" collection, Paris, 1991.
4. Joe McGiniss, *Cruelle incertitude. L'affaire Von Stein*, J'ai lu, Paris, 1993.
5. See the discussion of these cases hereafter.
6. Chuck Miller, "Stephen King goes to the Movies," in *Kingdom of Fear, 17 Essays on the Master of Horror*, Tim Underwood and Chuck Miller eds., New American Library, New York, 1987.
7. Stephen King, *The Shining*, Doubleday & Co., New York, 1977.
8. Stephen King, *Misery*, Hodder and Stoughton, London, 1987.
9. Stephen King, *Different Seasons*, Futura, London, 1982.
10. Stephen King, "The Raft," *Skeleton Crew*, Futura, London, 1986.
11. Stephen King, *Mist, Dark Forces*, 1980.
12. Stephen King, *Different Seasons*.
13. Stephen King, "The Boogeyman," *Night Shift*, New English Library, New York, 1978.
14. Stephen King, writing as Robert Bachman, *Thinner*, New American Library, New York, 1984.
15. Stephen King, writing as Robert Bachman, *Rage*, New English Library, London, 1977.
16. Stephen King, *Dolores Clairborne*, Penguin Books, Bergenfield, NJ, 1993.
17. Stephen King, *The Dark Tower*, Penguin Books, Bergenfield, NJ, 1991.
18. Stephen King, writing as Robert Bachman, *The Long Walk*, Penguin Books, Bergenfield, NJ, 1979.
19. Stephen King, *Running Man*, New English Library, London, 1982.
20. King, *Different Seasons*.
21. King, *Night Shift*.
22. Ibid.
23. King, *Different Seasons*.
24. King, *Night Shift*.

25. Ibid.

26. Miller, "Stephen King."

27. Harris, *Red Dragon*, p. 19.

28. Stephen King, *Carrie*, Coronet Books, Falmouth, 1974.

29. King, "The Ledge," *Night Shift*, p. 193.

30. There is a long list of film interpretations of the expression "to go berserk," a commonplace in Anglo-American culture. To take one example, Clive Barker's 1989 movie *NightBreed*, based on his own sadistic, satanic novel *Cabal* (Pocket Books, New York, 1995), contains a sort of blind, imprisoned mummy that wounds and devours its victims.

31. T.B. Benford and J.P. Johnson, *Reality Show. L'affaire John E. List*, "Crimes et enquêtes" collection, J'ai lu, Paris, 1993.

32. John McNaughton, *Henry: Portrait of a Serial Killer*, 1990.

33. King, "Mrs. Todd's Shortcut," *Night Shift*.

Chapter 3

1. Dennis McDougall, *Angel of Darkness*, New American Library, New York, 1991.

2. Jacques Finné, *La Bibliographie de Dracula*, L'Age d'Homme, Lausanne, 1986, p. 33.

3. One of the Gilbert and Sullivan operettas.

4. Mathieu Lindon, "Le sadique aux oeufs d'or, le scandale qui divise l'Amérique," *Libération*, 14 March 1991, pp. 22–3.

5. Bret Easton Ellis, *American Psycho*, Simon & Schuster, New York, 1991.

6. In Barker's *Hellraiser* series, the victims are held prisoner in another world, which is dominated by master torturers.

7. A 1992 film by Quentin Tarentino.

8. Edgar Allan Poe, "The Pit and the Pendulum" (*The Complete Works of Edgar Allan Poe*, J. Harrison, New York, 1965).

9. Michael McDowell, "The Unexpected and the Inevitable," in *Kingdom of Fear*.

10. Roger Zelazny and Thomas T. Thomas, *The Mask of Loki*, Baen Books, New York, 1990.

11. King, *Night Shift*.

12. See Schaefer's memoirs, *Diary of a Killer*, New American Library, New York.

13. Colin Turnbull, *Les Iks, survivre par la cruauté, Nord-Ouganda*, Stock, Paris, 1973.

14. A 1983 film by Ted Kotcheff, starring Sylvester Stallone.

15. James G. Frazer, *Adonis, Attis, Osiris*, London, 1907, and *The Golden Bough*, London, 1911–1915.

16. An interesting case of literary and criminal double identity is that of the Austrian Jack Unterweger, who killed eleven prostitutes, including one in Los

Angeles, and later became the darling of Viennese high society after publishing his prison novels (*Purgatory, The Writer in Prison*, etc.).

17. This recalls Orson Wells's superb film *A Touch of Evil*, which dealt with the same ambiguous relationship almost forty years ago.

Chapter 4

1. Kemper, quoted in Donald West, *Sacrifice unto Me*, Pyramid Books, New York, 1974, p. 199.

2. Harris, *The Silence of the Lambs*.

3. Harris, *Red Dragon*. As soon as the subject of cooking comes up, people's minds turn to France. Hence, for example, French writer Stéphane Bourgoin, obviously playing upon this stereotype, asked Toole whether he planned to publish the recipes for his cannibalistic feasts ("I hear you are going to write a cannibal cookbook, Ottis," *Serial Killers*, p. 235). Another famous case is that of Issei Sagawa, a young and very wealthy Japanese who came to Paris, where he killed and ate a Dutch girl. As far as we know, neither Landru nor Petiot, the two most notorious French killers, ever served up their victims with sautéed onions. In fact, cannibalistic habits, which are a far cry from gastronomic pleasure, seem more like a form of repression of the "fine art of cooking." But this remains to be proved. A brief word on the Japanese and Dutch cultures and cooking: some readers may be familiar with an amusing nineteenth-century Japanese tale that involves an "angel" descended from heaven (the daughter of a Dutch captain), who obliges a gallant young man named "White Dragon" to take her place in the kitchen for a month. This tale is very well known in Japan and may have acted like a time bomb in the confused mind of Sagawa, whose crime would appear to be an unconscious cultural retribution, incited more by paranoia than perversion.

4. Michael Tuchner, *Adam*, an American made-for-TV movie in 1983.

5. Bourgoin, *Serial Killers*.

6. His name is almost an anagram for "Cannibal Hitler."

7. *The Silence of the Lambs* (the book and the film).

8. Ibid.

9. "The zodiac killer" was the pseudonym of a murderer who struck in San Francisco in the 1970s. Suspected of dozens of crimes, he has never been positively identified.

10. Everything is relative: in *La Mascarade des sexes, Fétichisme, inversion et travestissement rituels* (Calmann-Lévy, Paris, 1980), Stéphane Breton shows that, in many societies, mythology is founded on a classification of similarities and differences between the sexes.

11. Hesiod, *Orphic Hymns*, 45, 3.
12. Particularly since an outbreak of mad-cow disease most certainly played a part in the sudden distaste for meat in British society.
13. *Alive*, a 1992 film by Frank Marshall.
14. Sherill Mulhern, "A la recherche du trauma perdu," *Chimères*, winter 1992.
15. Bourgoin, *Serial Killers*, p. 236.
16. Ibid.
17. Ibid.
18. *A Clockwork Orange*, a 1972 British film directed by Stanley Kubrick after the novel by Anthony Burgess (Pocket Books, New York, 1994), is the story of a criminal's psychological deconditioning from violent behavior, through stimulation of his reflexes of repulsion. The film shares the theme of Aldous Huxley's *Brave New World* (London, 1932), in which people are conditioned to love or hate certain activities through a form of training in which rewards are alternated with physical punishment.

Part II

Chapter 5

1. Bourgoin, *Serial Killers*.
2. Peter Straub, *Koko*, Penguin Books, New York, 1988.
3. To use Richard Sennett's terms, the "hidden injuries of class."
4. Charles Starkweather, "Rebellion," *Parade*, 4, 1959, pp. 10–14.
5. One cannot, however, deny the decisive importance of the sociological causes of violence, which are especially portentous in the United States.
6. As we shall see in the Richard Trenton Chase case.
7. Bourgoin, *Serial Killers*, pp. 164–5.
8. The director of *The Adams Family Values* (discussed later) uses the same idea to imagine how the Adams family children amuse themselves.
9. Bourgoin, *Serial Killers*, p. 163.
10. *Kämpe* means "champion" or "valiant knight" in German.
11. Bourgoin, *Serial Killers*, p. 168.
12. Leyton, *Hunting Humans*, p. 48.
13. A study of the famous nineteenth-century case of this young Frenchman, who killed his mother, was conducted under the direction of Michel Foucault. *Moi, Pierre Rivière, ayant éorgé ma mère, ma soeur, et mon frère. Un cas de parricide au XIX siècle présenté par Michel Foucault*, "Archives" collection, Gallimard/Julliard, Paris, 1975.

14. According to Leyton, *Hunting Humans*, a greater percentage of multiple killers have mothers who were married three or more times.
15. Leyton, *Hunting Humans*.
16. Ibid.
17. Margaret Cheney, *The Co-Ed Killer*, Walker, New York, 1976, p. 147.
18. Ibid., p. 143.
19. "I wanted those girls for myself, as possessions, [. . .] it was the only way for them to be mine," ibid., p. 108.
20. Donald West, *Sacrifice unto Me*, p. 196.
21. A 1982 film by George Roy Hill based on the novel by John Irving (*Le Monde selon Garp*, Le Seuil, Paris, 1980).
22. American film produced in 1989 and based on the novel by Barry Gifford.
23. We should not assume an air of horror with regard to modern times, when the most abundant source of murders of women is in fact the long line of matricides and infanticides that took place in antiquity: Agamemnon sacrificed his daughter, while Orestes executed his mother, Clytemnestra, and then plotted to kill Helen. There are also male warriors who killed or molested women, like Achilles, who attempted to rape Hemithea and slew Penthesilea, or Jason, who "fleeced" his wife Medea. In addition, there are tales of attacks on more or less demonized female figures: Perseus stealing the eye of the three hags and then decapitating the gorgon Medusa, who was raped as a maiden by Poseidon in the temple of Athena; Theseus killing the Crommyonian sow (the progeny of a tempest and a spider), wishing death on Hecate, and then killing the Amazons Molpadia and Antiope; Heracles slaying Hippolyte; the Hyacinthides being sacrificed to Athena; Cambles devouring his own wife, and so on. (See Nicole Loraux, *Façons tragiques de tuer une femme*, Hachette, Paris, 1985.)
24. Georges Zink, *Le Wunderer*, Aubier-Montaigne, Paris, 1949. Claude Lecouteux, *Fantômes et revenants au Moyen Age*, Imago, Paris, 1986; "Mara, Ephialtes, Incubus, le cauchemar chez les peuples germaniques," *Etudes germaniques*, 42, 1987, pp. 1–24.
25. *A Boy and his Dog*, 1975. Alvy Moore and L.Q. Jones also co-directed *The Witchmaker* (1969), which tells the story of a mad warrior (Luther the Berserk) who supplies a witch with fresh blood, and *The Brotherhood of Satan* (1971) about the leader of a satanic cult in California.
26. Bruce Gibney, *The Beauty Queen Killer*, 1984.
27. In *Mythologies*, Lévi-Strauss explains that there are equivalents between different Amerindian myths: the Jaguar in Latin America and the Coyote in North America, for example, are both drawn to women's menstrual blood.
28. See hereafter.
29. German film released in 1978.

Chapter 6

1. Lecouteux, *Petit dictionnaire de mythologie allemande*, p. 15. Exhibiting the strewn-about organs of victims of hanging is a frequently used technique in American horror film. The latest case in point is *The Silence of the Lambs*, which displays crucified victims who appear to have been draped in their own severed flesh by the terrible Hannibal Lecter.

2. "With the organized killer, the victims are personalized; the offender has enough verbal and other exchange with the victims to recognize them as individuals prior to killing them" (Ressler with Schachtman, *Whoever Fights Monsters*, p. 183). Here, we see that this is also the case with certain "random" killers, which indicates that this category is insufficient, a sign that police logic is limited to apparent behavior patterns.

3. Ressler with Schachtman, *Whoever Fights Monsters*.

4. V. Bugliosi and C. Gentry, *Helter Skelter, The True Story of the Manson Murders*, Bantam Books, New York, 1974, p. 256.

5. Lawrence Klausner, *Son of Sam* (see n. 6); D. Abrahamsen, "Confessions of Son of Sam," *Penthouse*, 15, 1983, pp. 58–194.

6. David Berkowitz, "Prison Diary", in Lawrence D. Klausner, *Son of Sam*, McGraw-Hill, New York, 1981 (quoted in Leyton, *Hunting Humans*, p. 199).

7. Ibid., p. 200.

8. Ibid., p. 186.

9. Graysmith, *The Crimes of the Zodiac*.

10. "Criminal poetry" has been used by detective writers, such as James Ellroy, whose serial killer character in *Blood on the Moon* (Mysterious Press, New York, 1984) is a puritanical poet who dismembers women "out of love" and leaves impassioned poems at the scene of the crime.

11. Bugliosi and Gentry, *Helter Skelter*, pp. 607–8.

12. Ibid., p. 247.

13. Ibid., pp. 292–3.

14. Ibid. It should also be pointed out that, in 1973, a clandestine African-American group, called the Death Angels, almost fulfilled Manson's prophesy by killing several dozen white victims.

15. These go back to a tradition in ancient Iranian religion, which is itself of Indian inspiration, and in particular to the theme of a succession of cosmic ages, each characterized by destruction and rebirth. (See Mircea Eliade, *Le Mythe de l'éternel retour*, Gallimard, Paris, 1969.)

16. Alain Pozzuoli (ed.), *Dictionnaire du fantastique*, Granché, Paris, 1992 (entry for '1979').

17. Arthur Lyons, *Satan Wants You: The Cult of Devil Worship in America*, Mysterious Press, New York, 1989.

18. Migene Gonzales Wippler, *Rituals and Spells of Santeria*, Original Publications, New York, 1984; *The Santeria Experience*, Prentice Hall, Englewood Cliffs, 1982.

19. Gérald Messadié, *Histoire générale du Diable*, Robert Laffont, Paris, 1993.

20. See Nicole Loraux, "La 'belle mort' Spartiate," *Ktèma*, 2, 1977.

21. The most recent armies of undead raised in film (*Army of Darkness, Evil Dead III*, 1991) are entirely constituted of skeletons clad in Viking armor and cleverly animated by state-of-the-art high technology.

22. Joe Dante's *Gremlins* films are based on the theme of a type of bestiality that grows as quickly as it is fed, like a weed.

23. This theme recalls the *Le Maître* comic book series by Christin and Mézières, published in the Valérian et Laureline collection by Dargaud, Paris, 1978.

Part III

Chapter 7

1. Noted by James Baldwin in *The Evidence of Things Not Seen*, 1985.

2. Peter Elkind, *The True Story of Nurse Genene Jones and the Texas Baby Murders*, Pocket Books, New York, 1983.

3. E. Franklin and W. Wright, *Les Péchés du père* (*The Sins of the Father*), J'ai lu, Paris, 1992.

4. *L'Avenir dure longtemps* and *Les Faits*, autobiography of Louis Althusser, with an introduction by Olivier Corpet and Yann Moulier-Boutang, eds., Stock/ Imec, Paris, April 1992.

5. Stephen King, *Night Shift*, New English Library, New York, 1978, p. 15.

6. Ibid., pp. 15–16.

7. Hilde Bruch, "Mass Murder, the Wagner Case," in *Violence, Causes and Solutions*, Renatus Hartogs and Eric Artzt, eds, Laurel Editions, New York, 1970.

8. Ibid., p. 266.

9. The documents consulted concerning this case are from Ressler with Schachtman, *Whoever Fights Monsters*, and Ray Biondi and Walt Hecox, *The Dracula Killer*, 1992.

10. Term also used by biographers Biondi and Hecox, ibid.

11. The metaphor of the extraterrestrial as a "material" representation of solitude is a popular one: "We are all extraterrestrials," said Abel Ferrara in an interview with Michel Field, broadcast on *Cercle de minuit* on 17 May 1993. Ferrara made a film about grave robbers whose bodies had been taken over by eel-like creatures from outer space capable of assuming the shape and appearance of the people they had killed.

12. Ressler with Schachtman, *Whoever Fights Monsters*.

13. Sigmund Freud, *Totem and Taboo*, The Penguin Freud Library, London, 1990.
14. My fellow researchers at the Centre National de Recherche Scientifique (CNRS) should not be concerned, however, about their own psychological dispositions. In general, despite the fact that they lend just as much importance to concrete proof as murderers do, "scientific" researchers are able to tell the difference between a human being and a laboratory rat. That said, without commenting on the myth of the mad scientist, one of the classic variations on the Jekyll-and-Hyde theme, researchers like myself would be well advised to realize that our desire for knowledge has strange origins, and that it should be kept in check so that we do not come to regard human beings as mere experimental subjects.
15. Stephen King, *The Bachman Books, Four Early Novels by Stephen King*, with an introduction by the author "Why I was Bachman," *Rage* (1977), *The Long Walk* (1979), *Roadwork* (1981), and *Running Man* (1982), Plume Books, New York, 1985.
16. King, "The Boogeyman," *Nightshift*.
17. King, *Different Seasons*: "Hope Springs Eternal: Rita Hayworth and the Shawshank Redemption," "Summer of Corruption: Apt Pupil, Fall from Innocence," "The Body, a Winter's Tale," "The Breathing Method."
18. King, *The Shining*, the book, and the 1980 film version by Stanley Kubrick, starring Jack Nicholson.

Chapter 8

1. Paul Verhoeven, *Basic Instinct*, 1992.
2. Roland Barthes, *Sade, Fourier, Loyola*, Le Seuil, Paris, 1971; Maurice Blanchot, *Sade et Restif de la Bretonne*, Complexe, Paris, 1986; Georges Bataille, *La Part maudite*, Minuit, Paris, 1967. Note, however, that Paul Auster, an "intellectual's" mystery novelist, translated the works of Maurice Blanchot.
3. Robert Cullen, *L'Ogre de Rostov*, Presses de la Cité, Paris, 1993, p. 185.
4. *Hamr* may have some relation to *Sraman*, an ancient Indian word meaning "ascetic," which has been transformed through Asiatic influences into *shaman*.
5. Stephen King, *The Dark Half*, Signet, New York, 1990, p. 10.
6. Hugh Hudson film (1984) with Christophe Lambert.
7. On modern hunting, see Monique and Michel Pinçon, *La Chasse à courre, ses rites et ses enjeux*, Payot, Paris, 1993.
8. King, *The Dark Half*.
9. *Rage* is the story of a child who takes his own class hostage; *The Long Walk* is about a race in which dropouts are (physically) eliminated in a fascist America

(although the country hasn't come to this . . . yet); *Roadwork* is a surreal description of an outbreak of paranoia in a modern city, etc.

10. *Carrie* (a girl with telekinetic powers), *Firestarter* (who can start a fire using his mental powers), *Thinner* (the effects of a spell cast by a magician), *Salem's Lot* (a haunted town), *Pet Sematary* (a cemetery that resuscitates the dead), *It* (King's version of the Cthuhlu), and *Needful Things* (the temptations of the devil) all belong to the realm of fantastic literature, while *The Shining* (a tale of a man's insanity in an isolated place), *Misery* (about a brutal nurse), *Cujo* (a friendly Saint Bernard that catches rabies), *Gerald's Game* (a woman who is bound and tied), etc. are closer to realism.

11. King, *The Dark Half*. A film version was released in 1992.

12. There is a true story of two brothers who were united in crime, one of whom was named Thaddeus: Gary Lewingdon and Thaddeus Charles killed ten persons in Columbus, Ohio, in the late 1970s.

13. Frank Norris is known for his masterpiece of "psychological lycanthropy," *Vandover and the Brute*, W. Heinemann, London, 1914.

14. *Alien*, a film by Ridley Scott, 1979. The alien is like the ichneumon fly, which is capable of "gouging its terebra through the bark of a tree and into the body of another insect, where it deposits its eggs, which devour their host as they develop" (Jean Bruno Renard, "Loups et félins dans le cinéma fantastique," in *Des fauves dans nos campagnes. Légendes, rumeurs et apparitions*, V. Campion-Vincent, ed., Imago, Paris, 1992).

15. Interview with Wes Craven, *Cahiers du cinéma*, 463, January 1993, p. 41 (by T. Jousse and N. Saada).

16. King, *The Shining*.

17. The father–son relationship is treated in Richard Benson's film *The Boy who Cried Werewolf* (Nathan Juran, 1973), the story of a boy who is saved by his father from a werewolf attack. But the wounded father then becomes a werewolf himself. Only the son knows the secret, as no one in their entourage notices the change.

18. It is not impossible to liken "Loki," from the Indo-European root word that becomes *lykos* in Greek, to *Ulf* (wolf) in the Germanic languages. A connection with notions of light, as in the forest "clearing" (and in Lug, the Celtic god, or in Lucifer, the "bringer of light"), has also been suggested. Light is associated with the Germanic and Celtic New Year's celebrations, which include the feast of Saint Lucia.

19. Zelarzny and Thomas, *Mask of Loki*, p. 362.

20. A popular theme in American fiction and "space operas," such as Dan Simmons's highly successful *Hyperion*.

Chapter 9

1. Clive Barker, *The Great and Secret Show, The First Book of Art*, Harper Collins, London, 1989, p. 673.
2. Jacqueline Carroy, *Les Personnalités doubles et multiples (entre science et fiction)*, Psychopathologie, PUF, Paris, 1993.
3. Gabriel Tarde, *Fragment d'histoire future*, Storck, Lyon, 1904.
4. Patrick Sabatier, "Saïpan. Une île en enfer," *Libération*, 7 April 1993, p. 41.
5. Renard, "Loups *et* félins."; Philippe Goergen, "Enragés et lycanthropes : les animalités contagieuses", and Alice Joisten and Robert Chanaud, "Le loup-garou dans les Alpes françaises ou les degrés du fantastique," *Des fauves*.
6. Quoted in Jean Théodorides, *Histoire de la rage*, Fondation Mérieux, Masson Editeur, Lyon, 1985.
7. See Pinçon and Pinçon, *Chasse à courre*.
8. A.D., "L'Homme au treillis," *Libération*, 15 juin, 1993.
9. Jacques Finné, *Trois saigneurs de la nuit*, Nouvelles Editions Oswald, Bruxelles, 1988.
10. A 1984 British film by Neil Jordan, who was Boorman's assistant during the making of *Excalibur*.
11. King, *Gerald's Game*.
12. King, *Cujo*. See also, *Cujo*, the 1983 film by Lewis Teague, after the novel by Stephen King.
13. Kurt Neumann, *The Fly*, 1958; Edward Bernds, *Return of the Fly*, 1959, 1965; Don Sharp, *The Curse of the Fly*, 1986; David Cronenberg, *The Fly*, 1989; Chris Walas, *The Fly II*, etc.
14. John Sanford, *Le Chien-Loup*, Belfond, Paris, 1992.
15. *The Curse of the Werewolf*, a 1961 film.
16. King, *Nightshift*.
17. In André Gide, *Les Caves du Vatican*, Gallimard, Paris, 1914.
18. Interview of Roger L. Depue (National Center for the Analysis of Violent Crime, NCAVC) by Bourgoin, *Serial Killers*, p. 90. Depue may not know that his ideas resemble those of a certain Dr. Laurent, who claimed, in the early days of criminal anthropology, that he could identify a murderer by the shape of his penis (Dr. Laurent, "La verge des criminels," *Archives d'anthropologie criminelle*, 3, 1892).
19. Edwy Plenel, "La bombe humaine," *Le Monde*, 16–17 May 1993.
20. My apologies for choosing this neologism over the scholarly term "lycan-thropic." On this literary genre, see Finné, *Bibliographie de Dracula*, p. 32.
21. Daniel Attias, *Peur bleue*, United States, 1985.

Chapter 10

1. *WaldeMacht*: the force of the dead.
2. Edgar Allan Poe, "The Case of Mr. Veldemar" (*The Complete Works of Edgar Allan Poe*, J. Harrison, New York, 1965).
3. By New Zealander Peter Jackson, 1992.
4. Bourgoin (interview with Ottis Toole), *Serial Killers*, p. 229.
5. In Latin countries, the myth still exists, but in a more repressed and disguised form, as in the miracle of Saint Xavier, whose coagulated blood becomes liquid again, in an allusion to sacrifices made for the New Year.
6. Bourgoin, *Serial Killers*, pp. 206 *et seq.*
7. Graysmith, *Crimes of the Zodiac*.
8. Barker, *Great and Secret Show*.
9. In 785, Charlemagne converted the Saxons. He issued the edict *Capitulatio de Paribus Saxioniae*, punishing by death those who interpreted the transubstantiation of the Eucharist literally, as an act of cannibalism.
10. Note that mythological figures, like those of dreams, are mutable: the bloodied aspect of a savaged corpse is transposed to the Harlequin or the Santa Claus costume; hunters (the living dead) can become the hunted (by a wild stag) or victims (as child figures), etc.
11. In ancient Greece, February was a time when madness returned during Anthesteria, one of the festivals composing the Dionysia that celebrated the arrival of the new flowers. Similarly, in mid-May the Roman gods Forculus and Forcula, respectively the guardian of doors and the protector of hinges, and Limentinus and Limentina, who guarded the threshold, became powerless to defend against the intrusion of the dead into people's homes. Had these visitors already begun entering by the chimney?
12. Bourgoin, *Serial Killers*, p. 233.
13. *Criblum* and *crimen* (Latin *crimen*, to judge) belong to the group *cernere* (to sort), derived from the Greek *Xpíω* (to combine materials for a mortar).

Chapter 11

1. Cullen, *L'Ogre*.
2. Gerald Frank, *The Boston Strangler*, New American Library, New York, 1967; G.W. Rae, *Confessions of the Boston Strangler*, Pyramid, New York, 1967.
3. Ressler with Schachtman, *Whoever Fights Monsters*, chapter 6, "Organized and disorganized crimes," pp. 179–211.
4. Graysmith, *Crimes of the Zodiac*.

5. This frantic chase is uncannily reminiscent of *Werewolf in a Girls' Dormitory*, an American film by Richard Benson, 1961.

6. James Cameron, *Terminator II, Judgment Day*, 1991.

7. Referring to himself in the third person is typical of Bundy's discourse, which is characterized by an inability to speak of his own acts in the first person.

8. Ted Bundy, letter to Ann Rule (17 May 1976, quoted in Ann Rule, *The Stranger Beside Me*, Warner Books, London, 1980, pp. 203–4).

9. Rule, *Stranger*, p. 397.

10. Leyton, *Hunting Humans*.

11. Ibid., p. 123.

12. A remake on the same theme was produced in 1991 by the Chiodo Brothers (*Killer Klowns from Outer Space*). This version is about horrible extraterrestrials whose clown disguise is really their natural form with a little makeup.

13. Games invented by B. Sperry and M. Legg and produced by the Virgin Company.

14. Don Davis, *L'Affaire Jeffrey Dahmer, le Monstre de Milwaukee*, J'ai lu, Paris, 1993. See also Stéphane Bourgoin, *Le Cannibale de Milwaukee*, Fleuve noir, Paris, 1993. Note that the "serial-killer" label not only applies to psychotic vagrants, but is also a fairly suitable description of the "category" of young male homosexuals who kill large numbers of unknown victims in succession. Such cases include those of Dennis Nilsen (fifteen victims between 1973 and 1983), John Joubert, John Wayne Gacy (more than thirty victims), Larry Eyler (twenty-three victims), Dean Corll (twenty-seven young boys slain), Juan Corona (twenty-five victims), and perhaps the Mourmelon killer in France, and so on. Here, the inability to deal with the twinned image of one's alter ego is reflected by the killers' homosexuality. The possibility that there is a connection between certain types of homosexuality and an extremely conflictual relationship has been treated by Richard Sennett (both indirectly in *The Fall of Public Man*, Alfred A. Knopf, New York, 1976, and more directly in his fiction writing).

15. Davis, *Jeffrey Dahmer*, p. 89.

16. Barker, *Great and Secret Show*, pp. 25–6.

17. David Riesman, N. Glazer, and R. Denney, *The Lonely Crowd*, Yale University Press, New Haven, 1950.

Part IV

Chapter 12

1. John Douglas, Robert Ressler, Ann Burgess, Carol Hartman, "Criminal profiling from crime scene analysis," *Behavioral Sciences and the Law*, 2, 1986.

2. Quoted in Bourgoin *Serial Killers*.

3. Ibid., p. 66.
4. Ressler with Schachtman, *Whoever Fights Monsters*, p. 137.
5. Ibid., p. 130.
6. Ibid., p. 129.
7. Ibid., p. 132.
8. One of the recent reinterpretations of the term "serial killer" is the use of the phrase by the right-to-life movement to describe women who have had more than one abortion.

Chapter 13

1. Centuries before antinuclear campaigns, the prospect of a long winter in association with a disastrous end of the world already existed in the Viking sagas: the *Fimbulvetr*, a harsh winter that lasted three years, was the sign that the end was near.
2. One should not be taken in by the suggestion that real atrocities are somehow becoming increasingly horrible. If one reads the French *Grand Guignol* plays from the beginning of this century, it becomes clear that authors were not squeamish then either. American film is designed to draw young groups who are no longer satisfied by Alfred Hitchcock's film sets or by plot lines by Dashiell Hammett or Raymond Chandler, which have become out of date. And yet these authors piled up bodies with such a generous hand that modern-day serial killers look like crude amateurs in comparison.
3. In Russia, another culture that was built in large part by the Vikings, people still drink a fermented molasses liquor called *kvass*.
4. Wes Craven inaugurated the Freddy Kruger (played by Robert Englund) series with *The Killer on Elm Street*. This violent zombie, whose face is covered with third-degree burns, has razor blades for fingernails, which he uses to lacerate his victims when he appears in their dreams. Highly popular among adolescent groups, the character was revived several times before Rachel Talalay finally "buried" him in 1991, after portraying him as the victim of an unhappy childhood and a psychopathic environment. The series is probably the most systematic of such "mad-killer" creations, oscillating between the fantastic, the "splatter film," and the "no-future" culture.
5. *A Boy and his Dog*, 1975.
6. Quoted in Brian J. Frost, *Book of the Werewolf*, Sphere Books, London, 1973 (introduction).
7. Adolf Hitler, *Mein Kampf*, Pimlico, London, 1992, p. 274.
8. Thomas Disch, *The Evil Caduceus*, Pocket Books, New York, 1994.
9. On "Western" women's hysterical neurotic habit of vilifying the father figure, see Marco Zafiropoulos's interesting article, "La haine inconsciente et le lien social," *Synapse*, 100, October 1993, and, in response, my letter to the editors (*Synapse*, February–March 1994).

10. *Wal* or *Val* means the dead on the battle field, and *kyrie* is related to the verb "to choose."

11. We have seen that the Nazi movement interests a number of violent (Huberty) or sadistic (Schaefer, Holmes, etc.), criminals; Brady (the male partner in a British sadistic "couple" in the 1960s) read works by the Nazis. Among followers of the occult, the Nazi movement is one of a set group of references.

12. Stephen King, *The Dead Zone*, Warner Books, London, 1979, p. 385.

13. Ibid., p. 386.

14. James Herbert, *The Spear*, Pocket Books, New York, 1992.

15. The myth of the eternal battle is very ancient. Called *Hjadningavig* (battle of the Odinic warriors), its structure is unchanging: a woman character incites the battle, which then begins anew every morning, because she raises the dead at night and sends them back to fight.

16. Robert Harris, *Fatherland*, Harper & Collins, New York, 1992.

Chapter 14

1. Susan Faludi, *Backlash*, Crown Publishers, New York, 1991.

2. John Updike, *The Witches of Eastwick*, Alfred A. Knopf, New York, 1984. Adapted for film by George Miller in 1987, with Jack Nicholson in the role of the devil, Deryl Van Horne.

3. Stephen King and Eric Lustbader are always very proud to remind us that they are professors of literature. The academic credentials of the makers of the most terrifying horror films are sometimes hard to believe.

4. William Blake, *The Marriage of Heaven and Hell*, 1793.

5. The word werewolf is derived from the Old English *werwulf*, meaning "man-wolf." The French term – *loup-garou* – contains a redundancy, since *garou*, from the Germanic root *wariwulf*, already means "man-wolf," while *loup* means wolf.

6. American film, 1993.

7. Translator's note: see Pierre Bourdieu, *La Distinction*, Minuit, Paris, 1979.

8. Immanuel Kant, *Idea for a Universal History with a cosmopolitan purpose* (1787), *Philosophical Writings*, Hans Reiss ed., Cambridge University Press, 1991, p. 45.

9. Davis, *Jeffrey Dahmer*.

10. Bourgoin, *Serial Killers*, interview with Roger L. Depue (FBI psychologist who helped to form VICAP), p. 83.

11. I should recall that Hitler also attributed the virtues of the nomadic life to the Aryan race: "We must bear in mind that in the time when the American continent was being opened up, numerous Aryans fought for their livelihood

as trappers, hunters, etc., and often, in larger troops with wife and children, always on the move, so that their existence was completely like that of the Nomads," *Mein Kampf*, p. 267.

12. Freud, *Totem and Taboo*, pp. 128–9.

13. Friedrich Nietzsche, *Thus Spake Zarathustra*.

14. Denis Duclos, *De la civilité, ou comment les sociétés apprivoisent la puissance*, La Découverte, Paris, 1993.

15. Nicolas Saada, "L'autre cinéma indépendant," *Cahiers du cinéma*, 463, January 1993, p. 37.

16. See, for example, Richard Lortz, *Dracula's Children*, Permanent Press, Sage Harbor, New York.

17. Margaret Mead, *Moeurs et sexualité en Océanie*, Plon, Paris, 1963. Mead demonstrated that ethnic groups in the South Sea Islands could have totally different mores depending on their culture's model for bringing up children: the Arapesh were friendly, the Mundugumor violent, the Samoans peaceful, etc. Several years ago, universities in New Zealand attempted to prove that the distinguished American anthropologist's findings were based on erroneous field studies, and that the "nonviolent" Arapesh society was in fact as violent as our own.

18. Directed by Martin Scorsese, 1976.

19. Marc Toullec, "Le fantôme de l'Opéra," *Ciné-Fantastique, Mad Movies*, 64, 1990, p. 15. This gibe is in the same register as the guffaws (or eloquent silences) that follow any mention of French rock music to American or British listeners.

20. The explosion of "anti-Japanese" fiction (typified by Eric Lustbader, despite his self-proclaimed admiration of the Ninja) is evidence of this.

Chapter 15

1. This is patently obvious in Margaret Thatcher's statement: "Society does not exist."

2. Let us not forget that the death toll from the religious wars in Europe, ten of which were in Germany alone, was in the millions.

3. Roy William Neill, *Frankenstein Meets the Werewolf*, 1943; Erle C. Kenton, *La Maison de Frankenstein*, 1944.

4. Vidal-Naquet, *Chasseur noir*.

Conclusion

1. "Militias, armed and dangerous," *The Economist*, 29 April 1996, p. 69.

2. Timothy McVeigh, letter to the *Union-Sun & Journal of Lockport*, New York, 1992.
3. Translator's note: Charles Maurras, right-wing French politician and writer (1868–1952), sentenced to life in confinement for supporting Mussolini and Franco and collaborating with the Pétain government. He was elected to the Académie Française in 1938, but the institution expelled him in 1945.

Index